P9-DGB-532

CASES AND MATERIALS ON FEDERAL CONSTITUTIONAL LAW

Volume II
Introduction to the Federal Executive Power
&
Separation of Powers Issues

LexisNexis Law School Publishing Advisory Board

Charles B. Craver
Freda H. Alverson Professor of Law
The George Washington University Law School

Richard D. Freer
Robert Howell Hall Professor of Law
Emory University School of Law

Craig Joyce
Andrews Kurth Professor of Law &
Co-Director, Institute for Intellectual Property and Information Law
University of Houston Law Center

Ellen S. Podgor
Professor of Law & Associate Dean of Faculty Development and Electronic Education
Stetson University College of Law

Paul F. Rothstein
Professor of Law
Georgetown University Law Center

Robin Wellford Slocum
Professor of Law & Director, Legal Research and Writing Program
Chapman University School of Law

Charles J. Tabb
Alice Curtis Campbell Professor of Law
University of Illinois College of Law

David I. C. Thomson
LP Professor & Director, Lawyering Process Program
University of Denver, Sturm College of Law

Judith Welch Wegner
Professor of Law
University of North Carolina School of Law

Modular Casebook Series

CASES AND MATERIALS ON FEDERAL CONSTITUTIONAL LAW

Volume II

Introduction to the Federal Executive Power
&
Separation of Powers Issues

Thomas H. Odom

VOLUME 2 ISBN: 978-1-4224-2206-9

Odom, Thomas H.
Introduction to interpretive methods & introduction to the federal judicial power / Thomas H. Odom.
p. cm. -- (Cases and materials on federal constitutional law ; v. 1)
Includes index.
ISBN 978-1-4224-2205-2 (soft cover)
1. Courts--United States. I. Title.
KF8718.O36 2008
347.73'1--dc22 2008036946

This publication is designed to provide accurate and authoritative information in regard to the subject matter covered. It is sold with the understanding that the publisher is not engaged in rendering legal, accounting, or other professional services. If legal advice or other expert assistance is required, the services of a competent professional should be sought.

LexisNexis, the knowledge burst logo, and Michie are trademarks of Reed Elsevier Properties Inc, used under license. Matthew Bender is a registered trademark of Matthew Bender Properties Inc.

Copyright © 2008 Matthew Bender & Company, Inc., a member of the LexisNexis Group.
All Rights Reserved.

No copyright is claimed in the text of statutes, regulations, and excerpts from court opinions quoted within this work. Permission to copy material exceeding fair use, 17 U.S.C. § 107, may be licensed for a fee of 25¢ per page per copy from the Copyright Clearance Center, 222 Rosewood Drive, Danvers, Mass. 01923, telephone (978) 750-8400.

NOTE TO USERS

To ensure that you are using the latest materials available in this area, please be sure to periodically check the LexisNexis Law School web site for downloadable updates and supplements at www.lexisnexis.com/lawschool.

Editorial Offices
744 Broad Street, Newark, NJ 07102 (973) 820-2000
201 Mission St., San Francisco, CA 94105-1831 (415) 908-3200
www.lexisnexis.com

MATTHEW BENDER

(2008–Pub.3262)

INTRODUCTION TO THE MODULAR CASEBOOK SERIES

By now you have realized that the course materials assigned by your instructor have a very different form than "traditional" casebooks. The *Modular Casebook Series* is intentionally designed to break the mold. Course materials consist of one or more separate volumes selected from among a larger and growing set of volumes. Each of those volumes is only about 225 to 250 in length so that an instructor may "mix and match" a suitable number of volumes for a course of varying length and focus. Each volume is designed to serve an instructional purpose rather than as a treatise. As a result, the volumes are published in soft cover. Publication of the separate volumes in soft cover also permits course materials to be revised more easily so that they will incorporate recent developments. Moreover, by purchasing only the assigned volumes for a given course, students are likely to recognize significant savings over the cost of a traditional casebook.

Traditional casebooks are often massive tomes, sometimes exceeding 1000 or even 1500 pages. Traditional casebooks are lengthy because they attempt to cover the entire breadth of material that might be useful to an instructor for a two-semester course of five or six credits. Even with six credits, different instructors may choose which portions of a traditional casebook do not fit within the time available. As a consequence, traditional casebooks may include a range of materials that would leave hundreds of unexplored in any particular six-credit class. For a student in a three or four credit course, such a book is hardly an efficient means for delivering the needed materials. Students purchase much more book than they need, at great expense. And students carry large, heavy books for months at a time.

Traditional casebooks are usually hard cover publications. It seems as though they are constructed so as to last as a reference work throughout decades of practice. In fact, as the presence of annual supplements to most casebooks makes clear, many casebooks are obsolete very shortly after publication. Treatises and hornbooks are designed to serve as reference works; casebooks serve a different purpose. Once again, the traditional format of casebooks seems to impose significant added costs on students without much reason.

The form of traditional casebooks increases the probability that the contents will become obsolete shortly after publication. The publication of lengthy texts in hardcover produces substantial delay between the time the author completes the final draft and the time the book reaches the hands of students. In addition, the broader scope of material addressed in a 1,000 or 1,500 page text means that portions of the text are more likely to be superceded by later developments than any particular narrowly-tailored volume in the *Modular Casebook Series*. Because individual volumes in the *Modular Casebook Series* may be revised without requiring revision of other volumes, the materials for any particular course will be less likely to require supplementation.

We hope you enjoy this innovative approach to course materials.

Dedication

For RDR: Scholar and friend.

Dedication

Acknowledgments

I would like to thank Dickinson School of Law and Pennsylvania State University for their financial support. I am indebted to my students whose daily interaction with me and the materials provide the impetus for constant improvement.

The hard work of numerous research assistants is reflected in this collection, notably: Michael Lynch, Justin Pickens, Chris VanLandingham, and Brian McMorrow.

I would like to express special appreciation to Peter J. Riebling for thoughtful exchanges regarding issues in separation of powers doctrine and to Anthony M. Bottenfield for his research in connection with the so-called "legislative veto."

Without the loving support of Janet this project would not have been completed.

All remaining errors and omissions are my own.

Preface to the First Edition

Technological improvements permit the compilation of resources in a manner unthinkable when I was a law student. Materials that permit further examination of assigned reading can be delivered in a cost-effective manner and in a format more likely to be useful in practice than reams of photocopies. The associated DVD-ROM contains full, searchable text of several of the most important resources for interpreting the Constitution, lowering the wall between doctrinal courses and research courses.

With regard to assigned reading, there is no good reason to burden students with stacks of hand-outs or expensive annual supplements. Publication through the *Modular Casebook Series* virtually ensures that even very recent developments may be incorporated prior to publication. Moreover, if important cases are decided after publication of the latest edition of the volume, they will be included on the DVD-ROM. Cases and materials that shed additional light on matter in the hard copy casebook are also included.

I welcome comments from readers so that I may make further improvements in the next edition of this publication.

THO

TECHNICAL NOTE FROM THE EDITOR

The cases and other materials excerpted in this volume have been edited in an effort to enhance readability. Case citation forms have been revised to include the year of decision and reference to the volume number of the United States Reports. Many citations to secondary sources have been expanded to include the full names of authors or editors, and to reference the date of publication. Citations of multiple cases for a single proposition have been shortened in many places to reference only one or two prominent authorities.

In some places archaic language or spelling has been revised.

Headings were added to some of the longer decisions to permit ease of reference to various parts of the opinion. Such headings may also assist the reader in identifying a transition from one point to another.

None of these changes were intended to substantively alter the original materials.

With the exception of one or two cases per Volume, cases have been edited to a length suitable for reading as a single assignment. In order to achieve that result, many interesting but tangential points have been omitted. The length of some opinions also hindered the inclusion of excerpts from concurring or dissenting opinions. Where such opinions have been omitted, it is noted in the text. These omissions are not intended to present a biased view of the doctrine under review. In most instances, a subsequent case will present significant points raised by the omitted concurring and dissenting opinions. Any remaining unintentional bias is solely the responsibility of the editor.

THO

Table of Contents

Table of Contents

CHAPTER 1
EXECUTIVE POWER — APPOINTMENT AND REMOVAL

The Constitution of the United States

We the People of the United States, in Order to form a more perfect Union, establish Justice, insure domestic Tranquility, provide for the common defence, promote the general Welfare, and secure the Blessings of Liberty to ourselves and our Posterity, do ordain and establish this Constitution for the United States of America.

Article I

Section 1. All legislative Powers herein granted shall be vested in a Congress of the United States, which shall consist of a Senate and House of Representatives.

Section 2. The House of Representatives shall be composed of Members chosen every second Year by the People of the several States, and the Electors in each State shall have the Qualifications requisite for Electors of the most numerous Branch of the State Legislature.

No person shall be a Representative who shall not have attained to the Age of twenty five Years, and been seven Years a Citizen of the United States, and who shall not, when elected, be an Inhabitant of that State in which he shall be chosen.

Representatives and direct Taxes shall be apportioned among the several States which may be included within this Union, according to their respective Numbers, which shall be determined by adding to the whole Number of free Persons, including those bound to Service for a Term of Years, and excluding Indians not taxed, three fifths of all other Persons. The actual Enumeration shall be made within three Years after the first Meeting of the Congress of the United States, and within every subsequent Term of ten Years, in such Manner as they shall by Law direct. The Number of Representatives shall not exceed one for every thirty Thousand, but each State shall have at Least one Representative; and until such enumeration shall be made, the State of New Hampshire shall be entitled to chuse three, Massachusetts eight, Rhode-Island and Providence Plantations one, Connecticut five, New-York six, New Jersey four, Pennsylvania eight, Delaware one, Maryland six, Virginia ten, North Carolina five, South Carolina five, and Georgia three.

When vacancies happen in the Representation from any State, the Executive Authority thereof shall issue Writs of Election to fill such Vacancies.

The House of Representatives shall chuse their Speaker and other Officers; and shall have the sole Power of Impeachment.

Section 3. The Senate of the United States shall be composed of two Senators from each State, chosen by the Legislature thereof, for six Years; and each Senator shall have one Vote.

Immediately after they shall be assembled in Consequence of the first Election, they shall be divided as equally as may be into three Classes. The Seats of the Senators of the first Class shall be vacated at the Expiration of the second Year, of the second Class at the Expiration of the fourth Year, and of the third Class at the Expiration of the sixth Year, so that one third may be chosen every second Year; and if Vacancies happen by Resignation, or otherwise, during the Recess of the

Legislature of any State, the Executive thereof may make temporary Appointments until the next Meeting of the Legislature, which shall then fill such Vacancies.

No Person shall be a Senator who shall not have attained to the Age of thirty Years, and been nine Years a Citizen of the United States, and who shall not, when elected, be an Inhabitant of that State for which he shall be chosen.

The Vice President of the United States shall be President of the Senate, but shall have no Vote, unless they be equally divided.

The Senate shall chuse their other Officers, and also a President pro tempore, in the Absence of the Vice President, or when he shall exercise the Office of President of the United States.

The Senate shall have the sole Power to try all Impeachments. When sitting for that Purpose, they shall be on Oath or Affirmation. When the President of the United States is tried, the Chief Justice shall preside: and no Person shall be convicted without the Concurrence of two thirds of the Members present.

Judgment in Cases of Impeachment shall not extend further than to removal from Office, and disqualification to hold and enjoy any Office of honor, Trust or Profit under the United States: but the Party convicted shall nevertheless be liable and subject to Indictment, Trial, Judgment and Punishment, according to Law.

Section 4. The Times, Places and Manner of holding Elections for Senators and Representatives, shall be prescribed in each State by the Legislature thereof; but the Congress may at any time by Law make or alter such Regulations, except as to the Places of chusing Senators.

The Congress shall assemble at least once in every Year, and such Meeting shall be on the first Monday in December, unless they shall by Law appoint a different Day.

Section 5. Each House shall be the Judge of the Elections, Returns and Qualifications of its own Members, and a Majority of each shall constitute a Quorum to do Business; but a smaller Number may adjourn from day to day, and may be authorized to compel the Attendance of absent Members, in such Manner, and under such Penalties as each House may provide.

Each House may determine the Rules of its Proceedings, punish its Members for disorderly Behaviour, and, with the Concurrence of two thirds, expel a Member.

Each House shall keep a Journal of its Proceedings, and from time to time publish the same, excepting such Parts as may in their Judgment require Secrecy; and the Yeas and Nays of the Members of either House on any question shall, at the Desire of one fifth of those Present, be entered on the Journal.

Section 6. The Senators and Representatives shall receive a Compensation for their Services, to be ascertained by Law, and paid out of the Treasury of the United States. They shall in all Cases, except Treason, Felony and Breach of the Peace, be privileged from Arrest during their Attendance at the Session of their respective Houses, and in going to and returning from the same; and for any Speech or Debate in either House, they shall not be questioned in any other Place.

No Senator or Representative shall, during the Time for which he was elected, be appointed to any civil Office under the Authority of the United States, which shall have been created, or the Emoluments whereof shall have been encreased during such time; and no Person holding any Office under the United States, shall be a Member of either House during his Continuance in Office.

Section 7. All Bills for raising Revenue shall originate in the House of Representatives; but the Senate may propose or concur with Amendments as on other Bills.

Every Bill which shall have passed the House of Representatives and the Senate, shall, before it become a Law, be presented to the President of the United States; If he approve he shall sign it, but if not he shall return it, with his Objections to that House in which it shall have originated, who shall enter the Objections at large on their Journal, and proceed to reconsider it. If after such Reconsideration two thirds of that House shall agree to pass the Bill, it shall be sent, together with the Objections, to the other House, by which it shall likewise be reconsidered, and if approved by two thirds of that House, it shall become a Law. But in all such Cases the Votes of both Houses shall be determined by yeas and Nays, and the Names of the Persons voting for and against the Bill shall be entered on the Journal of each House respectively. If any Bill shall not be returned by the President within ten days (Sundays excepted) after it shall have been presented to him, the Same shall be a Law, in like Manner as if he had signed it, unless the Congress by their Adjournment prevent its Return in which Case it shall not be a Law.

Every Order, Resolution, or Vote to which the Concurrence of the Senate and House of Representatives may be necessary (except on a question of Adjournment) shall be presented to the President of the United States; and before the Same shall take Effect, shall be approved by him, or being disapproved by him, shall be repassed by two thirds of the Senate and House of Representatives, according to the Rules and Limitations prescribed in the Case of a Bill.

Section 8. The Congress shall have Power To lay and collect Taxes, Duties, Imposts and Excises, to pay the Debts and provide for the common Defence and general Welfare of the United States; but all Duties, Imposts and Excises shall be uniform throughout the United States;

To borrow Money on the credit of the United States;

To regulate Commerce with foreign Nations, and among the several States, and with the Indian Tribes;

To establish an uniform Rule of Naturalization, and uniform Laws on the subject of Bankruptcies throughout the United States;

To coin Money, regulate the Value thereof, and foreign Coin, and fix the Standard of Weights and Measures;

To provide for the Punishment of counterfeiting the Securities and current Coin of the United States;

To establish Post Offices and post Roads;

To promote the Progress of Science and useful Arts, by securing for limited Times to Authors and Inventors the exclusive Right to their respective Writings and Discoveries;

To constitute Tribunals inferior to the supreme Court;

To define and punish Piracies and Felonies committed on the high Seas, and Offences against the Law of Nations;

To declare War, grant Letters of Marque and Reprisal, and make Rules concerning Captures on Land and Water;

To raise and support Armies, but no Appropriation of Money to that Use shall be for a longer Term than two Years;

To provide and maintain a Navy;

To make Rules for the Government and Regulation of the land and naval Forces;

To provide for calling forth the Militia to execute the Laws of the Union, suppress Insurrections and repel Invasions;

To provide for organizing, arming, and disciplining, the Militia, and for governing such Part of them as may be employed in the Service of the United States, reserving to the States respectively, the Appointment of the Officers, and the Authority of training the Militia according to the discipline prescribed by Congress;

To exercise exclusive Legislation in all Cases whatsoever, over such District (not exceeding ten Miles square) as may, by Cession of particular States, and the Acceptance of Congress, become the Seat of the Government of the United States, and to exercise like Authority over all Places purchased by the Consent of the Legislature of the State in which the Same shall be, for the Erection of Forts, Magazines, Arsenals, dock-Yards, and other needful Buildings; — And

To make all Laws which shall be necessary and proper for carrying into Execution the foregoing Powers, and all other Powers vested by this Constitution in the Government of the United States, or in any Department or Officer thereof.

Section 9. The Migration or Importation of such Persons as any of the States now existing shall think proper to admit, shall not be prohibited by the Congress prior to the Year one thousand eight hundred and eight, but a Tax or duty may be imposed on such Importation, not exceeding ten dollars for each Person.

The Privilege of the Writ of Habeas Corpus shall not be suspended, unless when in Cases of Rebellion or Invasion the public Safety may require it.

No Bill of Attainder or ex post facto Law shall be passed.

No Capitation, or other direct, Tax shall be laid, unless in Proportion to the Census or Enumeration herein before directed to be taken.

No Tax or Duty shall be laid on Articles exported from any State.

No Preference shall be given by any Regulation of Commerce or Revenue to the Ports of one State over those of another; nor shall Vessels bound to, or from, one State, be obliged to enter, clear, or pay Duties in another.

No Money shall be drawn from the Treasury, but in Consequence of Appropriations made by Law; and a regular Statement and Account of the Receipts and Expenditures of all public Money shall be published from time to time.

No Title of Nobility shall be granted by the United States: And no Person holding any Office of Profit or Trust under them, shall, without the Consent of the Congress, accept of any present, Emolument, Office, or Title, of any kind whatever, from any King, Prince, or foreign State.

Section 10. No State shall enter into any Treaty, Alliance, or Confederation; grant Letters of Marque and Reprisal; coin Money; emit Bills of Credit; make any Thing but gold and silver Coin a Tender in Payment of Debts; pass any Bill of Attainder, ex post facto Law, or Law impairing the Obligation of Contracts, or grant any Title of Nobility.

No State shall, without the Consent of the Congress, lay any Imposts or Duties on Imports or Exports, except what may be absolutely necessary for executing it's inspection Laws: and the net Produce of all Duties and Imposts, laid by any State on Imports or Exports, shall be for the Use of the Treasury of the United States; and all such Laws shall be subject to the Revision and Controul of the Congress.

No State shall, without the Consent of Congress, lay any Duty of Tonnage, keep Troops, or Ships of War in time of Peace, enter into any Agreement or Compact with another State, or with a foreign Power, or engage in War, unless actually invaded, or in such imminent Danger as will not admit of delay.

Article II

Section 1. The executive Power shall be vested in a President of the United States of America. He shall hold his Office during the Term of four Years, and, together with the Vice President, chosen for the same Term, be elected as follows

Each State shall appoint, in such Manner as the Legislature thereof may direct, a Number of Electors, equal to the whole Number of Senators and Representatives to which the State may be entitled in the Congress: but no Senator or Representative, or Person holding an Office of Trust or Profit under the United States, shall be appointed an Elector.

The Electors shall meet in their respective States, and vote by Ballot for two Persons, of whom one at least shall not be an Inhabitant of the same State with themselves. And they shall make a List of all the Persons voted for, and of the Number of Votes for each; which List they shall sign and certify, and transmit sealed to the Seat of the Government of the United States, directed to the President of the Senate. The President of the Senate shall, in the Presence of the Senate and House of Representatives, open all the Certificates, and the Votes shall then be counted. The Person having the greatest Number of Votes shall be the President, if such Number be a Majority of the whole Number of Electors appointed; and if there be more than one who have such Majority, and have an equal Number of Votes, then the House of Representatives shall immediately chuse by Ballot one of them for President; and if no Person have a Majority, then from the five highest on the List the said House shall in like Manner chuse the President. But in chusing the President, the Votes shall be taken by States, the Representation from each State having one Vote; A quorum for this Purpose shall consist of a Member or Members from two thirds of the States, and a Majority of all the States shall be necessary to a Choice. In every Case, after the Choice of the President, the Person having the greatest Number of Votes of the Electors shall be the Vice President. But if there should remain two or more who have equal Votes, the Senate shall chuse from them by Ballot the Vice President.

The Congress may determine the Time of chusing the Electors, and the Day on which they shall give their Votes; which Day shall be the same throughout the United States.

No Person except a natural born Citizen, or a Citizen of the United States, at the time of the Adoption of this Constitution, shall be eligible to the Office of President; neither shall any Person be eligible to that Office who shall not have attained to the Age of thirty five Years, and been fourteen Years a Resident within the United States.

In the Case of the Removal of the President from Office, or of his Death, Resignation, or Inability to discharge the Powers and Duties of the said Office, the Same shall devolve on the Vice President, and the Congress may by Law provide for the Case of Removal, Death, Resignation or Inability, both of the President and Vice President, declaring what Officer shall then act as President, and such Officer shall act accordingly, until the Disability be removed, or a President shall be elected.

The President shall, at stated Times, receive for his Services, a Compensation, which shall neither be encreased nor diminished during the Period for which he shall have been elected, and he shall not receive within that Period any other Emolument from the United States, or any of them.

Before he enter on the Execution of his Office, he shall take the following Oath or Affirmation: — "I do solemnly swear (or affirm) that I will faithfully execute the

Office of the President of the United States, and will to the best of my Ability, preserve, protect and defend the Constitution of the United States."

Section 2. The President shall be the Commander in Chief of the Army and Navy of the United States, and of the Militia of the several States, when called into the actual service of the United States; he may require the Opinion, in writing, of the principal Officer in each of the executive Departments, upon any Subject relating to the Duties of their respective Offices, and he shall have Power to grant Reprieves and Pardons for Offenses against the United States, except in Cases of Impeachment.

He shall have Power, by and with the Advice and Consent of the Senate, to make Treaties, provided two thirds of the Senators present concur; and he shall nominate, and by and with the Advice and Consent of the Senate, shall appoint Ambassadors, other public Ministers and Consuls, Judges of the supreme Court, and all other Officers of the United States, whose Appointments are not herein otherwise provided for, and which shall be established by Law but the Congress may by Law vest the Appointment of such inferior Officers, as they think proper, in the President alone, in the Courts of Law, or in the Heads of Departments.

The President shall have Power to fill up all Vacancies that may happen during the Recess of the Senate, by granting Commissions which shall expire at the End of their next Session.

Section 3. He shall from time to time give to the Congress Information of the State of the Union, and recommend to their Consideration such Measures as he shall judge necessary and expedient; he may, on extraordinary Occasions, convene both Houses, or either of them, and in Case of Disagreement between them, with Respect to the Time of Adjournment, he may adjourn them to such Time as he shall think proper; he shall receive Ambassadors and other public Ministers; he shall take Care that the Laws be faithfully executed, and shall Commission all the Officers of the United States.

Section 4. The President, Vice President and all civil Officers of the United States, shall be removed from Office on Impeachment for, and Conviction of, Treason, Bribery, or other high Crimes and Misdemeanors.

Article III

Section 1. The judicial Power of the United States, shall be vested in one supreme Court, and in such inferior Courts as the Congress may from time to time ordain and establish. The Judges, both of the supreme and inferior Courts, shall hold their Offices during good Behaviour, and shall, at stated Times, receive for their Services, a Compensation, which shall not be diminished during their Continuance in Office.

Section 2. The judicial Power shall extend to all Cases, in Law and Equity, arising under this Constitution, the Laws of the United States, and Treaties made, or which shall be made, under their Authority; — to all Cases affecting Ambassadors, other public Ministers and Consuls; — to all Cases of admiralty and maritime Jurisdiction; — to Controversies to which the United States shall be a Party; — to Controversies between two or more States; — between a State and Citizens of another State; — between Citizens of different States; — between Citizens of the same State claiming Lands under Grants of different States, and between a State, or the Citizens thereof, and foreign States, Citizens or Subjects.

In all cases affecting Ambassadors, other public Ministers and Consuls, and those in which a State shall be a Party, the supreme Court shall have original Jurisdiction. In all the other Cases before mentioned, the supreme Court shall have appellate Jurisdiction, both as to Law and Fact, with such Exceptions, and under such Regulations as the Congress shall make.

The Trial of all Crimes, except in Cases of Impeachment, shall be by Jury; and such Trial shall be held in the State where the said Crimes shall have been committed; but when not committed within any State, the Trial shall be at such Place or Places as the Congress may by Law have directed.

Section 3. Treason against the United States, shall consist only in levying War against them, or in adhering to their Enemies, giving them Aid or Comfort. No Person shall be convicted of Treason unless on the Testimony of two Witnesses to the same overt Act, or on Confession in open Court.

The Congress shall have Power to declare the Punishment of Treason, but no Attainder of Treason shall work Corruption of Blood, or Forfeiture except during the Life of the Person attainted.

Article IV

Section 1. Full Faith and Credit shall be given in each State to the public Acts, Records, and judicial Proceedings of every other State. And the Congress may by general Laws prescribe the Manner in which such Acts, Records and Proceedings shall be proved, and the Effect thereof.

Section 2. The Citizens of each State shall be entitled to all Privileges and Immunities of Citizens in the several States.

A Person charged in any State with Treason, Felony, or other Crime, who shall flee from Justice, and be found in another State, shall on Demand of the executive Authority of the State from which he fled, be delivered up, to be removed to the State having Jurisdiction of the Crime.

No Person held to Service or Labour in one State, under the Laws thereof, escaping into another, shall, in Consequence of any Law or Regulation therein, be discharged from such Service or Labour, but shall be delivered up on Claim of the Party to whom such Service or Labour may be due.

Section 3. New States may be admitted by the Congress into this Union; but no new State shall be formed or erected within the Jurisdiction of any other State; nor any State be formed by the Junction of two or more States, or Parts of States, without the Consent of the Legislatures of the States concerned as well as of the Congress.

The Congress shall have Power to dispose of and make all needful Rules and Regulations respecting the Territory or other Property belonging to the United States; and nothing in this Constitution shall be so construed to Prejudice any Claims of the United States, or of any particular State.

Section 4. The United States shall guarantee to every State in this Union a Republican Form of Government, and shall protect each of them against Invasion; and on Application of the Legislature, or of the Executive (when the Legislature cannot be convened) against domestic Violence.

Article V

The Congress, whenever two thirds of both Houses shall deem it necessary, shall propose Amendments to this Constitution, or, on the Application of the Legislatures of two thirds of the several States, shall call a Convention for proposing Amendments, which, in either Case, shall be valid to all Intents and Purposes, as Part of this Constitution, when ratified by the Legislatures of three fourths of the several States, or by Conventions in three fourths thereof, as the one or the other Mode of Ratification may be proposed by the Congress; provided that no Amendment which may be made prior to the Year One thousand eight hundred and eight shall in any Manner affect the first and fourth Clauses in the Ninth Section of the first Article; and that no State, without its Consent, shall be deprived of it's equal Suffrage in the Senate.

Article VI

All Debts contracted and Engagements entered into, before the adoption of this Constitution, shall be as valid against the United States under this Constitution, as under the Confederation.

This Constitution, and the Laws of the United States which shall be made in Pursuance thereof; and all Treaties made, or which shall be made, under the Authority of the United States, shall be the supreme Law of the Land; and the Judges in every State shall be bound thereby, any Thing in the Constitution or Laws of any State to the Contrary notwithstanding.

The Senators and Representatives before mentioned, and the members of the several State Legislatures, and all executive and judicial Officers, both of the United States and of the several States, shall be bound by Oath or Affirmation, to support this Constitution; but no religious Test shall ever be required as a Qualification to any Office or public Trust under the United States.

Article VII

The Ratification of the Conventions of nine States, shall be sufficient for the Establishment of this Constitution between the States so ratifying the Same.

Go. Washington — Presidt.
And deputy from Virginia

New Hampshire
John Langdon
Nicholas Gilman

New Jersey
Wil: Livingston
David Brearley
Wm. Paterson
Jona: Dayton

Massachusetts
Nathaniel Gorham
Rufus King
Connecticut
Wm. Saml. Johnson
Roger Sherman
New York
Alexander Hamilton

Pennsylvania
B Franklin
Thomas Mifflin
Robt. Morris
Geo. Clymer
Thos. Fitzsimons
Jared Ingersoll
James Wilson
Gouv Morris

Delaware
Geo: Read
Cunning Bedford jun
John Dickinson
Richard Bassett
Jaco: Broom

North Carolina
Wm: Blount
Richd. Dobbs Spaight.
Hu Williamson

Maryland
James McHenry
Dan of St. Thos. Jenifer
Danl. Carroll

South Carolina
J. Rutledge
Charles Cotesworth Pinckney
Pierce Butler.

Virginia
John Blair —
James Madison Jr.

Georgia
William Few
Abr Baldwin

The Bill of Rights
(1791)

Amendment I

Congress shall make no law respecting an establishment of religion, or prohibiting the free exercise thereof; or abridging the freedom of speech, or of the press; or the right of the people peaceably to assemble, and to petition the government for a redress of grievances.

Amendment II

A well regulated militia, being necessary to the security of a free state, the right of the people to keep and bear arms, shall not be infringed.

Amendment III

No soldier shall, in time of peace be quartered in any house, without the consent of the owner, nor in time of war, but in a manner to be prescribed by law.

Amendment IV

The right of the people to be secure in their persons, houses, papers, and effects, against unreasonable searches and seizures, shall not be violated, and no warrants shall issue, but upon probable cause, supported by oath or affirmation, and particularly describing the place to be searched, and the persons or things to be seized.

Amendment V

No person shall be held to answer for a capital, or otherwise infamous crime, unless on a presentment or indictment of a grand jury, except in cases arising in the land or naval forces, or in the militia, when in actual service in time of war or public danger; nor shall any person be subject for the same offense to be twice put in jeopardy of life or limb; nor shall be compelled in any criminal case to be a witness against himself, nor be deprived of life, liberty, or property, without due process of law; nor shall private property be taken for public use, without just compensation.

Amendment VI

In all criminal prosecutions, the accused shall enjoy the right to a speedy and public trial, by an impartial jury of the state and district wherein the crime shall have been committed, which district shall have been previously ascertained by law, and to be informed of the nature and cause of the accusation; to be confronted with the witnesses against him; to have compulsory process for obtaining witnesses in his favor, and to have the assistance of counsel for his defense.

Amendment VII

In suits at common law, where the value in controversy shall exceed twenty dollars, the right of trial by jury shall be preserved, and no fact tried by a jury, shall be otherwise reexamined in any court of the United States, then according to the rules of the common law.

Amendment VIII

Excessive bail shall not be required, nor excessive fines imposed, nor cruel and unusual punishments inflicted.

Amendment IX

The enumeration in the Constitution, of certain rights, shall not be construed to deny or disparage others retained by the people.

Amendment X

The powers not delegated to the United States by the Constitution, nor prohibited by it to the states, are reserved to the states respectively, or to the people.

Later Amendments

Amendment XI

(1798)

The judicial power of the United States shall not be construed to extend to any suit in law or equity, commenced or prosecuted against one of the United States by Citizens of another State, or by Citizens or Subjects of any Foreign State.

Amendment XII

(1804)

The Electors shall meet in their respective states and vote by ballot for President and Vice-President, one of whom, at least, shall not be an inhabitant of the same state with themselves; they shall name in their ballots the person voted for as President, and in distinct ballots the person voted for as Vice-President, and they shall make distinct lists of all persons voted for as President, and of all persons voted for as Vice-President, and of the number of votes for each, which lists they shall sign and certify, and transmit sealed to the seat of the government of the United States, directed to the President of the Senate; — The President of the Senate shall, in the presence of the Senate and House of Representatives, open all the certificates and the votes shall then be counted; — the person having the greatest number of votes for President, shall be the President, if such number be a majority of the whole number of Electors appointed; and if no person have such majority, then from the persons having the highest numbers not exceeding three on the list of those voted for as President, the House of Representatives shall choose immediately, by ballot, the President. But in choosing the President, the votes shall be taken by states, the representation from each state having one vote; a quorum for this purpose shall consist of a member or members from two-thirds of the states, and a majority of all the states shall be necessary to a choice. And if the House of Representatives shall not choose a President whenever the right of choice shall devolve upon them, before the fourth day of March next following, then the Vice-President shall act as President, as in the case of the death or other constitutional disability of the President. The person having the greatest number of votes as Vice-President, shall be the Vice-President, if such number be a majority of the whole number of Electors appointed, and if no person have a majority, then from the two highest numbers on the list, the Senate shall choose the Vice-President; a quorum for the purpose shall consist of two-thirds of the whole number of Senators, and a majority of the whole number shall be necessary to a choice. But no person constitutionally ineligible to the office of President shall be eligible to that of Vice-President of the United States.

Amendment XIII

(1865)

Section 1. Neither slavery nor involuntary servitude, except as a punishment for crime whereof the party shall have been duly convicted, shall exist within the United States, or any place subject to their jurisdiction.

Section 2. Congress shall have power to enforce this article by appropriate legislation.

Amendment XIV

(1868)

Section 1. All persons born or naturalized in the United States, and subject to the jurisdiction thereof, are citizens of the United States and of the State wherein they reside. No State shall make or enforce any law which shall abridge the privileges or immunities of citizens of the United States; nor shall any State deprive any person of life, liberty, or property, without due process of law; nor deny to any person within its jurisdiction the equal protection of the laws.

Section 2. Representatives shall be apportioned among the several States according to their respective numbers, counting the whole number of persons in each State, excluding Indians not taxed. But when the right to vote at any election for the choice of electors for President and Vice President of the United States, Representatives in Congress, the Executive and Judicial officers of a State, or the members of the Legislature thereof, is denied to any of the male inhabitants of such State, being twenty-one years of age, and citizens of the United States, or in any way abridged, except for participation in rebellion, or other crime, the basis of representation therein shall be reduced in the proportion which the number of such male citizens shall bear to the whole number of male citizens twenty-one years of age in such State.

Section 3. No person shall be a Senator or Representative in Congress, or elector of President and Vice President, or hold any office, civil or military, under the United States, or under any State, who, having previously taken an oath, as a member of Congress, or as an officer of the United States, or as a member of any State legislature, or as an executive or judicial officer of any State, to support the Constitution of the United States, shall have engaged in insurrection or rebellion against the same, or given aid or comfort to the enemies thereof. But Congress may by a vote of two-thirds of each House, remove such disability.

Section 4. The validity of the public debt of the United States, authorized by law, including debts incurred for payment of pensions and bounties for services in suppressing insurrection or rebellion, shall not be questioned. But neither the United States nor any State shall assume or pay any debt or obligation incurred in aid of insurrection or rebellion against the United States, or any claim for the loss or emancipation of any slave; but all such debts, obligations and claims shall be held illegal and void.

Section 5. The Congress shall have power to enforce, by appropriate legislation, the provisions of this article.

Amendment XV

(1870)

Section 1. The right of citizens of the United States to vote shall not be denied or abridged by the United States or by any State on account of race, color, or previous condition of servitude.

Section 2. The Congress shall have power to enforce this article by appropriate legislation.

Amendment XVI

(1913)

The Congress shall have power to lay and collect taxes on incomes, from whatever source derived, without apportionment among the several States, and without regard to any census or enumeration.

Amendment XVII

(1913)

The Senate of the United States shall be composed of two Senators from each State, elected by the people thereof, for six years; and each Senator shall have one vote. The electors in each State shall have the qualifications requisite for electors of the most numerous branch of the State legislature.

When vacancies happen in the representation of any State in the Senate, the executive authority of such State shall issue writs of election to fill such vacancies: *Provided*, That the legislature of any State may empower the executive thereof to make temporary appointments until the people fill the vacancies by election as the legislature may direct.

This amendment shall not be so construed as to effect the election or term of any Senator chosen before it becomes valid as part of the Constitution.

Amendment XVIII

(1919)

Section 1. After one year from the ratification of this article the manufacture, sale, or transportation of intoxicating liquors within, the importation thereof into, or the exportation thereof from the United States and all territory subject to the jurisdiction thereof for beverage purposes is hereby prohibited.

Section 2. The Congress and the several States shall have concurrent power to enforce this article by appropriate legislation.

Section 3. This article shall be inoperative unless it shall have been ratified as an amendment to the Constitution by the legislatures of the several States, as provided in the Constitution, within seven years from the date of the submission hereof to the States by the Congress.

Amendment XIX

(1920)

The right of citizens of the United States to vote shall not be denied or abridged by the United States or by any State on account of sex.

Congress shall have power to enforce this article by appropriate legislation.

Amendment XX

(1933)

Section 1. The terms of the President and Vice President shall end at noon on the 20th day of January, and the terms of Senators and Representatives at noon on the 3d day of January, of the years in which such terms would have ended if this article had not been ratified; and the terms of their successors shall then begin.

Section 2. The Congress shall assemble at least once in every year, and such meeting shall begin at noon on the 3d day of January, unless they shall by law appoint a different day.

Section 3. If, at the time fixed for the beginning of the term of the President, the President elect shall have died, the Vice President elect shall become President. If a President shall not have been chosen before the time fixed for the beginning of his term, or if the President elect shall have failed to qualify, then the Vice President elect shall act as President until a President shall have qualified; and the Congress may by law provide for the case wherein neither a President elect nor a Vice President elect shall have qualified, declaring who shall then act as President, or the manner in which one who is to act shall be selected, and such person shall act accordingly until a President or Vice President shall have qualified.

Section 4. The Congress may by law provide for the case of the death of any of the persons from whom the House of Representatives may choose a President whenever the right of choice shall have devolved upon them, and for the case of the death of any of the persons from whom the Senate may choose a Vice President whenever the right of choice shall have devolved upon them.

Section 5. Sections 1 and 2 shall take effect on the 15th day of October following the ratification of this article.

Section 6. This article shall be inoperative unless it shall have been ratified as an amendment to the Constitution by the legislatures of three-fourths of the several States within seven years from the date of its submission.

Amendment XXI

(1933)

Section 1. The eighteenth article of amendment to the Constitution of the United States is hereby repealed.

Section 2. The transportation or importation into any State, territory, or possession of the United States for delivery or use therein of intoxicating liquors, in violation of the laws thereof, is hereby prohibited.

Section 3. This article shall be inoperative unless it shall have been ratified as an amendment to the Constitution by conventions in the several States, as provided in the Constitution, within seven years from the date of the submission hereof to the States by the Congress.

Amendment XXII

(1951)

Section 1. No person shall be elected to the office of the President more than twice, and no person who has held the office of President, or acted as President, for more than two years of a term to which some other person was elected President shall be elected to the office of the President more than once. But this article shall not apply to any person holding the office of President when this article was proposed by the Congress, and shall not prevent any person who may be holding the office of President, or acting as President, during the term within which this article becomes operative from holding the office of President or acting as President during the remainder of such term.

Section 2. This article shall be inoperative unless it shall have been ratified as an amendment to the Constitution by the legislatures of three-fourths of the several States within seven years from the date of its submission to the States by the Congress.

Amendment XXIII

(1961)

Section 1. The District constituting the seat of government of the United States shall appoint in such manner as the Congress may direct:

A number of electors of President and Vice President equal to the whole number of Senators and Representatives in Congress to which the District would be entitled if it were a State, but in no event more than the least populous State; they shall be in addition to those appointed by the States, but they shall be considered, for the purposes of the election of the President and Vice President, to be electors appointed by a State; and they shall meet in the District and perform such duties as provided by the twelfth article of amendment.

Section 2. The Congress shall have power to enforce this article by appropriate legislation.

Amendment XXIV

(1964)

Section 1. The right of citizens of the United States to vote in any primary or other election for President or Vice President, for electors for President or Vice President, or for Senator or Representative in Congress, shall not be denied or abridged by the United States or any State by reason of failure to pay any poll tax or other tax.

Section 2. The Congress shall have the power to enforce this article by appropriate legislation.

Amendment XXV

(1967)

Section 1. In case of the removal of the President from office or his death or resignation, the Vice President shall become President.

Section 2. Whenever there is a vacancy in the office of the Vice President, the President shall nominate a Vice President who shall take office upon confirmation by a majority vote of both Houses of Congress.

Section 3. Whenever the President transmits to the President pro tempore of the Senate and the Speaker of the House of Representatives his written declaration that he is unable to discharge the powers and duties of his office, and until he transmits to them a written declaration to the contrary, such powers and duties shall be discharged by the Vice President as Acting President.

Section 4. Whenever the Vice President and a majority of either the principal officers of the executive departments or such other body as Congress may by law provide, transmit to the President pro tempore of the Senate and the Speaker of the House of Representatives their written declaration that the President is unable to discharge the powers and duties of his office, the Vice President shall immediately assume the powers and duties of the office as Acting President.

Thereafter, when the President transmits to the President pro tempore of the Senate and the Speaker of the House of Representatives his written declaration that no inability exists, he shall resume the powers and duties of his office unless the Vice President and a majority of either the principal officers of the executive department or of such other body as Congress may by law provide, transmit within four days to the President pro tempore of the Senate and the Speaker of the House of Representatives their written declaration that the President is unable to discharge the powers and duties of his office. Thereupon Congress shall decide the issue, assembling within forty-eight hours for that purpose if not in session. If the Congress, within twenty-one days after receipt of the latter written declaration, or, if Congress is not in session, within twenty-one days after Congress is required to assemble, determine by two-thirds vote of both Houses that the President is unable to discharge the powers and duties of his office, the Vice President shall continue to discharge the same as Acting President; otherwise, the President shall resume the powers and duties of his office.

Amendment XXVI

(1971)

Section 1. The right of citizens of the United States, who are 18 years of age or older, to vote, shall not be denied or abridged by the United States or any State on account of age.

Section 2. The Congress shall have the power to enforce this article by appropriate legislation.

Amendment XXVII

(1992)

No law varying the compensation for the services of the Senators and Representatives shall take effect until an election of Representatives shall have intervened.

Volume I in this series introduced five commonly-accepted forms of argument in problems involving interpretation of the Constitution: (1) the broad *structure* of government established by the Constitution, (2) the *historical setting* from which the Constitution emerged and its explication during the ratification process and early implementation, (3) the *text* of the Constitution itself, (4) the *tradition* or historical precedent of understanding the Constitution in a particular matter, and (5) the weight of *judicial precedent* in light of the doctrine of *stare decisis.* Those forms of argument were introduced through materials primarily directed to the structure and power of the federal judiciary. All the same forms of argument are available to address other questions of constitutional law.

Each of the five forms of argument were introduced in Volume I with materials selected to support the different forms of argument, including ratification debates, legislation from the First Congress, letters illustrating early interpretations of the Constitution, and early judicial precedents. The next step beyond understanding the various forms of argument is the identification and use of source material to support one or more arguments.

Exercise 1:

Apply the first four forms of argument to questions regarding the scope of the executive power, particularly with respect to the power to appoint officers and to remove them from office.

(1) If Volume I was assigned prior to this Volume, re-read the description of government prepared in *Volume I, Exercise 1.* Regardless of whether you previously performed that exercise, consider what the *structure* of government suggests is the scope of the President's power of appointment and removal. Conversely, what does the structure of government suggest about the power of Congress to limit the President's ability to appoint or remove officers? What role, if any, does Congress have in the appointment and removal of officers?

(2) (Re)read the U.S. Constitution. What does the *text* of the Constitution provide as to the scope of the President's power of appointment and removal? Conversely, what does the text suggest about the power of Congress to limit the President's ability to appoint or remove officers? What role, if any, does Congress have in the appointment and removal of officers?

(3) (Re)read the statutes enacted by the First Congress creating Departments and establishing the judiciary. Excerpts of these materials appear in Volume I, Chapter 2. The full text of those statutes are included on the DVD-ROM. What does the text of these post-ratification *historical* sources reveal regarding the scope of the President's power of appointment and removal, as derived from the Constitution directly rather than from legislation? Conversely, what do these sources suggest about the power of Congress to limit the President's ability to appoint or remove officers? (Re)read the Act Concerning the District of Columbia and consider whether it changes your view. An excerpt of that Act appears in Volume 1 in connection with *Marbury v. Madison* and the full text of that statute is included on the DVD-ROM.

(4) The DVD-ROM associated with these printed materials contains additional "Tools for Textualists" that may permit you to frame additional textual arguments. You may want to examine the partial concordance or a dictionary that defines terms that may have been more-familiar to those who drafted and ratified the Constitution. If you do so, does the additional information change your view?

(5) The DVD-ROM contains additional "Tools for Originalists" including the text of many essays written to influence the decision of whether to ratify the Constitution. You may want to examine those materials to support an argument

regarding the shared public understanding of the Constitution. If you do so, does the additional information change your view?

(6) The DVD-ROM contains additional "Tools for Traditionalists" including the full text of multiple early treatises on the Constitution. St. George Tucker taught law at William and Mary in the 1790s. He adapted his notes from his course in constitutional law into his *View of the Constitution,* published in 1803. Henry Baldwin, as Associate Justice of the U.S. Supreme Court, published his one volume treatise on constitutional law in 1837. Joseph Story, an Associate Justice of the U.S. Supreme Court, first published his multi-volume treatise on constitutional law in 1833. You may want to examine one or more of those treatises to ascertain the traditional understanding of the appointment and removal powers prior to the controversies addressed in the case law later in this chapter.

MYERS v. UNITED STATES

272 U.S. 52 (1926)

CHIEF JUSTICE TAFT delivered the Opinion of the Court.

This case presents the question whether under the Constitution the President has the exclusive power of removing executive officers of the United States whom he has appointed by and with the advice and consent of the Senate.

[I]

[Frank S.] Myers . . . was on July 21, 1917, appointed by the President, by and with the advice and consent of the Senate, to be a postmaster of the first class at Portland, Or[egon], for a term of four years. On January 20, 1920, Myers' resignation was demanded. He refused the demand. On February 2, 1920, he was removed from office by order of the Postmaster General, acting by direction of the President. . . . He protested to the department against his removal, and continued to do so until the end of his term. . . . On April 21, 1921, he brought this suit in the Court of Claims for his salary from the date of his removal,. . . $8,838.71. In August, 1920, the President made a recess appointment of one Jones, who took office September 19, 1920.

The Court of Claims gave judgment against Myers and this is an appeal from that judgment. The court held that he had lost his right of action because of his delay in suing, citing *Arant v. Lane,* 249 U.S. 367 (1919), *Nicholas v. United States,* 257 U.S. 71 (1921), and *Norris v. United States,* 257 U.S. 77 (1921). These cases show that when a United States officer is dismissed, whether in disregard of the law or from a mistake as to the facts of his case, he must promptly take effective action to assert his rights. But we do not find that Myers failed in this regard. He was constant in his efforts at reinstatement. . . . Indeed, the Solicitor General, while not formally confessing error in this respect, conceded at the bar that no laches has been shown.

By the sixth section of the Act of Congress of July 12, 1876, ch. 179, 19 Stat. 80, 81, under which Myers was appointed with the advice and consent of the Senate as a first-class postmaster, it is provided that:

> Postmasters of the first, second, and third classes shall be appointed and may be removed by the President by and with the advice and consent of the Senate, and shall hold their offices for four years unless sooner removed or suspended according to law.

The Senate did not consent to the President's removal of Myers during his term. If this statute in its requirement that his term should be four years unless sooner removed by the President by and with the advice and consent of the Senate is valid, the appellant, Myers' administratrix, is entitled to recover his unpaid salary for his full term and the judgment of the Court of Claims must be reversed. The government maintains that the requirement is invalid, for the reason that under Article II of the Constitution the President's power of removal of executive officers appointed by him with the advice and consent of the Senate is full and complete without consent of the Senate. If this view is sound, the removal of Myers by the President without the Senate's consent was legal, and the judgment of the Court of Claims against the appellant was correct, and must be affirmed, though for a different reason from [that] given by that court. We are therefore confronted by the constitutional question and cannot avoid it.

[II]

[A]

[The Court's quotation of Article II and Article III, section 1, of the Constitution are omitted.]

The question where the power of removal of executive officers appointed by the President by and with the advice and consent of the Senate was vested, was presented early in the first session of the First Congress. There is no express provision respecting removals in the Constitution, except . . . for removal from office by impeachment. The subject was not discussed in the Constitutional Convention. Under the Articles of Confederation, Congress was given the power of appointing certain executive officers of the Confederation, and during the Revolution and while the articles were given effect, Congress exercised the power of removal. . . .

[B]

Consideration of the executive power was initiated in the Constitutional Convention by the seventh resolution in the Virginia Plan introduced by Edmund Randolph. Max Farrand, Records of the Federal Convention of 1787, p. 21 (1911). It gave to the executive "all the executive powers of Congress under the Confederation," which would seem therefore to have intended to include the power of removal which had been exercised by that body as incident to the power of appointment. As modified by the committee of the whole this resolution declared for a national executive of one person to be elected by the Legislature, with the power to carry into execution the national laws and to appoint to offices in cases not otherwise provided for. It was referred to the committee on detail (1 Max Farrand, *supra*, at 230), which recommended that the executive powers should be vested in a single person to be styled the President of the United States, that he should take care that the laws of the United States be duly and faithfully executed, and that he should commission all the officers of the United States and appoint officers in all cases not otherwise provided by the Constitution (2 Max Farrand, *supra*, at 185). The committee further recommended that the Senate be given power to make treaties, and to appoint ambassadors, and judges of the Supreme Court.

After the great compromises of the convention — the one giving the states equality of representation in the Senate, and the other placing the election of the President, not in Congress, as once voted, but in an electoral college, in which the influence of larger states in the selection would be more nearly in proportion to their population — the smaller states led by Roger Sherman, fearing that under the second compromise the President would constantly be chosen from one of the larger states, secured a change by which the appointment of all officers, which theretofore had been left to the President without restriction, was made subject to the Senate's advice and consent, and the making of treaties and the appointments of ambassadors, public ministers, consuls, and judges of the Supreme Court were transferred to the President, but made subject to the advice and consent of the Senate. . . . Although adopted finally without objection by any state in the last days of the convention, members from the larger states, like [James] Wilson and others, criticized this limitation of the President's power of appointment of executive officers and the resulting increase of the power of the Senate. 2 MAX FARRAND, *supra*, at 537–539.

[C]

[1]

In the House of Representatives of the First Congress, on Tuesday, May 18, 1789, Mr. Madison moved in the committee of the whole that there should be established three executive departments, one of Foreign Affairs, another of the Treasury, and a third of War, at the head of each of which there should be a Secretary, to be appointed by the President by and with the advice and consent of the Senate, and to be removable by the President. The committee agreed to the establishment of a Department of Foreign Affairs, but a discussion ensued as to making the Secretary removable by the President. 1 ANNALS OF CONGRESS 370–371. "The question was now taken and carried, by a considerable majority, in favor of declaring the power of removal to be in the President." 1 ANNALS OF CONGRESS 383.

On June 16, 1789, the House resolved itself into a committee of the whole on a bill proposed by Mr. Madison for establishing an executive department to be denominated the Department of Foreign Affairs, in which the first clause, after stating the title of the officer and describing his duties, had these words "to be removable from office by the President of the United States." 1 ANNALS OF CONGRESS 455. After a very full discussion the question was put; Shall the words "to be removable by the President" be struck out? It was determined in the negative — yeas, 20, nays 34. 1 ANNALS OF CONGRESS 576.

On June 22, in the renewal of the discussion:

> Mr. Benson moved to amend the bill, by altering the second clause, so as to imply the power of removal to be in the President alone. The clause enacted that there should be a chief clerk, to be appointed by the Secretary of Foreign Affairs, and employed as he thought proper, and who, in case of vacancy, should have the charge and custody of all records, books, and papers appertaining to the department. The amendment proposed that the chief clerk, "whenever the said principal officer shall be removed from office by the President of the United States, or in any other case of vacancy," should during such vacancy, have the charge and custody of all records, books, and papers appertaining to the department.

1 ANNALS OF CONGRESS 578.

> Mr. Benson stated that his objection to the clause "to be removable by the President" arose from an idea that the power of removal by the President hereafter might appear to be exercised by virtue of a legislative grant only, and consequently be subjected to legislative instability, when he was well

> satisfied in his own mind that it was fixed by a fair legislative construction of the Constitution.

1 Annals of Congress 579.

> Mr. Benson declared, if he succeeded in this amendment, he would move to strike out the words in the first clause, "to be removable by the President," which appeared somewhat like a grant. Now the mode he took would evade that point and establish a legislative construction of the Constitution. He also hoped his amendment would succeed in reconciling both sides of the House to the decision, and quieting the minds of gentlemen.

1 Annals of Congress 578.

Mr. Madison admitted the objection made by the gentleman near him (Mr. Benson) to the words of the bill. He said:

> They certainly may be construed to imply a legislative grant of power. He wished everything like ambiguity expunged, and the sense of the House explicitly declared, and therefore seconded the motion. Gentlemen have all along proceeded on the idea that the Constitution vests the power in the President, and what arguments were brought forward respecting the convenience or inconvenience of such disposition of the power were intended only to throw light upon what was meant by the compilers of the Constitution. Now, as the words proposed by the gentleman from New York expressed to his mind the meaning of the Constitution, he should be in favor of them, and would agree to strike out those agreed to in the committee.

1 Annals of Congress 578, 579.

Mr. Benson's first amendment to alter the second clause by the insertion of the italicized words, made that clause read as follows:

> That there shall be in the State Department an inferior officer to be appointed by the said principal officer, and to be employed therein as he shall deem proper, to be called the chief clerk in the Department of Foreign Affairs, *and who, whenever the principal officers shall be removed from office by the President of the United States,* or in any other case of vacancy, shall, during such vacancy, have charge and custody of all records, books and papers appertaining to said department.

The first amendment was then approved by a vote of 30 to 18. 1 Annals of Congress 580. Mr. Benson then moved to strike out in the first clause the words "to be removable by the President," in pursuance of the purpose he had already declared, and this second motion of his was carried by a vote of 31 to 19. 1 Annals of Congress 585.

The bill as amended was ordered to be engrossed, and read the third time the next day, June 24, 1789, and was then passed by a vote of 29 to 22, and the clerk was directed to carry the bill to the Senate and desire their concurrence. 1 Annals of Congress 591.

It is very clear from this history that the exact question which the House voted upon was whether it should recognize and declare the power of the President under the Constitution to remove the Secretary of Foreign Affairs without the advice and consent of the Senate. That was what the vote was taken for. Some effort has been made to question whether the decision carries the result claimed for it, but there is not the slightest doubt after an examination of the record, that the vote was, and was intended to be, a legislative declaration that the power to remove officers appointed by the President and the Senate vested in the President alone, and until the Johnson impeachment trial in 1868 its meaning was not doubted, even by those who questioned its soundness.

The discussion was a very full one. Fourteen out of the 29 who voted for the passage of the bill and 11 of the 22 who voted against the bill took part in the discussion. Of the members of the House, 8 had been in the Constitutional Convention, and of these 6 voted with the majority, and 2, Roger Sherman and Elbridge Gerry, the latter of whom had refused to sign the Constitution, voted in the minority. After the bill as amended had passed the House, it was sent to the Senate, where it was discussed in secret session, without report. The critical vote there was upon the striking out of the clause recognizing and affirming the unrestricted power of the President to remove. The Senate divided . . ., requiring the deciding vote of the Vice President, John Adams, who voted against striking out, and in favor of the passage of the bill as it had left the House. . . . The bill, having passed as it came from the House, was signed by President Washington and became a law. Act of July 27, 1789, ch. 4, 1 Stat. 28.

. . . .

[2]

It is convenient in the course of our discussion of this case to review the reasons advanced by Mr. Madison and his associates for their conclusion, supplementing them, so far as may be, by additional considerations which lead this court to concur therein.

[a]

First. Mr. Madison insisted that Article II by vesting the executive power in the President was intended to grant him the power of appointment and removal of executive officers except as thereafter expressly provided in that Article. He pointed out that one of the chief purposes of the convention was to separate the legislative from the executive functions. He said:

> If there is a principle in our Constitution, indeed in any free Constitution more sacred than another, it is that which separates the legislative, executive and judicial powers. If there is any point in which the separation of the legislative and executive powers ought to be maintained with great caution, it is that which relates to officers and offices.

1 Annals of Congress 581.

Their union under the Confederation had not worked well, as the members of the convention knew. Montesquieu's view that the maintenance of independence, as between the legislative, the executive and the judicial branches, was a security for the people had their full approval. 2 Max Farrand, *supra*, at 56 (statement of James Madison); *Kendall v. United States*, 37 U.S. 524, 610 (1838). Accordingly the Constitution was so framed as to vest in the Congress all legislative powers therein granted, to vest in the President the executive power, and to vest in one Supreme Court and such inferior courts as Congress might establish the judicial power. From this division on principle, the reasonable construction of the Constitution must be that the branches should be kept separate in all cases in which they were not expressly blended, and the Constitution should be expounded to blend them no more than it affirmatively requires. 1 Annals of Congress 497 (statement of James Madison). This rule of construction has been confirmed by this court . . . .

The debates in the Constitutional Convention indicated the intention to create a strong executive, and after a controversial discussion the executive power of the government was vested in one person and many of his important functions were specified so as to avoid the humiliating weakness of the Congress during the Revolution and under the Articles of Confederation. 1 MAX FARRAND, *supra*, at 66–67.

Mr. Madison and his associates in the discussion in the House dwelt at length upon the necessity there was for construing Article II to give the President the sole power of removal in his responsibility for the conduct of the executive branch, and enforced this by emphasizing his duty expressly declared in the third section of the Article to "take care that the laws be faithfully executed." 1 ANNALS OF CONGRESS 496, 497 (statement of James Madison).

The vesting of the executive power in the President was essentially a grant of the power to execute the laws. But the President alone and unaided could not execute the laws. He must execute them by the assistance of subordinates. This view has since been repeatedly reaffirmed by this court. . . . As he is charged specifically to take care that they be faithfully executed, the reasonable implication, even in the absence of express words, was that as part of his executive power he should select those who were to act for him under his direction in the execution of the laws. The further implication must be, in the absence of any express limitation respecting removals, that as his selection of administrative officers is essential to the execution of the laws by him, so must be his power of removing those for whom he cannot continue to be responsible. 1 ANNALS OF CONGRESS 474 (statement of Fisher Ames). It was urged that the natural meaning of the term "executive power" granted the President included the appointment and removal of executive subordinates. If such appointments and removals were not an exercise of executive power, what were they? They certainly were not the exercise of legislative or judicial power in government as usually understood.

It is quite true that, in state and colonial governments at the time of the Constitutional Convention, power to make appointments and removals had sometimes been lodged in the Legislatures or in the courts, but such a disposition of it was really vesting part of the executive power in another branch of government. In the British system, the crown, which was the executive, had the power of appointment and removal of executive officers, and it was natural, therefore, for those who framed our Constitution to regard the words "executive power" as including both. *Ex parte Grossman*, 267 U.S. 87 (1925). . . .

The requirement of the second section of Article II that the Senate should advise and consent to the presidential appointments, was to be strictly construed. The words of section 2, following the general grant of executive power under section 1, were either an enumeration and emphasis of specific functions of the executive, not all inclusive, or were limitations upon the general grant of the executive power, and as such, being limitations, should not be enlarged beyond the words used. 1 ANNALS OF CONGRESS 462, 463, 464 (statement of James Madison). The executive power was given in general terms strengthened by specific terms where emphasis was regarded as appropriate, and was limited by direct expressions where limitation was needed, and the fact that no express limit was placed on the power of removal by the executive was convincing indication that none was intended. This is the same construction of Article II as that of Alexander Hamilton quoted *infra*.

[b]

Second. The view of Mr. Madison and his associates was that not only did the grant of executive power to the President in the first section of Article II carry with it the power of removal, but the express recognition of the power of appointment in the second section enforced this view on the well-approved principle of constitutional and statutory construction that the power of removal of executive officers was incident to the power of appointment. It was agreed by the opponents of the bill, with only one or two exceptions, that as a constitutional principle the power of appointment carried with it the power of removal. 1 ANNALS OF CONGRESS 491 (statement of Roger Sherman). . . . The reason for the principle is that those in charge of and responsible for administering functions of government, who select their executive subordinates, need in meeting their responsibility to have the power to remove those whom they appoint.

Under section 2 of Article II, however, the power of appointment by the executive is restricted in its exercise by the provision that the Senate, a part of the legislative branch of the government, may check the action of the executive by rejecting the officers he selects. Does this make the Senate part of the removing power? And this, after the whole discussion in the House is read attentively, is the real point which was considered and decided in the negative by the vote already given.

The history of the clause by which the Senate was given a check upon the President's power of appointment makes it clear that it was not prompted by any desire to limit removals. . . . This was made apparent by the remarks of Abraham Baldwin, of Georgia, in the debate in the First Congress. He had been a member of the Constitutional Convention. In opposing the construction which would extend the Senate's power to check appointments to removals from office, he said:

> I am well authorized to say that the mingling of the powers of the President and Senate was strongly opposed in the convention which had the honor to submit to the consideration of the United States and the different States the present system for the government of the Union. Some gentlemen opposed it to the last, and finally it was the principal ground on which they refused to give it their signature and assent. . . .

1 ANNALS OF CONGRESS 557.

Madison said:

> Perhaps there was no argument urged with more success or more plausibly grounded against the Constitution under which we are now deliberating than that founded on the mingling of the executive and legislative branches of the government in one body. . . .

1 ANNALS OF CONGRESS 380.

. . . The Senate has full power to reject newly proposed appointees whenever the President shall remove the incumbents. Such a check enables the Senate to prevent the filling of offices with bad or incompetent men, or with those against whom there is tenable objection.

The power to prevent the removal of an officer who has served under the President is different from the authority to consent to or reject his appointment. When a nomination is made, it may be presumed that the Senate is, or may become, as well advised as to the fitness of the nominee as the President, but in the nature of things the defects in ability or intelligence or loyalty in the administration of the laws of one who has served as an officer under the President are facts as to which the President, or his trusted subordinates, must be better informed than the Senate, and the power to remove him may therefor be regarded as confined for very sound and practical reasons, to the governmental authority which has administrative control. . . .

Oliver Ellsworth was a member of the Senate of the First Congress, and was active in securing the imposition of the Senate restriction upon appointments by the President. He was the author of the Judiciary Act in that Congress . . . and subsequently Chief Justice of the United States. His view as to the meaning of this Article of the Constitution, upon the point as to whether the advice of the Senate was necessary to removal, like that of Madison, formed and expressed almost in the very atmosphere of the convention, was entitled to great weight. What he said in the discussion in the Senate was reported by Senator William Patterson, as follows:

> The three distinct powers, legislative, judicial and executive should be placed in different hands. . . . To turn a man out of office is an exercise neither of legislative nor judicial power; it is like a tree growing upon land that has been granted. The advice of the Senate does not make the appointment. The President appoints. There are certain restrictions in certain cases, but the restriction is as to the appointment, and not as to the removal.

2 George Bancroft, History of the Constitution of the United States 192.

. . . .

Another argument advanced in the First Congress against implying the power of removal in the President alone from its necessity in the proper administration of the executive power was that all embarrassment in this respect could be avoided by the President's power of suspension of officers, disloyal or incompetent, until the Senate could act.

To this, Mr. Benson said:

> . . . Surely gentlemen do not pretend that the President has the power of suspension granted expressly by the Constitution . . . . If they are willing to allow a power of suspending, it must be because they construe some part of the Constitution in favor of such a grant. The construction in this case must be equally unwarrantable. But admitting it proper to grant this power, what then? When an officer is suspended, does the place become vacant? May the President proceed to fill it up? Or must the public business be likewise suspended? When we say an officer is suspended, it implies that the place is not vacant; but the parties may be heard, and, after the officer is freed from the objections that have been taken to his conduct, he may proceed to execute the duties attached to him. What would be the consequence of this? If the Senate, upon its meeting, were to acquit the officer, and replace him in his station, the President would then have a man forced on him whom he considered as unfaithful . . . . Without a confidence in the Executive Department, its operations would be subject to perpetual discord, and the administration of the government become impracticable.

1 Annals of Congress 506.

Mr. Vining said:

> . . . .
>
> The gentlemen say the President may suspend. They were asked if the Constitution gave him this power any more than the other? Do they contend the one to be a more inherent power than the other? If they do not,

> why shall it be objected to us that we are making a Legislative construction of the Constitution, when they are contending for the same thing?

1 ANNALS OF CONGRESS 512.

In the case before us, the same suggestion has been made for the same purpose, and we think it is well answered in the foregoing. The implication of removal by the President alone is no more a strained construction of the Constitution than that of suspension by him alone and the broader power is much more needed and more strongly to be implied.

[c]

Third. Another argument urged against the constitutional power of the President alone to remove executive officers appointed by him with the consent of the Senate is that, in the absence of an express power of removal granted to the President, power to make provision for removal of all such officers is vested in the Congress by section 8 of Article I.

[i]

Mr. Madison, mistakenly thinking that an argument like this was advanced by Roger Sherman, took it up and answered it as follows:

> He seems to think (if I understand him rightly) that the power of displacing from office is subject to legislative discretion, because, it having a right to create, it may limit or modify as it thinks proper. I shall not say but at first view this doctrine may seem to have some plausibility. But when I consider that the Constitution clearly intended to maintain a marked distinction between the legislative, executive and judicial powers of government, and when I consider that, if the Legislature has a power such as is contended for, they may subject and transfer at discretion powers from one department of our government to another, they may, on that principle, exclude the President altogether from exercising any authority in the removal of officers, they may give to the Senate alone, or the President and Senate combined, they may vest it in the whole Congress, or they may reserve it to be exercised by this House. When I consider the consequences of this doctrine, and compare them with the true principles of the Constitution, I own that I cannot subscribe to it. . . .

1 ANNALS OF CONGRESS 495, 496.

Of the 11 members of the House who spoke from amongst the 22 opposing the bill, 2 insisted that there was no power of removing officers after they had been appointed, except by impeachment, and that the failure of the Constitution expressly to provide another method of removal involved this conclusion. Eight of them argued that the power of removal was in the President and the Senate; that the House had nothing to do with it; and most of these were very insistent in this view in establishing their contention that it was improper for the House to express in legislation any opinion on the constitutional question whether the President could remove without the Senate's consent.

[ii]

The constitutional construction that excludes Congress from legislative power to provide for the removal of superior officers finds support in the second section of

Article II. By it the appointment of all officers, whether superior or inferior, by the President is declared to be subject to the advice and consent of the Senate. In the absence of any specific provision to the contrary, the power of appointment to executive office carries with it, as a necessary incident, the power of removal. Whether the Senate must concur in the removal is aside from the point we now are considering. That point is that by the specific constitutional provision for appointment of executive officers with its necessary incident of removal, the power of appointment and removal is clearly provided for by the Constitution, and the legislative power of Congress in respect to both is excluded save by the specific exception as to inferior officers in the clause that follows. This is "but the Congress may by law vest the appointment of such inferior officers, as they think proper, in the President alone, in the Courts of Law, or in the Heads of Departments." These words, it has been held by this Court, give to Congress the power to limit and regulate removal of such inferior officers by heads of departments when it exercises its constitutional power to lodge the power of appointment with them. *United States v. Perkins,* 116 U.S. 483 (1886). Here then is an express provision introduced in words of exception for the exercise by Congress of legislative power in the matter of appointments and removals in the case of inferior executive officers. The phrase, "But Congress may by law vest," is equivalent to "excepting that Congress may by law vest." By the plainest implication it excludes congressional dealing with appointments or removals of executive officers not falling within the exception and leaves unaffected the executive power of the President to appoint and remove them.

A reference of the whole power of removal to general legislation by Congress is quite out of keeping with the plan of government devised by the framers of the Constitution. It could never have been intended to leave to Congress unlimited discretion to vary fundamentally the operation of the great independent executive branch of government and thus most seriously to weaken it. . . .

[iii]

It is reasonable to suppose also that had it been intended to give Congress power to regulate or control removals in the manner suggested, it would have been included among the specifically enumerated legislative powers in Article I, or in the specified limitations on the executive power in Article II. The difference between the grant of legislative power under Article I to Congress which is limited to the powers therein enumerated, and the more general grant of executive power to the President under Article II is significant. The fact that the executive power is given in general terms strengthened by specific terms where emphasis is appropriate, and limited by direct expressions where limitation is needed, and that no express limit is placed on the power of removal by the executive is a convincing indication that none was intended.

[iv]

It is argued that the denial of the legislative power to regulate removals in some way involves the denial of power to prescribe qualifications for office, or reasonable classification for promotion, and yet that has been often exercised. We see no conflict between the latter power and that of appointment and removal, provided of course that the qualifications do not so limit selection and so trench upon executive choice as to be in effect legislative designation. As Mr. Madison said in the First Congress:

> The powers relative to offices are partly legislative and partly executive. The Legislature creates the office, defines the powers, limits its duration,

> and annexes a compensation. This done, the legislative power ceases. They ought to have nothing to do with designating the man to fill the office. That I conceive to be of an executive nature. . . .

1 ANNALS OF CONGRESS 581, 582.

The legislative power here referred to by Mr. Madison is the legislative power of Congress under the Constitution, not legislative power independently of it. Article II expressly and by implication withholds from Congress power to determine who shall appoint and who shall remove except as to inferior offices. To Congress under its legislative power is given the establishment of offices, the determination of their functions and jurisdiction, the prescribing of reasonable and relevant qualifications and rules of eligibility of appointees, and the fixing of the term for which they are to be appointed and their compensation — all except as otherwise provided by the Constitution.

[v]

An argument in favor of full congressional power to make or withhold provision for removals of all appointed by the President is sought to be found in an asserted analogy between such a power in Congress and its power in the establishment of inferior federal courts. . . . It is clear that the mere establishment of a federal inferior court does not vest that court with all the judicial power of the United States as conferred in the second section of Article III, but only that conferred by Congress specifically on the particular court. It must be limited territorially and in the classes of cases to be heard, and the mere creation of the courts does not confer jurisdiction except as it is conferred in the law of its creation or its amendments. It is said that similarly in the case of the executive power, which is "vested in the President," the power of appointment and removal cannot arise until Congress creates the office and its duties and powers, and must accordingly be exercised and limited only as Congress shall in the creation of the office prescribe.

We think there is little or no analogy between the two legislative functions of Congress in the cases suggested. . . . The duty of Congress . . . to make provision for the vesting of the whole federal judicial power in federal courts, were it held to exist, would be one of imperfect obligation and unenforceable. On the other hand, the moment an office and its powers and duties are created, the power of appointment and removal, as limited by the Constitution, vests in the executive. The functions of distributing jurisdiction to courts and the exercise of it when distributed and vested are not at all parallel to the creation of an office, and the mere right of appointment to, and of removal from, the office which at once attaches to the executive by virtue of the Constitution.

[d]

Fourth. Mr. Madison and his associates pointed out with great force the unreasonable character of the view that the convention intended . . . to give to Congress or the Senate . . . the means of thwarting the executive in the exercise of his great powers . . . by fastening upon him, as subordinate executive officers, men who by their inefficient service under him, by their lack of loyalty to the service, or by their different views of policy might make his taking care that the laws be faithfully executed most difficult or impossible.

As Mr. Madison said in the debate in the First Congress:

> Vest this power in the Senate jointly with the President, and you abolish at once that great principle of unity and responsibility in the executive

> department, which was intended for the security of liberty and the public good. If the President should possess alone the power of removal from office, those who are employed in the execution of the law will be in their proper situation, and the chain of dependence be preserved; the lowest officers, the middle grade, and the highest will depend, as they ought, on the President, and the President on the community.

1 ANNALS OF CONGRESS 499.

Mr. Boudinot of New Jersey said upon the same point:

> . . . Does not this set the Senate over the head of the President? But suppose they shall decide in favor of the officer, what a situation is the President then in, surrounded by officers with whom, by his situation, he is compelled to act, but in whom he can have no confidence . . . ?

1 ANNALS OF CONGRESS 468.

. . . .

Made responsible under the Constitution for the effective enforcement of the law, the President needs as an indispensable aid to meet it the disciplinary influence upon those who act under him of a reserve power of removal. But it is contended that executive officers appointed by the President with the consent of the Senate are bound by the statutory law, and are not to do his will . . . . Each head of a department is and must be the President's alter ego in the matters of that department where the President is required by law to exercise authority.

. . . .

In all such cases, the discretion to be exercised is that of the President in determining the national public interest and in directing the action to be taken by his executive subordinates to protect it. In this field his cabinet officers must do his will. He must place in each member of his official family, and his chief executive subordinates, implicit faith. The moment that he loses confidence in the intelligence, ability, judgment, or loyalty of any one of them, he must have the power to remove him without delay. . . .

. . . There is nothing in the Constitution which permits a distinction between the removal of the head of a department or a bureau, when he discharges a political duty of the President or exercises his discretion, and the removal of executive officers engaged in the discharge of their normal duties. The imperative reasons requiring an unrestricted power to remove the most important of his subordinates in their most important duties must therefore control the interpretation of the Constitution as to all appointed by him.

But this is not to say that there are not strong reasons why the President should have a like power to remove his appointees charged with other duties than those above described. . . . Laws are often passed with specific provisions for adoption of regulations by a department or bureau head to make the law workable and effective. The ability and judgment manifested by the official thus empowered, as well as his energy and stimulation of his subordinates, are subjects which the President must consider and supervise in his administrative control. Finding such officers to be negligent and inefficient, the President should have the power to remove them. Of course there may be duties so peculiarly and specifically committed to the discretion of a particular officer as to raise a question whether the President may overrule or revise the officer's interpretation of his statutory duty in a particular instance. Then there may be duties of a *quasi* judicial character imposed on executive officers and members of executive tribunals whose decisions after hearing affect interests of individuals, the discharge of which the President cannot in a particular case properly influence or control. But even in such a case he may consider the decision after its rendition as a reason for removing the officer, on the ground that the discretion regularly entrusted to that officer by statute has not been on the whole intelligently or wisely exercised. Otherwise he does not discharge his own constitutional duty of seeing that the laws be faithfully executed.

[3]

We have devoted much space to this discussion and decision of the question of the presidential power of removal in the First Congress, not because a congressional conclusion on a constitutional issue is conclusive, but first because of our agreement with the reasons upon which it was avowedly based, second because this was the decision of the First Congress on a question of primary importance in the organization of the government made within two years after the Constitutional Convention and within a much shorter time after its ratification, and third because that Congress numbered among its leaders those who had been members of the convention. It must necessarily constitute a precedent upon which many future laws supplying the machinery of the new government would be based and, if erroneous, would be likely to evoke dissent and departure in future Congresses. . . . [I]t was soon accepted as a final decision of the question by all branches of the government.

. . . .

[a]

A typical case of such acquiescence was that of Alexander Hamilton. In this discussion in the House of Representatives in 1789, Mr. White and others cited the opinion of Mr. Hamilton in respect to the necessity for the consent of the Senate to the removals . . . .

> It has been mentioned as one of the advantages to be expected from the co-operation of the Senate in the business of appointments, that it would contribute to the stability of the administration. The consent of that body would be necessary to displace as well as to appoint. A change of the Chief Magistrate, therefore, would not occasion so violent or so general a revolution in the officers of the government as might be expected if he were the sole disposer of offices.

1 Annals of Congress 456 (quoting Federalist No. 77 (Alexander Hamilton)).

Hamilton changed his view of this matter during his incumbency as Secretary of the Treasury in Washington's Cabinet, as is shown by his view of Washington's first proclamation of neutrality in the war between France and Great Britain. That proclamation was at first criticized as an abuse of executive authority. . . . [Hamilton defended the Administration and based his argument on] Article II of the Constitution . . . and followed exactly the reasoning of Madison and his associates as to the executive power upon which the legislative decision of the First Congress as to Presidential removal depends, and he cites it as authority. He said:

> [Article II] of the Constitution of the United States, section first, establishes this general proposition, that 'the Executive Power shall be vested in a President of the United States of America.'
>
> The same Article, in a succeeding section, proceeds to delineate particular cases of executive power. . . .

> It would not consist with the rules of sound construction, to consider this enumeration of particular authorities as derogating from the more comprehensive grant in the general clause, further than as it may be coupled with express restrictions or limitations, as in regard to the co-operation of the Senate in the appointment of officers and the making of treaties . . . . The difficulty of a complete enumeration of all the cases of executive authority would naturally dictate the use of general terms, and would render it improbable that a specification of certain particulars was designed as a substitute for those terms, when antecedently used. The different mode of expression employed in the Constitution, in regard to the two powers, the legislative and the executive, serves to confirm this inference. In the Article which gives the legislative powers of the government, the expressions are 'All legislative powers herein granted shall be vested in a congress of the United States.' In that which grants the executive power, the expressions are 'The executive power shall be vested in a President of the United States.'
>
> The enumeration ought therefore to be considered, as intended merely to specify the principle articles implied in the definition of executive power; leaving the rest to flow from the general grant of that power, interpreted in conformity with other parts of the Constitution, and with the principles of free government.
>
> The general doctrine of our Constitution then is that the executive power of the nation is vested in the President, subject only to the exceptions and qualifications, which are expressed in the instrument.
>
> . . . This mode of construing the Constitution has indeed been recognized by Congress in formal acts upon full consideration and debate, of which the power of removal from office is an important instance. . . .

7 J.C. HAMILTON, WORKS OF HAMILTON 80, 81 (1851).

[b]

The words of a second great constitutional authority quoted as in conflict with the congressional decision are those of Chief Justice Marshall. They were used by him in *Marbury v. Madison,* 5 U.S. 137 (1803). The judgment in that case is one of the great landmarks in the history of the construction of the Constitution of the United States, and is of supreme authority first in respect to the power and duty of the Supreme Court and other courts to consider and pass upon the validity of acts of Congress enacted in violation of the limitations of the Constitution when properly brought before them in cases in which the rights of the litigating parties require such consideration and decision, and second in respect to the lack of power of Congress to vest in the Supreme Court original jurisdiction to grant the remedy of mandamus in cases in which by the Constitution it is given only appellate jurisdiction. But it is not to be regarded as such authority in respect of the power of the President to remove officials appointed by the advice and consent of the Senate, for that question was not before the court.

[i]

. . . The rule was discharged by the Supreme Court, for the reason that the court had no jurisdiction in such a case to issue a writ of mandamus.

. . . .

. . . [T]he opinion assumed that in the case of a removable office the writ would fail on the presumption that there was in such a case discretion of the appointing power to withhold the commission. And so the Chief Justice proceeded to express an opinion on the question whether the appointee was removable by the President. . . .

There was no answer by Madison to the rule issued in the case. The case went by default. It did not appear even by avowed opposition to the issue of the writ that the President had intervened in the matter at all. It would seem to have been quite consistent with the case as shown that this was merely an arbitrary refusal by the Secretary to perform his ministerial function, and therefore that the expression of opinion that the officer was not removable by the President was necessary, even to the conclusion that a writ in a proper case could issue. . . . [T]he whole statement was certainly *obiter dictum* with reference to the judgment actually reached. The question whether the officer was removable was not argued to the court by any counsel contending for that view. Counsel for [Marbury], who made the only argument, contended that the officer was not removable by the President, because he held a judicial office and under the Constitution could not be deprived of his office for the five years of his term by presidential action. The opinion contains no wider discussion of the question than that quoted above.

. . . .

In such a case we may well recur to the Chief Justice's own language in *Cohens v. Virginia*, 19 U.S. 264 (1821), in which, in declining to yield to the force of his previous language in *Marbury v. Madison*, which was unnecessary to the judgment in that case and was *obiter dictum* . . . [explained that such statements are not binding].

[ii]

The weight of this *dictum* of the Chief Justice as to presidential removal in *Marbury v. Madison*, was considered by this Court in *Parsons v. United States*, 167 U.S. 324 (1897). It was a suit by Parsons against the United States for the payment of the balance due for his salary and fees as United States district attorney for Alabama. He had been commissioned as such under the statute for the term of four years from the date of the commission, subject to the conditions prescribed by law. There was no express power of removal provided. Before the end of the four years he was removed by the President. He was denied recovery.

The language of the court in *Marbury v. Madison*, already referred to, was pressed upon this court to show that Parsons was entitled, against the presidential action of removal, to continue in office. If it was authoritative, and stated the law as to an executive office, it ended the case; but this court did not recognize it as such, for the reason that the Chief Justice's language relied on was not germane to the point decided in *Marbury v. Madison*. If his language was more than a dictum and a decision, then *Parsons'* case overrules it.

Another distinction suggested by Mr. Justice Peckham in *Parsons'* case was that the remarks of the Chief Justice were in reference to an office in the District of Columbia, over which by [Article I, Section 8, Clause 17], Congress had exclusive jurisdiction in all cases, and might not apply to offices outside of the District in respect to which the constant practice and congressional decision had been the other way. 167 U.S. at 335. How much weight should be given to this distinction . . . we need not consider.

[iii]

If the Chief Justice in *Marbury v. Madison* intended to express an opinion for the court inconsistent with the legislative decision of 1789, it is enough to observe that he changed his mind, for otherwise it is inconceivable that he should have written and printed his full account of the discussion and decision in the First Congress and his acquiescence to it [in the biography of George Washington that he authored].

He concluded his account as follows:

> . . . To obviate any misunderstanding of the principle on which the question had been decided, Mr. Benson (later) moved in the House, when the report of the committee of the whole was taken up, to amend the second clause in the bill so as clearly to imply the power of removal to be solely in the President. . . . As the bill passed into a law, it has ever been considered as a full expression of the sense of the Legislature on this important part of the American Constitution.

5 John Marshall, The Life of George Washington 192–200 (1805–07). This language was first published in 1807, four years after the judgment in *Marbury v. Madison*, and the edition was revised by the Chief Justice in 1832. 3 Albert J. Beveridge, The Life of John Marshall 248, 252, 272, 273 (1916).

[D]

[1]

Congress in a number of acts followed and enforced the legislative decision of 1789 for 74 years. In the act of the First Congress, which adapted to the Constitution the ordinance of 1787 for the government of the Northwest Territory, which had provided for the appointment and removal of executive territorial officers by the Congress under the Articles of Confederation, it was said

> in all cases where the United States in Congress assembled, might, by the said ordinance, revoke any commission or remove from any office, the President is hereby declared to have the same powers of revocation and removal.

Ch. 8, 1 Stat. 53. This was approved 11 days after the act establishing the Department of Foreign Affairs and was evidently in form a declaration in accord with the constitutional construction of the latter act. In the provision for the Treasury and War Departments, the same formula was used as occurred in the act creating the Department of Foreign Affairs, but it was omitted from other creative acts only because the decision was thought to be settled constitutional construction. *In re Hennen*, 38 U.S. 230 (1839).

Occasionally we find that Congress thought it wiser to make express what would have been understood. Thus in the Judiciary Act of 1789 we find it provided in section 27:

> That a marshall shall be appointed in and for each district for the term of four years, but shall be removable . . . at pleasure, whose duty it shall be to attend the District and Circuit Courts.

Ch. 20, 1 Stat. 87. That act became a law on September 24. It was formulated by a Senate committee of which Oliver Ellsworth was chairman and which presumably was engaged in drafting it during the time of the congressional debate on removals. Section 35 of the same act provided for the appointment of an attorney for the United States to prosecute crimes and conduct civil actions on behalf of the United States, but nothing was said as to his term of office or of his removal. The difference in the two cases was evidently to avoid any inference from the fixing of the term that a conflict with the legislative decision of 1789 was intended.

In the Act of May 15, 1820, Ch. 102, 3 Stat. 582, Congress provided that thereafter all district attorneys, collectors of customs [and numerous other specified officers], to be appointed under the laws of the United States shall be appointed for the term of four years, but shall be removable from office at pleasure.

It is argued that these express provisions for removal at pleasure indicate that without them no such power would exist in the President. We cannot accede to this view. Indeed the conclusion that they were adopted to show conformity to the legislative decision of 1789 is authoritatively settled by a specific decision of this court.

In *Parsons v. United States,* 167 U.S. 324 (1897), . . . [t]his court held that the [statutory provision at issue] should be construed as having been passed in light of the acquiescence of Congress in the decision of 1789, and therefore included the power of removal by the President, even though the clause for removal was omitted. This reasoning was essential to the conclusion reached and makes the construction by this court of the act of 1820 authoritative. . . .

> The provision for a removal from office at pleasure was not necessary for the exercise of that power by the President, because of the fact that he was then regarded as being clothed with such power in any event. Considering the construction of the Constitution in this regard as given by the Congress of 1789, and having in mind the constant and uniform practice of the government in harmony with such construction, we must construe this act as providing absolutely for the expiration of the term of office at the end of four years, and not as giving a term that shall last, at all events, for that time, and we think the provision that the officials were removable from office at pleasure was but a recognition of the construction thus almost universally adhered to and acquiesced in as to the power of the President to remove.

167 U.S. at 339.

In the Act of July 17, 1862, ch. 200, § 17, 12 Stat. 596, Congress actually requested the President to make removals in the following language:

> The President of the United States be, and hereby is, authorized and requested to dismiss and discharge from the military service . . . any officer for any cause which, in his judgment, either renders such officer unsuitable for, or whose dismiss[al] would promote, the public service.

Attorney General Devens (15 Op. A.G. 421) said of this act that, so far as it gave authority to the President, it was simply declaratory of the long-established law; that the force of the act was to be found in the word "requested," by which it was intended to re-enforce strongly this power in the hands of the President at a great crisis of the state — a comment by the Attorney General which was expressly approved by this court in *Blake v. United States,* 103 U.S. 227, 234 (1880).

The acquiescence in the legislative decision of 1789 for nearly three-quarters of a century by all branches of the government has been affirmed by this court in unmistakable terms. In *Parsons v. United States* . . . this court . . . said:

> Many distinguished lawyers originally had very different opinions in regard to this power from the one arrived at by this Congress, but when the question was alluded to in the after years they recognized that the decision of Congress in 1789, and the universal practice of the government under it, had settled the question beyond any power of alteration.

167 U.S. at 330.

[2]

We find this confirmed by Chancellor Kent's and Mr. Justice Story's comments. . . .

. . . .

In his Commentaries, referring to this question, the Chancellor said:

> This question has never been made the subject of judicial decision; and the construction given to the Constitution in 1789 has continued to rest on this loose, incidental, declaratory opinion of Congress, and the sense and practice of government since that time. It may now be considered as firmly and definitely settled, and there is good sense and practical utility in the construction.

1 JAMES KENT, COMMENTARIES ON AMERICAN LAW 310 (1830).

. . . .

[Justice Story, in his treatise first published in 1833, found] that until . . . the administration of President Jackson, the power of unrestricted removal had been exercised by all the Presidents, but that moderation and forbearance had been shown; that under President Jackson, however, an opposite course had been pursued extensively and brought again the executive power of removal to a severe scrutiny. The learned author then says:

> If there has been any aberration from the true constitutional exposition of the power of removal (which the reader must decide for himself), it will be difficult, and perhaps impracticable, after 40 years' experience, to recall the practice to correct theory. But, at all events, it will be a consolation to those who love the Union, and honor a devotion to the patriotic discharge of duty, that in regard to 'inferior officers' (which appellation probably includes ninety-nine out of a hundred of the lucrative offices in the government), the remedy for any permanent abuse is still within the power of Congress, by the simple expedient of requiring the consent of the Senate to removals in such cases.

2 JOSEPH STORY, COMMENTARIES ON THE CONSTITUTION OF THE UNITED STATES § 1544.

In an article by Mr. Fish contained in an American Historical Association Reports, for 1899, removals from office, not including presidential removals in the Army and the Navy, in the administrations from Washington to Johnson are stated to have been as follows . . . . These, we may infer, were all made in conformity to the legislative decision of 1789.

[3]

Mr. [Daniel] Webster is cited as opposed to the views of the decision of the First Congress. His views were evoked by the controversy between the Senate and

President Jackson. The alleged general use of patronage for political purposes by the President and his dismissal of Duane, Secretary of the Treasury, without reference to the Senate, upon Duane's refusal to remove government deposits from the United States Bank, awakened bitter criticism in the Senate, and led to an extended discussion of the power of removal by the President. In a speech, May 7, 1834, . . . Mr. Webster asserted that the power of removal, without the consent of the Senate, was in the President alone, according to the established construction of the Constitution, and that Duane's dismissal could not be justly said to be a usurpation. 4 DANIEL WEBSTER, THE WORKS OF DANIEL WEBSTER 103–105 (1857). A year later, in February, 1835, Mr. Webster seems to have changed his views somewhat . . . . He closed his speech thus:

> But I think the decision of 1789 has been established by practice, and recognized by subsequent laws, as the settled construction of the Constitution, and that it is our duty to act upon the case accordingly for the present, without admitting that Congress may not, hereafter, if necessity shall require it, reverse the decision of 1789.

Id. at 179, 198.

Mr. Webster denied that the vesting of the executive power in the President was a grant of power. It amounted, he said, to no more than merely naming the department. Such a construction, although having the support of as great an expounder of the Constitution as Mr. Webster, is not in accord with the usual canon of interpretation of that instrument, which requires that real effect should be given to all the words it uses. . . . Nor can we concur in Mr. Webster's apparent view that when Congress, after full consideration and with the acquiescence and long practice of all the branches of the government, has established the construction of the Constitution, it may by its mere subsequent legislation reverse such construction. It is not given power by itself thus to amend the Constitution. It is not unjust to note that Mr. Webster's final conclusion on this head was after pronounced political controversy with General Jackson, which he concedes may have affected his judgment and attitude on the subject.

Mr. [Henry] Clay and Mr. [John C.] Calhoun, acting upon a like impulse, also vigorously attacked the decision, but no legislation of any kind was adopted in that period to reverse the established constitutional construction, while its correctness was vigorously asserted and acted on by the executive. . . .

In *Ex parte Hennen,* 38 U.S. 230 (1839), the prevailing effect of the legislative decision of 1789 was fully recognized. The question there was of the legality of removal from office by a United States District Court of its clerk, appointed by it under Section 7 of the Judiciary Act [of 1789]. The case was ably argued and the effect of the legislative decision of the First Congress was much discussed. The court said:

> The Constitution is silent with respect to the power of removal from office, where the tenure is not fixed. . . . It cannot, for a moment, be admitted that it was the intention of the Constitution that those offices which are denominated inferior offices should be held during life. And if removable at pleasure, by whom is such removal to be made? In the absence of all constitutional provision or statutory regulation, it would seem to be a sound and necessary rule to consider the power of removal as incident to the power of appointment. . . . No one denied the power of the President and Senate, jointly, to remove, where the tenure of the office was not fixed by the Constitution, which was a full recognition of the principle that the power of removal was incident to the power of appointment. But it was very

> early adopted as the practical construction of the Constitution that this power was vested in the President alone. And such would appear to have been the legislative construction of the Constitution. . . .

38 U.S. at 258–59.

[4]

The legislative decision of 1789 and this court's recognition of it was followed in 1842 by Attorney General Legare in the administration of President Tyler (4 Op. A.G. 1), in 1847 by Attorney General Clifford in the administration of President Polk (4 Op. A.G. 603), by Attorney General Crittenden in the administration of President Fillmore (5 Op. A.G. 288, 290), and by Attorney General Cushing in the Administration of President Buchanan (6 Op. A.G. 4), all of whom delivered opinions of a similar tenor.

[E]

[1]

[The Court addressed congressional creation of "courts" outside the scope of Article III staffed by "judges" who do not receive the constitutionally-guaranteed tenure of judges commissioned to serve on courts created under Article III.] The argument is that, as there is no express constitutional restriction as to the removal of such judges, they come within the same class as executive officers, and that statutes and practice in respect to them may properly be used to refute the authority of the legislative decision of 1789 and acquiescence therein.

The fact seems to be that judicial removals were not considered in the discussion in the First Congress, and that the First Congress (*see* Act of Aug. 7, 1789, ch. 8, 1 Stat. 50–53) and succeeding Congresses until 1804, assimilated the judges appointed for the territories to those appointed under Article III, and provided life tenure for them, while other officers of those territories were appointed for a term of years unless sooner removed. . . . In *American Insurance Co. v. Canter,* 26 U.S. 511 (1828), it was held that the territorial judges were not judges of constitutional courts, on which the judicial power conferred by the Constitution on the general government could be deposited. After some 10 or 15 years, the judges in some territories were appointed for a term of years, and the Governor and other officers were appointed for a term of years unless sooner removed. . . .

After 1804 removals were made by the President of territorial judges appointed for terms of years before the ends of their terms. They were sometimes suspended and sometimes removed. Between 1804 and 1867 there were 10 removals of such judges . . . . The Executive Department seemed then to consider that territorial judges were subject to removal just as if they had been executive officers under the legislative decision of 1789. . . . Since 1867, territorial judges have been removed by the President . . . .

The question of the President's power to remove such a judge . . . came before this court in *United States v. Guthrie,* 58 U.S. 284 (1854). The relator, Goodrich, who had been removed by the President from his office as a territorial judge, sought by mandamus to compel the Secretary of the Treasury to draw his warrant for the relator's salary for the remainder of his term after removal . . . . This court did not decide this issue, but held that it had no power to issue a writ of mandamus in such a case. . . .

In . . . *McAllister v. United States*, 141 U.S. 174 (1891), a judge of the District Court of Alaska it was held could be deprived of a right to salary as such by his suspension under Revised Statutes § 1768. That section gave the President in his discretion authority to suspend any civil officer appointed by and with advice and consent of the Senate, except judges of the courts of the United States . . . . It was held that the words "except judges of the courts of the United States" applied to judges appointed under Article III and did not apply to territorial judges, and that the President under section 1768 had power to suspend a territorial judge . . . and no recovery could be had for salary during that suspended period. Mr. Justice Field with Justices Gray and Brown dissented on the ground that in England . . . it had become established law that judges should hold their offices independent of executive removal, and that our Constitution expressly makes such limitation as to the only judges specifically mentioned in it, and should be construed to carry such limitation as to other judges appointed under its provisions.

. . . .

The questions, first, whether a judge appointed by the President with the consent of the Senate under an act of Congress, not under authority of Article III of the Constitution, can be removed by the President alone without the consent of the Senate; second, whether the legislative decision of 1789 covers such a case; and, third, whether Congress may provide for his removal in some other way — present considerations different from those which apply in the removal of executive officers, and therefore we do not decide them.

[2]

We come now to consider an argument . . . that this case concerns only the removal of . . . an inferior officer, and that such an office was not included within the legislative decision of 1789, which related only to superior officers to be appointed by the President by and with the advice and consent of the Senate. This, it is said, is the distinction which Chief Justice Marshall had in mind in *Marbury v. Madison* in the language already discussed in respect to the President's power of removal of a District of Columbia justice of the peace appointed and confirmed for a term of years. . . . It cannot be certainly affirmed whether the conclusion there stated was based on a dissent from the legislative decision of 1789, or on the fact that the office was created under the special power of Congress exclusively to legislate for the District of Columbia, or on the fact that the office was a judicial one, or on the circumstance that it was an inferior office. In view of the doubt as to what was really the basis of the remarks relied on and their *obiter dictum* character, they can certainly not be used to give weight to the argument that the 1789 decision only related to superior officers.

The very heated discussions during General Jackson's administration, except as to the removal of Secretary Duane, related to . . . the distribution of offices, which were most of them inferior offices, and it was the operation of the legislative decision of 1789 upon the power of removal of incumbents of such offices that led the General to refuse to comply with the request of the Senate that he give his reasons for the removals therefrom. It was to such inferior offices that Chancellor Kent's . . . commentaries on the decision of 1789 [applied, specifically] with reference to the removal of United States marshals. It was such inferior offices that Mr. Justice Story conceded to be covered by the legislative decision in his treatise on the Constitution . . . . It was with reference to removals from such inferior offices that the already cited opinions of the Attorneys General, in which the legislative decision of 1789 was referred to as controlling authority, were delivered. . . . Finally,

Parsons' case, where it was the point in judgment, conclusively establishes for this court that the legislative decision of 1789 applied to a United States attorney, an inferior officer.

It is further pressed on us that, even though the legislative decision of 1789 included inferior officers, yet under the legislative power given Congress with respect to such officers it might directly legislate as to the method of their removal without changing their method of appointment by the President with the consent of the Senate. We do not think the language of the Constitution justifies such a contention.

. . . .

. . . In *United States v. Perkins,* 116 U.S. 483 (1886), a cadet engineer, a graduate of the Naval Academy, brought suit to recover his salary for the period after his removal by the Secretary of the Navy. It was decided that his right was established . . . . The Court of Claims . . . said:

> Whether or not Congress can restrict the power of removal incident to the power of appointment of those officers who are appointed by the President . . . does not arise in this case and need not be considered. We have no doubt that, when Congress by law vests the appointment of inferior officers in the heads of departments it may limit and restrict the power of removal as it deems best for the public interest. . . . The head of a department has no constitutional prerogative of appointment to offices independently of the legislation of Congress, and by such legislation he must be governed, not only in making appointments, but in all that is incident thereto.

This language of the Court of Claims was approved by this court and the judgment was affirmed.

. . . The authority of Congress given by the excepting clause to vest the appointment of such inferior officers in the heads of departments carries with it authority incidentally to invest the heads of departments with power to remove. It has been the practice of Congress to do so and this court has recognized that power. The court also has recognized in the *Perkins* case that Congress, in committing the appointment of such inferior officers to the heads of departments, may prescribe incidental regulations controlling and restricting the latter in the exercise of the power of removal. . . .

Assuming, then, the power of Congress to regulate removals as incidental to the exercise of its constitutional power to vest appointments of inferior officers in the heads of departments, certainly so long as Congress does not exercise that power, the power of removal must remain where the Constitution places it, with the President, as part of the executive power . . . .

Whether the action of Congress in removing the necessity for the advice and consent of the Senate and putting the power of appointment in the President alone would make his power of removal in such case any more subject to Congressional legislation than before is a question this court did not decide in the *Perkins* case. . . . [I]t is not before us and we do not decide it.

. . . If [Congress] does not choose to entrust the appointment of such inferior officers to less authority than the President with the consent of the Senate, it has no power of providing for their removal. . . .

[F]

[1]

. . . .

We come now to a period in the history of the government when both houses of Congress attempted to reverse this constitutional construction, and to subject the power of removing executive officers appointed by the President and confirmed by the Senate to the control of the Senate, indeed finally to the assumed power in Congress to place the removal of such officers anywhere in the government.

This reversal grew out of the serious political difference between . . . Congress and President [Andrew] Johnson. There was a two-thirds majority of the republican party, in control of each house of Congress, which resented what it feared would be Mr. Johnson's obstructive course in the enforcement of the reconstruction measures in respect to the states whose people had lately been at war against the national government. This led the two houses to enact legislation to curtail the then acknowledged powers of the President. . . . The real challenge to the decision of 1789 was begun by the Act of July 13, 1866 forbidding dismissals of Army and Navy officers in time of peace without a sentence by court-martial, which this court . . . attributed to the growing difference between President Johnson and Congress.

Another measure having the same origin and purpose was a rider of the Army Appropriation Act of March 2, 1867 . . . which . . . directed that all orders relating to military operations by the President or Secretary of War should be issued through the General of the Army, who should not be removed, suspended, or relieved of command, or assigned to duty elsewhere, except at his own request, without the previous approval of the Senate . . . .

But the chief legislation in support of the reconstruction policy of Congress was the Tenure of Office Act of March 2, 1867, providing that all officers appointed by and with the consent of the Senate should hold their offices until their successors should have in like manner been appointed and qualified; that certain heads of departments, including the Secretary of War, should hold their offices during the term of the President by whom appointed and one month thereafter, subject to removal by consent of the Senate. The Tenure of Office Act was vetoed, but it was passed over the veto. The House of Representatives preferred articles of impeachment against President Johnson for refusal to comply with, and for conspiracy to defeat, the legislation above referred to, but he was acquitted for lack of a two-thirds vote for conviction in the Senate.

. . . .

The extreme provisions of all this legislation were a full justification for the considerations, so strongly advanced by Mr. Madison and his associates in the First Congress, for insisting that the power of removal of executive officers by the President alone was essential in the division of powers between the executive and legislative bodies. It exhibited in a clear degree the paralysis to which a partisan Senate and Congress could subject the executive arm, and destroy the principle of executive responsibility, and separation of the powers sought for by the framers of our government, if the President had no power of removal save by consent of the Senate. It was an attempt to redistribute the powers and minimize those of the President.

[2]

After President Johnson's term ended, the injury and invalidity of the Tenure of Office Act in its radical innovation were immediately recognized by the executive and objected to. General Grant, succeeding Mr. Johnson in the presidency, earnestly recommended in his first message the total repeal of the act . . . .

While in response to this a bill for repeal of that act passed the House, it failed in the Senate, and, though the law was changed, it still limited the presidential power of removal. The feeling growing out of the controversy with President Johnson retained the act on the statute book until 1887, when it was repealed. Ch. 353, 24 Stat. 500. During this interval, on June 8, 1872, Congress passed an act reorganizing and consolidating the Post Office Department, and provided that the Postmaster General and his three assistants should be appointed by the President by and with the advice and consent of the Senate, and might be removed in the same manner. Ch. 335, § 2, 17 Stat. 284. In 1876 the act here under discussion was passed, making the consent of the Senate necessary both to the appointment and removal of first, second, and third class postmasters. Ch. 179, § 6, 19 Stat. 80.

In the same interval, in March, 1886, President Cleveland, in discussing the requests which the Senate had made for his reasons for removing officials, and the assumption that the Senate had the right to pass upon those removals and thus to limit the power of the President, said:

> I believe the power to remove or suspend such officials is vested in the President alone by the Constitution, which in express terms provides that "the executive power shall be vested in a President of the United States of America," and that "he shall take care that the laws be faithfully executed."
>
> . . . When the Constitution by express provision superadded to its legislative duties the right to advise and consent to appointments to office and to sit as a court of impeachment, it conferred upon that body all the control and regulation of executive action supposed to be necessary for the safety of the people; and this express and special grant of such extraordinary powers . . . should be held, under a familiar maxim of construction, to exclude every other right of interference with executive functions.

11 Messages and Papers of the Presidents 4964.

[3]

[a]

The attitude of the Presidents on this subject has been unchanged and uniform to the present day whenever an issue has clearly been raised. [President Wilson in 1920 and President Coolidge in 1924, both reaffirmed Presidential power of removal in formal messages to Congress.]

[b]

In spite of the foregoing presidential declarations, it is contended that, since the passage of the Tenure of Office Act, there has been general acquiescence by the executive in the power of Congress to forbid the President alone to remove executive officers, an acquiescence which has changed any formerly accepted constitutional construction to the contrary. Instances are cited of the signed approval by President Grant and other Presidents of legislation in derogation of such construction. We think these are all to be explained, not by acquiescence therein, but by reason of the otherwise valuable effect of the legislation approved. Such is doubtless the explanation of the executive approval of the act of 1876, which we are considering, for it was an appropriation act on which the section here in question was imposed as a rider.

[i]

In the use of congressional legislation to support or change a particular construction of the Constitution by acquiescence, its weight for the purpose must depend not only upon the nature of the question, but also upon the attitude of the executive and judicial branches of the government, as well as upon the number of instances in the execution of the law in which opportunity for objection in the courts or elsewhere is afforded. When instances which actually involve the question are rare or have not in fact occurred, the weight of the mere presence of acts on the statute book for a considerable time as showing general acquiescence in the legislative assertion of a questioned power is minimized. No instance is cited to us where any question has arisen respecting a removal of a Postmaster General or one of his assistants. The President's request for resignation of such offices is generally complied with. The same thing is true of the postmasters. There have been many executive removals of them and but few protests or objections. Even when there has been a refusal by a postmaster to resign, removal by the President has been followed by a nomination of a successor and the Senate's confirmation has made unimportant the inquiry as to the necessity for the Senate's consent to the removal.

[ii]

Other acts of Congress are referred to which contain provisions said to be inconsistent with the 1789 decision. Since the provision for an Interstate Commerce Commission in 1887, many administrative boards have been created whose members are appointed by the President, by and with the advice and consent of the Senate, and in the statutes creating them have been provisions for the removal of the members for specified causes. Such provisions are claimed to be inconsistent with the independent power of removal by the President. This, however, is shown to be unfounded by the case of *Shurtleff v. United States,* 189 U.S. 311 (1903). That concerned an act creating a board of general appraisers . . . and provided for their removal for inefficiency, neglect of duty, or malfeasance in office. The President removed an appraiser without notice or hearing. It was forcibly contended that the affirmative language of the statute implied the negative of the power to remove except for cause and after a hearing. . . . [T]he court held that, in the absence of constitutional or statutory provision otherwise, the President could by virtue of his general power of appointment remove an officer . . . notwithstanding specific provisions for his removal for cause, on the ground that the power of removal inhered in the power to appoint. This is an indication that many of the statutes cited are to be reconciled to the unrestricted power of the President to remove, if he chooses to exercise his power.

There are other later acts pointed out in which doubtless the inconsistency with the independent power of the President to remove is clearer, but these cannot be said to have really received the acquiescence of the executive branch of the government. Whenever there has been a real issue made in respect to the question of presidential removals, the attitude of the executive in Congressional message has been clear and positive against the validity of such legislation. . . .

[G]

The fact seems to be that all departments of the government have constantly had in mind, since the passage of the Tenure of Office Act, that the question of power of removal by the President of officers appointed by him with the Senate's consent has not been settled adversely to the legislative action of 1789, but, in spite of congressional action, has remained open until the conflict should be subjected to judicial investigation and decision.

The actions of this court cannot be said to constitute assent to a departure from the legislative decision of 1789, when the *Parsons* and *Shurtleff* cases, one decided in 1897, and the other in 1903, are considered for they certainly leave the question open. . . . Those cases indicate no tendency to depart from the view of the First Congress. This court has since the Tenure of Office Act manifested an earnest desire to avoid a final settlement of the question until it should be inevitably presented, as it is here.

An argument . . . has been made against our conclusion . . . that it will open the door to a reintroduction of the spoils system. The evil of the spoils system aimed at in the Civil Service Law and its amendments is in respect to inferior officers. It has never been attempted to extend that law beyond them. . . . Reform in the federal civil service was begun by the Civil Service Act of 1883. It has been developed from that time, so that the classified service now includes a vast majority of all the civil officers. . . . The independent power of removal by the President alone under present conditions works no practical interference with the merits system. Political appointments of inferior officers are still maintained in one important class, that of the first, second, and third class postmasters, collectors of internal revenue, marshals, collectors of customs, and other officers of that kind distributed through the country. They are appointed by the President with the consent of the Senate. It is the intervention of the Senate in their appointment . . . which prevents their classification into the merit system. If such appointments were vested in the heads of departments to which they belong, they could be entirely removed from politics, and that is what a number of Presidents have recommended. . . .

. . . This court has repeatedly laid down the principle that a contemporaneous legislative exposition of the Constitution, when the founders of our government and framers of our Constitution were actively participating in public affairs, acquiesced in for a long term of years, fixes the construction to be given its provisions. *See Stuart v. Laird*, 5 U.S. 299 (1803); . . . *Cohens v. Virginia*, 19 U.S. 264 (1821). . . .

We are now asked to set aside this construction thus buttressed and adopt an adverse view, because the Congress of the United States did so during a heated political difference of opinion between the then President and the majority leaders of Congress over the reconstruction measures adopted as a means of restoring to their proper status the states which attempted to withdraw from the Union at the time of the Civil War. The extremes to which the majority in both Houses carried legislative measures in that matter are now recognized by all . . . . Without animadverting on the character of the measures taken, we are certainly justified in saying that they should not be given the weight affecting proper constitutional construction to be accorded to that reached by the First Congress . . . during a political calm and acquiesced in by the whole government for three-quarters of a century, especially when the new construction contended for has never been acquiesced in by either the executive or the judicial departments. . . .

For the reasons given, we must therefore hold that the provisions of the law of 1876 by which the unrestricted power of removal of first-class postmasters is denied to the President is in violation of the Constitution and invalid. This leads to an affirmance of the judgment of the Court of Claims.

. . . .

Judgment affirmed.

[The dissenting opinions of Justices McReynolds, Brandeis, and Holmes are omitted.]

Exercise 2:

Consider how the Court in *Myers v. United States* resolves questions regarding the scope of the executive power, particularly with respect to the power to appoint officers and to remove them from office. In addition to the doctrinal answers, note the forms of argument and supporting sources the Court found persuasive. Specifically, consider:

(1) In Part I, the Court summarized the factual and procedural background of this dispute. In doing so, the Court observed that the Court of Claims ruled against Myers on the basis of his delay in seeking judicial relief. The Supreme Court summarized its precedents as establishing "that when a United States officer is dismissed, . . . he must promptly take action to assert his rights." President Jefferson took office on March 4, 1801, Marbury never entered into service as a justice of the peace, and Marbury did not file in the Supreme Court his request for his commission until December 17, 1801. Does that chronology suggest an additional basis for denying the requested writ in that case without reaching any of the constitutional issues?

(2) In Part I, the Supreme Court found that the Court of Claims was in error in determining that Myers failed to promptly and diligently assert his rights. In light of the fact that the Court of Claims based its judgment on that erroneous determination, how could the Supreme Court affirm? Should the Supreme Court have taken a different approach to the case?

(3) In Part II(A), the Supreme Court asserted that the Constitution contains no express provision governing removals from office other than the provision for impeachment. Is that correct? What inference regarding removal should be drawn based upon the impeachment provision? Are there any other textual provisions that support an inference regarding the removability of officers other than judges appointed to Article III courts?

(4) In Part II(B), the Supreme Court addressed the drafting history of Article II of the Constitution. What light, if any, does the drafting history shed on the meaning of the President's powers and the authority of Congress to limit those powers? What weight should be given to the drafting history?

(5) In Part II(C)(1), the Supreme Court reviewed the actions of the First Congress in establishing the first executive department and the first principal officer of an executive department. Is it clear that Congress declared its interpretation of the Constitution as vesting in the President the unilateral and unlimited power to remove the Secretary of Foreign Affairs? Or, is there some other explanation for the historical materials? If the First Congress did so express its understanding of the Constitution, should that view fix the meaning of the Constitution? Why or why not?

(6) Assume that when, in September 1789, Congress expanded the duties of the Secretary of Foreign Affairs and his executive department — which resulted in the more-appropriate name "State" being substituted for "Foreign Affairs" — Con-

gress expressly provided that the Secretary would "serve in office for a period of two years unless previously removed by the President with the concurrence of the Senate." If several years later, President Adams unilaterally removed from office his Secretary of State, Timothy Pickering, less than two years into Pickering's term, would Pickering have a claim to his salary for the unexpired term?

(7) Does the answer to the previous question depend at all on whether President Washington signed the legislation rather than it being passed over his veto? Why or why not?

(8) According to the historical materials summarized by the Court in Parts II(C)(2)(a)–(b) of its opinion, did the Framers (or, at least, the Framers as understood by the First Congress) draw any pertinent distinction between the President's power unilaterally to remove the Secretary of State and:

(a) any other principal, executive officer?

(b) any other principal officer other than judges appointed to Article III courts?

(c) any inferior, executive officer?

(9) In Part II(C)(2)(a) of its opinion, the Court asserted that "the reasonable construction of the Constitution must be that the branches should be kept separate in all cases in which they were not expressly blended, and the Constitution should be expounded to blend them no more than it affirmatively requires." Do you agree with that principle of construction?

(10) In the final paragraph of Part II(C)(2)(a), the Supreme Court referenced James Madison's explanation in the First Congress of the meaning of the first sentence of Article II in conjunction with more specific provisions in subsequent sections of that Article. What are the implications of that explanation for unenumerated or "inherent" powers of the President?

(11) In Part II(C)(2)(c) of its opinion, the Supreme Court addressed the argument that the "greater power" to create an office implies the "lesser power" to prescribe conditions for removal from office. Is the lesser power implied? If so, does it not equally follow that the power to dictate the mode of appointment flows from the power to create the office? Under that reasoning, could Congress create the office of Commissioner of the Internal Revenue and vest appointment to that office in the Speaker of the House of Representatives? Why or why not?

(12) Does the "greater power" to create an office imply the "lesser power" to prescribe qualifications for the office? Could Congress create the office of Attorney General and require that only individuals admitted to the practice of law for twenty years be eligible to fill the office? If so, could Congress create a group of offices (for example, all the judgeships for the U.S. Supreme Court) and, in order to "moderate" the partisan influence in selecting officers, require that the President name no more than a bare majority of nominees of the same political party? Or, to limit geographic concentration of power, could Congress require that no two of the group of officers reside in the same State? Would it make any difference if the offices were not in the Article III judiciary?

(13) In Part II(C)(2)(c)(ii) of its opinion, the Court drew a distinction between the power of Congress to limit removal of inferior officers appointed by the President with Senate confirmation and the power of Congress to limit removal of inferior officers the appointment of whom Congress vested in the "Heads of Departments." Does that distinction follow from the constitutional text? Does that distinction find support in the views of the Framers and/or the views of the First Congress?

(14) Based on the rationale of Part II(C)(2)(c)(ii) of the Court's opinion, would Congress have the authority to limit the removal of inferior officers appointed by the President alone, without Senate confirmation? Why or why not?

(15) In Part II(C)(2)(c)(iv) of its opinion, the Court quoted Madison regarding the power of Congress to play a role in selecting the individual to fill an office it creates. Assume Congress enacted legislation prohibiting the President from appointing to any office a member of his own family, expressly defining the relations so disqualified. Should the Court enforce such a prohibition?

(16) In Part II(C)(2)(c)(v) of its opinion, the Court rejected an analogy. Should it have done so? Assume that the First Congress failed to establish any judicial offices, even rejecting any obligation to provide for the Supreme Court's number of judges, jurisdiction, places of meeting, or compensation. Would Congress have violated some obligation? In what manner, if any, would that obligation have been enforceable? In what way are issues of appointment and removal of officers, other than judges to Article III courts, any more enforceable against Congress?

(17) In Part II(C)(2)(d) of its opinion, the Court explored some policy reasons articulated by Madison (and others) for finding unlimited and unilateral power of removal in the President. Do those reasons support any pertinent distinction between the President's power unilaterally to remove the Secretary of State and:

(a) any other principal, executive officer?

(b) any other principal officer other than judges appointed to Article III courts?

(c) any inferior, executive officer?

(18) Do the reasons considered in Question 17 support any pertinent distinction between inferior officers appointed by the President with the advice and consent of the Senate and:

(a) inferior officers appointed by the President alone?

(b) inferior officers appointed by the Heads of Departments?

(19) In Part II(C)(2)(d) of its opinion, the Court referred to "executive officers and members of executive tribunals" who have "duties of a *quasi* judicial character." Are officers with such duties properly classified as "executive"? Or, should all officers engaged in such activities be classified as part of the judiciary? If such officers are part of the judiciary, must they be provided with the tenure and other protections specified in Article III? If so, no issue would arise regarding Presidential removal of such officers. On the other hand, if such officers are not considered part of the judiciary and not protected as specified in Article III, executive officers are performing adjudication. How is that fact consistent with the separation of powers advocated by the Framers?

(20) In Part II(C)(3)(a) of its opinion, the Court quoted a statement of Alexander Hamilton in THE FEDERALIST to the effect that Senate approval would be required for a President to remove officers. Should that source receive more or less weight than the debates in the Constitutional Convention, discussed in Part II(A) of the Court's opinion? Why?

(21) In Part II(C)(3)(a) of its opinion, the Court quoted Alexander Hamilton's defense of President Washington's action in proclaiming neutrality in the war between France and Great Britain. Why should a matter subsequent to ratification of the Constitution be considered in interpreting the meaning of its terms?

(22) In Part II(C)(3)(b) of its opinion, the Court addressed the precedent established by *Marbury v. Madison*. Did the Court fairly characterize the holding

of *Marbury*? Should *Marbury* be viewed as applicable precedent to the issue before the Court?

(23) In Part II(D)(1) of its opinion, the Court addressed its precedent in *Parsons*. In that case, the Court had construed a statute under which an inferior officer was appointed for a term of four years as not limiting the power of the President to remove the officer prior to the expiration of that term. Does the reasoning of *Parsons* deny any meaning to the statutory term of four years? If Volume I was assigned prior to this Volume, consider whether the reasoning of *Parsons* illustrates the seventh of the rules identified by Justice Brandeis in *Ashwander v. TVA*. Under a statutory construction parallel to that followed in *Parsons*, would President Jefferson have had authority to remove Marbury from office even if James Marshall had delivered Marbury's commission (and, if so, how does that changed premise affect Chief Justice Marshall's rationale)?

(24) In Part II(D)(2) of its opinion, the Court quoted Justice Story — who simultaneously served on the U.S. Supreme Court and held an appointment as a law professor at Harvard and published leading treatises and expositions of the law — as believing that the historical precedent of 1789 did not limit Congress with respect to inferior officers. Was Justice Story correct?

(25) In Part II(E)(1) of its opinion, the Court acknowledged that Congress created tribunals "for the territories" which Congress called "courts" and staffed the tribunals with officers it called "judges." With the first statute creating such offices, in 1789, Congress provided for life tenure. Congress continued to do so in a series of statutes for more than fifteen years. Why did that practice not establish an interpretation of the Constitution that required Congress to grant officers wielding "*quasi* judicial" powers life tenure, like Article III judges vested with the only "judicial power" expressly identified in the Constitution? As a corollary, why did that practice not establish an interpretation of the Constitution that prohibited Presidents from removing such officers?

(26) In *Myers*, the Court declined to address the removal of such *quasi* judicial officers. Should the Court have expressed its views with respect to such officers so as to provide greater guidance to the executive?

(27) In Part II(E)(2) of its opinion, the Court addressed the argument that the congressional interpretation of the Constitution recognizing unlimited Presidential power of removal applied only to principal officers. Did the Court convincingly demonstrate a historical understanding that inferior officers were subject to Presidential removal?

(28) In Part II(E)(2) of its opinion, the Court described its precedent in *United States v. Perkins*. In what way did that case modify the doctrine regarding the power of Congress to limit the removability of non-judicial officers? What are the textual and historical bases for the interpretation adopted in *Perkins?*

(29) In Part II(F) of its opinion, the Court detailed legislation through which Congress sought to limit the President's power to remove non-judicial officers. At the time it was enacted, did the Tenure of Office Act violate the text and/or historical understanding of the Constitution? At the time it was enacted, did the Tenure of Office Act violate any Supreme Court precedent?

(30) Some of the legislation addressed in Part II(F) of the Court's opinion was enacted with Presidential approval while other legislation was enacted over Presidential veto. Should judicial determination of whether legislation limiting Presidential authority is constitutional consider whether the legislation was approved by the President? Why or why not?

(31) In Part II(F)(3)(b)(i) of its opinion, the Court suggested some criteria by which one might determine which legislative precedents (or, perhaps, historical precedents more broadly) properly fix the meaning to be given to the Constitution. Do these criteria establish meaningful and appropriate principles? If so, in a case where the criteria are satisfied, should the Court adhere to legislative precedent despite contrary constitutional text or ascertainable views of the Framers? What if *both* constitutional text and the views of the Framers are opposed to the legislative precedent?

(32) In Part II(F)(3)(b)(ii) of its opinion, the Court addressed the Interstate Commerce Act of 1887 and other subsequent legislation which created various federal administrative agencies. The Court acknowledged that those statutes purported to provide the officers who head those agencies with tenure for fixed terms of years subject to earlier removal by the President only for specified causes, usually limited to "inefficiency, neglect of duty, or malfeasance in office." Assume that in such a statute, Congress clearly expressed its intent to limit the President's power to remove an officer, other than a judge of an Article III court, who had been appointed by the President with the advice and consent of the Senate. If the Supreme Court could not avoid the constitutional issue through any other interpretation of the statute, does *Myers* (and/or the judicial precedents discussed therein) hold that the President nonetheless retains unlimited power of removal?

(33) In Part II(G) of its opinion, the Court addressed the consistency of the Civil Service Act of 1883 with its view of the removal power. How can the Court assert that the Civil Service Act can limit the ability to remove an officer but the Act at issue in *Myers* does not? What is the distinction? Does the distinction find any support in constitutional text and/or the statements of the Framers and/or the debates in the First Congress? Could the distinction be expanded to limit the power to remove a principal officer?

(34) After reviewing the entire majority decision in *Myers*, consider what constitutionally-permissible measures were available to Congress to respond to disagreements with the actions

(a) of President Jackson's aggressive use of the "spoils system" of political patronage, and

(b) of President Johnson's approach to Reconstruction after the Civil War.

A NOTE CONCERNING THE "COMPTROLLER"

Some question has been raised as to the strength of the so-called "decision of 1789" discussed in *Myers*. When considering the bill that established the Department of the Treasury (excerpted in Volume 1, Chapter 2, and reproduced in full text on the DVD-ROM), one might observe first that the First Congress did not formally denominate the agency as an "Executive Department," as it had with the Department of Foreign Affairs. In addition, the various offices established by that bill included the "Comptroller" which was not granted a term of years and as to which no protection from unlimited Presidential removal was specified.

A point raised by James Madison on the floor of the House of Representatives with regard to the prospective office of Comptroller has been cited in support of inferences regarding the views of the First Congress. Madison briefly suggested that the officer be treated differently than the offices that the House had considered up to that point in time. On June 29, 1789, with the House of Representatives meeting as a committee of the whole, Madison

. . . observed, that the Committee [of the Whole] had gone through the bill [to create the Department of the Treasury] without making any provision respecting the tenure by which the Comptroller is to hold his office. He thought it was a point worthy of consideration, and would, therefore, submit a few observations upon it.

It will be necessary, said he, to consider the nature of this office, to enable us to come to a right decision on the subject; in analyzing its properties, we shall easily discover they are not purely of an executive nature. It seems to me that they partake of a judiciary quality as well as executive; perhaps the latter obtains in the greatest degree. The principal duty seems to be deciding upon the lawfulness and justice of the claims and accounts subsisting between the United States and particular citizens: this partakes strongly of the judicial character, and there may be strong reasons why an officer of this kind should not hold his office at the pleasure of the executive branch of the Government. I am inclined to think that we ought to consider him something in the light of an arbitrator between the public and individuals, and that he ought to hold his office by such a tenure as will make him responsible to the public generally; then again it may be thought, on the other side, that some persons ought to be authorized on behalf of the individual, with the usual liberty of referring to a third person, in case of disagreement, which may throw some embarrassment in the way of the first idea.

Whatever, Mr. Chairman, may be my opinion with respect to the tenure by which an executive officer may hold his office according to the meaning of the Constitution, I am very well satisfied, that a modification by the Legislature may take place in such as partake of the judicial qualities, and that the legislative power is sufficient to establish this office on such a footing as to answer the purposes for which it is prescribed.

With this view he would move a proposition, to be inserted in the bill; it was that the Comptroller should hold his office during ___ years, unless sooner removed by the President: he will always be dependent upon the Legislature, by reason of the power of impeachment; but he might be made still more so, when the House took up the Salary bill. He would have the person re-appointable at the expiration of the term, unless he was disqualified by a conviction on an impeachment before the Senate; by this means the Comptroller would be dependent upon the President, because he can be removed by him; he will be dependent upon the Senate, because they must consent to his election for every term of years; and he will be dependent upon this House, through the means of impeachment, and the power we shall reserve over his salary; by which means we shall effectually secure the dependence of this officer upon the Government. But making him thus thoroughly dependent, would make it necessary to secure his impartiality, with respect to the individual [claimant]. This might be effected by giving any person, who conceived himself aggrieved, a right to petition the Supreme Court for redress, and they should be empowered to do right therein; this will enable the individual to carry his claim before an independent tribunal.

A provision of this kind exists in two of the United States at this time and is found to answer a very good purpose. He mentioned this, that gentlemen might not think it altogether novel. The committee [of the whole], he hoped, would take a little time to examine the idea.

1 Annals of Congress 635–36 (statement of James Madison).[1] Because Madison proposed both to specify a term of office for the Comptroller and qualified that term with the phrase "unless sooner removed by the President" it is not clear that Madison intended to limit Presidential removal.[2] But Madison had introduced the proposal because he thought that the officer should not hold his office at the pleasure of the executive branch.

Several Members of the House immediately spoke against Madison's proposal as inconsistent with the settled interpretation established in connection with the Secretary of the first executive department. Congressman Sedgwick explained "that a majority of the House had decided that all officers concerned in executive business should depend upon the will of the President for their continuance in office; and with good reason." *Id.* at 637. He viewed the Comptroller as exercising "important executive duties" so that the officer should "be dependent upon the President." *Id.* at 638. Congressman Benson, likewise, expressed opposition to any measure that could be understood to undermine the prior decision:

> Mr. Benson did not like the object of the motion, because it was, in some measure, setting afloat the question which had already been carried.
>
> He wished there might be some certainty in knowing what was the tenure of offices; he thought they were well fixed now, if nothing more was done with the question. The judges hold theirs during good behavior, as established by the constitution; all others, during pleasure. He was afraid the present motion would lead to a different construction from the one lately adopted; by devices of this kind, he apprehended the Legislature might overthrow the executive power; he would therefore vote against it, if it were not withdrawn.

Id. at 638. The next day, Madison withdrew his proposal. *Id.* at 639.

Whatever one may make of Madison's internally inconsistent statements with respect to the tenure appropriate to a *quasi*-judicial officer,[3] his comments drew objections and Madison quickly relented. One might read the incident as strengthening the commitment to the "decision of 1789" and illustrating that it applied equally to officers subordinate to the Heads of Departments as well as the Heads of Departments themselves, and to officers engaged in a combination of *quasi*-judicial and executive functions as well as purely executive officers.

More than a century later, in 1921, Congress established the General Accounting Office to be headed by the "Comptroller General of the United States" who was to be appointed by the President for a single term of fifteen years. That officer has very different duties and, as discussed in *Bowsher v. Synar,* has been considered as an officer of Congress rather than as an Executive (or independent) officer. Despite the similarity of titles, the Court in *Humphrey's Executor* was not addressing this office of then-recent creation; the sole citation supporting the Court's discussion is a reference to Madison's statement discussed above.

---

[1] This source is a reconstruction of early congressional debate prior to the publication of the Congressional Record. (The Annals of Congress are vailable in digital format at http://memory.loc.gov/ammem/amlaw/lwaclink.html).

[2] The Supreme Court, in fact, interpreted legislation enacted decades later that specified a term of office as not limiting Presidential removal. *See Shurtleff v. United States,* 189 U.S. 311 (1903) (discussed in *Myers v. United States,* 272 U.S. 52 (1926)).

[3] The role of the Comptroller, as described by Madison, seems very like the role of the "judges" of the Court of Claims described in *Myers* and *Humphrey's Executor.*

HUMPHREY'S EXECUTOR v. UNITED STATES

295 U.S. 602 (1935)

JUSTICE SUTHERLAND delivered the Opinion of the Court.

Plaintiff brought suit in the Court of Claims against the United States to recover a sum of money alleged to be due the deceased as salary as a Federal Trade Commissioner from October 8, 1933, when the President undertook to remove him from office, to the time of his death on February 14, 1934. . . .

William E. Humphrey, the decedent, on December 10, 1931, was nominated by President Hoover to succeed himself as a member of the Federal Trade Commission, and he was confirmed by the United States Senate. He was duly commissioned for a term of seven years, expiring September 25, 1938; and, after taking the required oath of office, entered upon his duties. On July 25, 1933, President Roosevelt addressed a letter to the commissioner asking for his resignation, on the ground "that the aims and purposes of the Administration with respect to the work of the Commission can be carried out most effectively with personnel of my own selection," but disclaiming any reflection upon the commissioner or upon his services.

. . . .

The commissioner declined to resign; and on October 7, 1933, the President wrote him: "Effective as of this date you are hereby removed from the office of Commissioner of the Federal Trade Commission."

Humphrey never acquiesced in this action, but continued thereafter to insist that he was still a member of the commission, entitled to perform its duties and receive the compensation provided by law at the rate of $10,000 per annum. . . .

. . . .

The Federal Trade Commission Act, ch. 311, §§ 1, 2, 38 Stat. 717, 718 (codified as 15 U.S.C. §§ 41, 42), creates a commission of five members to be appointed by the President by and with the advice and consent of the Senate, and section 1 provides:

> Not more than three of the commissioners shall be members of the same political party. The first commissioners appointed . . . but their successors shall be appointed for terms of seven years, except that any person chosen to fill a vacancy shall be appointed only for the unexpired term of the commissioner whom he shall succeed. . . . Any commissioner may be removed by the President for inefficiency, neglect of duty, or malfeasance in office. . . .

. . . .

[I]

First. The question first to be considered is whether, by the provisions of section 1 of the Federal Trade Commission Act already quoted, the President's power is limited to removal for the specific causes enumerated therein. The negative contention of the government is based principally upon the decision of this court in *Shurtleff v. United States,* 189 U.S. 311 (1903). [The 1890 statute at issue in that case provides that the President could remove from office a general appraiser of merchandise for "inefficiency, neglect of duty, or malfeasance in office."] That opinion, after saying that no term of office was fixed by the act and that, with the exception of judicial officers provided for by the Constitution, [observed that] no civil officers had ever held office by life tenure since the foundation of the government . . . .

. . . .

. . . In the face of the unbroken precedent against life tenure, except in the case of the judiciary, the conclusion that Congress intended that, from among all other civil officers, appraisers alone should be selected to hold office for life was so extreme as to forbid, in the opinion of the court, any ruling which would produce that result if it reasonably could be avoided. The situation here presented is plainly and wholly different. The statute fixes a term of office . . . . The words of the act are definite and unambiguous.

. . . [T]he fixing of a definite term subject to removal for cause, unless there be some countervailing provision or circumstance indicating the contrary, which here we are unable to find, is enough to establish the legislative intent that the term is not to be curtailed in the absence of such cause. . . .

The commission is to be nonpartisan; and it must, from the very nature of its duties, act with entire impartiality. . . . Its duties are neither political nor executive, but predominantly quasi judicial and quasi legislative. Like the Interstate Commerce Commission, its members are called upon to exercise the trained judgment of a body of experts "appointed by law and informed by experience."

The legislative reports in both houses of Congress clearly reflect the view that a fixed term was necessary to the effective and fair administration of the law. . . .

. . . .

Thus, the language of the act, the legislative reports, and the general purposes of the legislation as reflected in the debates, all combine to demonstrate the congressional intent to create a body of experts who shall gain experience by length of service; a body which shall be independent of executive authority, except in its selection, and free to exercise its judgment without the leave or hindrance of any other official or any department of the government. To the accomplishment of these purposes, it is clear that Congress was of opinion that length and certainty of tenure would vitally contribute. . . .

We conclude that the intent of the act is to limit the executive power of removal to the causes enumerated, the existence of none of which is claimed here . . . .

[II]

Second. To support its contention that the removal provision of section 1, as we have just construed it, is an unconstitutional interference with the executive power of the President, the government's chief reliance is *Myers v. United States,* 272 U.S. 52 (1926). That case has been so recently decided, and the prevailing and dissenting opinions so fully review the general subject of the power of executive removal, that further discussion would add little of value to the wealth of material there collected. These opinions examine at length the historical, legislative, and judicial data bearing upon the question, beginning with what is called "the decision of 1789" in the first Congress and coming down almost to the day when the opinions were delivered. They occupy 243 pages of the volume in which they are printed. Nevertheless, the narrow point actually decided was only that the President had power to remove a postmaster of the first class, without the advice and consent of the Senate as required by act of Congress. In the course of the opinion of the court, expressions occur which tend to sustain the government's contention, but those are beyond the point involved and, therefore, do not come within the rule of stare decisis. In so far as they are out of harmony with the views here set forth, these expressions are disapproved. A like situation was presented in the case of *Cohens v. Virginia*, 19 U.S. 264 (1821), in respect of certain general expressions in the opinion in *Marbury v. Madison*, 5 U.S. 137 (1803). Chief Justice Marshall, who delivered the opinion in the *Marbury* case, speaking again for the court in the *Cohens* case, said:

> It is a maxim, not to be disregarded, that general expressions, in every opinion, are to be taken in connection with the case in which those expressions are used. If they go beyond the case, they may be respected, but ought not to control the judgment in a subsequent suit, when the very point is presented for decision. The reason of this maxim is obvious. The question actually before the court is investigated with care, and considered in its full extent. Other principles which may serve to illustrate it, are considered in their relation to the case decided, but their possible bearing on all other cases is seldom completely investigated.

. . . .

The office of a postmaster is so essentially unlike the office now involved that the decision in the *Myers* case cannot be accepted as controlling our decision here. A postmaster is an executive officer restricted to the performance of executive functions. He is charged with no duty at all related to either the legislative or judicial power. The actual decision in the *Myers* case finds support in the theory that such an officer is merely one of the units in the executive department and, hence, inherently subject to the exclusive and illimitable power of removal by the Chief Executive, whose subordinate and aid he is. Putting aside *dicta*, which may be followed if sufficiently persuasive but which are not controlling, the necessary reach of the decision goes far enough to include all purely executive officers. It goes no farther; much less does it include an officer who occupies no place in the executive department and who exercises no part of the executive power vested by the Constitution in the President.

The Federal Trade Commission is an administrative body created by Congress to carry into effect legislative policies embodied in the statute in accordance with the legislative standard therein prescribed, and to perform other specified duties as a legislative or as a judicial aid. Such a body cannot in any proper sense be characterized as an arm or an eye of the executive. Its duties are performed without executive leave and, in the contemplation of the statute, must be free from executive control. In administering the provisions of the statute in respect of "unfair methods of competition," that is to say, in filling in and administering the details embodied by that general standard, the commission acts in part quasi legislatively and in part quasi judicially. In making investigations and reports thereon for the information of Congress under section 6, in aid of the legislative power, it acts as a legislative agency. Under section 7, which authorizes the commission to act as a master in chancery under rules prescribed by the court, it acts as an agency of the judiciary. To the extent that it exercises any executive function, as distinguished from executive power in the constitutional sense, it does so in the discharge and effectuation of its quasi legislative or quasi judicial powers, or as an agency of the legislative or judicial departments of the government. . . .

If Congress is without authority to prescribe causes for removal of members of the trade commission and limit executive power of removal accordingly, that power at once becomes practically all-inclusive in respect of civil officers with the exception of the judiciary provided for by the Constitution. The Solicitor General, at the bar, apparently recognizing this to be true, with commendable candor, agreed that his view in respect of the removability of members of the Federal Trade Commission necessitated a like view in respect of the Interstate Commerce Commission and the Court of Claims. We are thus confronted with the serious question whether not only the members of these quasi legislative and quasi judicial bodies, but the judges of the legislative Court of Claims, exercising judicial power . . . continue in office only at the pleasure of the President.

We think it plain under the Constitution that illimitable power of removal is not possessed by the President in respect of officers of the character of those just named. The authority of Congress, in creating quasi legislative or quasi judicial agencies, to require them to act in discharge of their duties independently of executive control cannot well be doubted; and that authority includes, as an appropriate incident, power to fix the period during which they shall continue, and to forbid their removal except for cause in the meantime. For it is quite evident that one who holds his office only during the pleasure of another cannot be depended upon to maintain an attitude of independence against the latter's will.

The fundamental necessity of maintaining each of the three general departments of government entirely free from the control or coercive influence, direct or indirect, of either of the others, has often been stressed and is hardly open to serious question. So much is implied in the very fact of the separation of powers of these departments by the Constitution; and in the rule which recognizes their essential coequality. The sound application of a principle that makes one master in his own house precludes him from imposing his control in the house of another who is master there. James Wilson, one of the Framers of the Constitution and a former justice of this court, said that the independence of each department required that its proceedings "should be free from the remotest influence, direct or indirect, of either of the other two powers." James DeWitt Andrews, 1 The Works of James Wilson 367 (1896). . . .

The power of removal here claimed for the President falls within this principle, since its coercive influence threatens the independence of a commission, which is not only wholly disconnected from the executive department, but which, as already fully appears, was created by Congress as a means of carrying into operation legislative and judicial powers, and as an agency of the legislative and judicial departments.

In light of the question now under consideration, we have re-examined the precedents referred to in the *Myers* case, and find nothing in them to justify a conclusion contrary to that which we have reached. The so-called "decision of 1789" had relation to a bill proposed by Mr. Madison to establish an executive Department of Foreign Affairs. The bill provided that the principal officer was "to be removable from office by the President of the United States." This clause was changed to read "whenever the principal officer shall be removed from office by the President of the United States," certain things would follow, thereby, in connection with the debates, recognizing and confirming, as the court thought in the *Myers* case, the sole power of the President in the matter. We shall not discuss the subject further, since it is so fully covered by the opinions in the *Myers* case, except to say that the office under consideration by Congress was not only purely executive, but the officer one who was responsible to the President, and to him alone, in a very definite sense. A reading of the debates shows that the President's illimitable power of removal was not considered in respect of other than executive officers. And it is pertinent to observe that when, at a later time, the tenure of office for the Comptroller of the Treasury was under consideration, Mr. Madison quite evidently thought that, since the duties of that office were not purely of an executive nature but partook of the judiciary quality as well, a different rule in respect of executive removal might well apply. . . .

In *Marbury v. Madison*, 5 U.S. at 162, 165–66, it is made clear that Chief Justice Marshall was of opinion that a justice of the peace for the District of Columbia was not removable at the will of the President; and that there was a distinction between such an officer and officers appointed to aid the President in the performance of his constitutional duties. In the latter case, the distinction he saw was that "their acts are his acts" and his will, therefore, controls; and, by way of illustration, he adverted to the act establishing the Department of Foreign Affairs, which was the subject of the "decision of 1789."

The result of what we now have said is this: Whether the power of the President to remove an officer shall prevail over the authority of Congress to condition the power by fixing a definite term and precluding a removal except for cause will depend upon the character of the office; the *Myers* decision, affirming the power of the President alone to make the removal, is confined to purely executive officers; and as to officers of the kind here under consideration, we hold that no removal can be made during the prescribed term for which the officer is appointed, except for one or more of the causes named in the applicable statute.

. . . .

JUSTICE MCREYNOLDS, concurring in the judgement.

[Omitted.]

Exercise 3:

Consider the following questions in connection with *Humphrey's Executor v. United States:*

(1) The Court recited that in creating the Federal Trade Commission, Congress purported to require the President to select Commissioners on the basis of partisan political affiliation. Is that limitation on the President's appointment authority consistent with pertinent constitutional text and/or the views of the Framers (discussed at length in *Myers*) and/or the views expressed by a majority in the First Congress (also discussed at length in *Myers*)?

(2) Is this purported limitation on the President's appointment power consistent with any legislative precedent referenced in *Myers*?

(3) Are Commissioners of the Federal Trade Commission "principal" or "inferior" officers? Does that make any difference to the Court's analysis in *Myers* or any of the judicial precedents discussed therein? Does the Court in *Humphrey's Executor* place any significance on such classification?

(4) The Court recited that in enacting the Federal Trade Commission Act, Congress purported to limit the President's authority to remove Commissioners before expiration of a term of office. In light of the fact that Congress required that the Commissioners be appointed with Senate confirmation, what, if anything, would *Myers* indicate regarding whether that limitation was constitutional? Which, if any, of the following matters supports or rejects the constitutionality of the limitation:

(a) the text of the Constitution (itself or as viewed by the majority in *Myers*);

(b) the views of the Framers (discussed at length in *Myers*);

(c) the views expressed by a majority in the First Congress (also discussed at length in *Myers*)?

(5) In Part I of its opinion, the Court discussed its precedent in *Shurtleff v. United States*. Was the Court's view of the case consistent with the characterization of that precedent in *Myers*?

(6) In Part I of its opinion, the Court asserted that Congress intended that the FTC "be nonpartisan," that the FTC's duties "are neither political nor executive," and that Congress designed the FTC to be "independent of executive authority, except in its selection." Assuming that the Court correctly discerned the intent of Congress, does Congress have constitutional authority to create offices other than (1) legislative officers, like the Speaker of the House or the President pro tempore of the Senate (*see* Art. I, § 2, ¶ 5; Art. I, § 3, ¶ 5); (2) judges, clerks, and marshals of the federal courts contemplated by Article III (*see* Art. I, § 8, cl. 9); (3) military officers (*see* Art. I, § 8, cl.12-14); (4) officers for the District of Columbia, like justices of the peace, and other land within States purchased by the federal government, like park police (*see* Art. I, § 8, cl.17); (5) officers "in each of the executive Departments" (*see* Art. II, § 2, ¶ 1), including "Ambassadors . . . and Consuls" (*see* Art. II, § 2, ¶ 2); and (6) territorial officers for lands within the jurisdiction of the United States but not located within any State, such as the governor of the Northwest Territories (*see* Art. IV, § 3, ¶ 2)? If so, what is the textual basis for that authority?

(7) In the view of the Framers (discussed at length in *Myers*), were federal civil (not military) officers exercising nationwide authority (not limited to the territories or other federal enclaves), to be exclusively divided into legislative, executive, and judicial departments? If so, what purposes were to be served by such division?

(8) In Part II of its opinion, the Court acknowledged that *Myers* constituted the primary precedent upon which the President relied for his removal authority. *Myers* had been decided in 1926, just nine years prior to the decision in *Humphrey's Executor*. In *Myers*, the Court ruled, by a 6-3 margin, that the President had removal authority. In *Humphrey's Executor*, the Court ruled 9-0 against the President's removal authority and "disapproved" any portion of *Myers* inconsistent with its decision. If the Court in *Humphrey's Executor* determined that *Myers* was incorrectly decided, would *stare decisis* favor following *Myers*? Why or why not?

(9) In Part II of its opinion, the Court asserted that, in *Myers*, "the narrow point actually decided was only that the President had the power to remove a postmaster of the first class, without the advice and consent of the Senate as required by act of Congress." If Humphrey had been a postmaster of the second class, rather than a Commissioner of the Federal Trade Commission, would *Myers* have constituted controlling precedent? Why or why not? If Humphrey had been a non-postmaster, inferior officer serving in the State Department who had been appointed by the President with Senate confirmation, would *Myers* have constituted controlling precedent? Why or why not?

(10) In Part II of its opinion, the Court distinguished between the office from which Myers was removed and the office from which Humphrey was removed. In terms of promoting the policy of the President, which of the two officers does the President most need to control?

(11) In Part II of its decision, the Court asserted that "the necessary reach of" its prior decision in *Myers* "goes far enough to include *all* purely executive officers." Does that mean that an inferior, "purely executive" officer must be subject to unlimited power of Presidential removal even if the officer was appointed without Senate confirmation? If so, is the Civil Service Act of 1883 (discussed in *Myers*) subject to constitutional attack?

(12) The same quote from Part II of the Court's decision raises the question whether there are any "purely" executive officers. Do all executive officers wield some incidental *quasi*-legislative or *quasi*-judicial powers? When the Secretary of State promulgates regulations regarding procedures for applications for a passport, is he engaged in *quasi*-legislative activities? When the Secretary of State decides whether to issue a travel advisory regarding a foreign nation and/or when he selects among competing contractors to operate a facility, is he engaged in *quasi*-judicial activities?

(13) If the Federal Trade Commission "occupies no place in the executive department" where does it fit within the constitutional design? Section 3 of the Act creating the FTC indicates that the Commission replaces an earlier agency — the Bureau of Corporations — which was subject to the supervision of the Secretary of Commerce. "All pending investigations and proceedings of the Bureau" were transferred to the Commission as were the clerks and employees, the records and papers and property, and appropriations and unexpended funds. Do those provisions affect your answer?

(14) In Part II of its decision, the Court distinguished *Myers* as involving no officer "who exercises no part of the executive power vested by the Constitution in the President." Is it true that the Federal Trade Commission exercises no "executive power"? The Court acknowledged that the FTC did exercise some "executive function[s]" but asserted that those functions did not constitute "executive power in the constitutional sense" and such functions were merely ancillary to the FTC's *quasi*-legislative or *quasi*-judicial activities. Section 5 of the Act creating the FTC indicates that the Commission had the authority to draft and file a "complaint stating its charges" that the named party was using "any unfair method of competition in commerce" which would then initiate adjudicatory proceedings. Is the decision whether and when to bring a complaint a function of the executive (as distinguished from the legislature or judiciary)? In the criminal context, are the prosecutor's duties ancillary to the legislature's criminalization of certain conduct and/or the judiciary's trial of the defendant? Or is prosecution a core function of the executive that the Framers would have separated from legislative and judicial power? How, if at all, is the FTC's role in identifying parties and charges different from that of a prosecutor?

(15) In Part II of its decision, the Court asserted that if Congress was not permitted to limit the President's power to remove Commissioners of the FTC, the President's constitutional power of removal "at once becomes practically all-inclusive in respect of civil officers with the exception of the judiciary." Is there no limiting principle available? Would a ruling that President Roosevelt had constitutional authority to remove Humphrey from office logically require that the President have unlimited authority to remove inferior officers appointed by the heads of Executive Departments? Is there any argument that Congress could have limited the President's power to remove the head of the Bureau of Corporations even if it could not limit the President's power to remove an FTC Commissioner?

(16) With respect to the asserted lack of a limiting principle, the Court stated that if President Roosevelt had constitutional authority to remove Humphrey from office, that would logically require that he had unlimited authority to remove Commissioners of the Interstate Commerce Commission and "judges" of the Court of Claims (which is not a "court" within the meaning of Article III). Is there, in fact, any basis to distinguish among those officers?

(17) Assuming the Court in *Humphrey's Executor* perceived no readily-apparent limiting principle, how should that fact influence the Court's decision?

Should the Court decide the fate of Humphrey's claim in the shadow of a hypothetical Presidential removal of a judge of the Court of Claims? Or, should the Court ignore the potential broader consequences of its ruling and consider only the specific circumstance of Humphrey's removal?

(18) In Part II of its decision, the Court asserted that the power of Congress to create agencies that operate independent of executive control (except for appointment of the officers) and which wield powers that are not wholly legislative or wholly judicial "cannot well be doubted." Do you agree? Why or why not?

(19) In Part II of its decision, the Court asserted that when the First Congress established its interpretation of the Constitution with respect to the President's power to remove officers, it addressed only the context of executive officers. If the only officers contemplated by the Framers were those in classes identified in the constitutional text — referenced above in Question 6 — does the failure to consider officers like Humphrey represent the intent to exempt such officers from "the decision of 1789" or doubt that such officers were constitutionally permitted?

(20) In Part II of its decision, the Court suggested that "the decision of 1789" might not have been so firm by purporting to reference James Madison's views regarding the tenure of the "Comptroller of the Treasury." Consider the *Note Concerning the "Comptroller"* and determine whether that source supports or undermines the position of the majority of the Court.

(21) Assuming the administration had foreseen the result in *Humphrey's Executor*, how might President Roosevelt, acting unilaterally, have obtained an FTC populated with officers of his own selection without establishing adverse judicial precedent? President Roosevelt came into office with majorities in both Houses of Congress of his own party. Working together with Congress, how might President Roosevelt have obtained his goal without setting an adverse Supreme Court precedent?

The Importance of the Removal Question

Professors Steven G. Calabresi and Christopher S. Yoo have recently published a significant treatise on Presidential power entitled THE UNITARY EXECUTIVE: PRESIDENTIAL POWER FROM WASHINGTON TO BUSH. As they observe, the matter is not limited to historical battles that shaped our Constitution. Rather the removal power presents "one of the biggest issues of our time" because it concerns "how to establish better control over big, unresponsive government bureaucracies." *Id.* at 6.

The extensive compilation of Professors Calabresi and Yoo provides "a comprehensive historical chronicle of the struggles between the president and Congress over control of execution of federal law." *Id.* at 14. As such, it is an important resource for arguments in this field premised upon tradition as distinguished from text, structure, and ratification history. One important caveat is that the authors expressly limit their presentation to "*presidential claims* about the unitary executive debate." *Id.* at 18 (emphasis added). To counterbalance the self-interest of the Executive in such matters, it will be appropriate to consult the scholarship addressing congressional efforts to limit Executive power.

In the course of their work, Professors Calabresi and Yoo address the various historical episodes referenced in the *Myers* opinion, including:

- The Preratification Origins of the Unitary Executive Debate and the Decision of 1789, *see id.* at 30–36;
- President Jackson's aggressive use of the removal power, *see id.* at 99–104, and the controversy over his removal of the Treasury Secretary, *see id.* at

105–12;

- The Tenure of Office Act and the Impeachment of President Andrew Johnson, *see id.* at 179–87; and
- President Wilson's instruction of the removal of Frank S. Myers himself, *see id.* at 255–56.

They also address President Franklin D. Roosevelt's attempted removal of William E. Humphrey and the litigation it prompted. *See id.* at 283–88.

CHAPTER 2

CONFLICTS BETWEEN EXECUTIVE AND LEGISLATIVE POWER

The previous Chapter introduced cases addressing conflicts between the Executive and Legislative branches of the central government in the context of the appointment and removal of officers. While that context is a fertile ground for exploration of such conflicts, it is not the only area where the scope of constitutional powers — as distinguished from statutory and political constraints — arise.

YOUNGSTOWN SHEET & TUBE CO. v. SAWYER

343 U.S. 579 (1952)

JUSTICE BLACK delivered the opinion of the Court.

We are asked to decide whether the President was acting within his constitutional power when he issued an order directing the Secretary of Commerce to take possession of and operate most of the Nation's steel mills. The mill owners argue that the President's order amounts to lawmaking, a legislative function which the Constitution has expressly confided to the Congress and not to the President. The Government's position is that the order was made on findings of the President that his action was necessary to avert a national catastrophe which would inevitably result from a stoppage of steel production, and that in meeting this grave emergency the President was acting within the aggregate of his constitutional powers as the Nation's Chief Executive and the Commander in Chief of the Armed Forces of the United States. The issue emerges here from the following series of events:

In the latter part of 1951, a dispute arose between the steel companies and their employees over terms and conditions that should be included in new collective bargaining agreements. Long-continued conferences failed to resolve the dispute. . . . The Federal Mediation and Conciliation Service then intervened in an effort to get labor and management to agree. . . . On April 4, 1952, the Union gave notice of a nation-wide strike called to begin at 12:01 a.m. April 9. The indispensability of steel as a component of substantially all weapons and other war materials led the President to believe that the proposed work stoppage would immediately jeopardize our national defense and that governmental seizure of the steel mills was necessary in order to assure the continued availability of steel. Reciting these considerations for his action, the President, a few hours before the strike was to begin, issued Executive Order 10340 . . . . The order directed the Secretary of Commerce to take possession of most of the steel mills and keep them running. The Secretary immediately issued his own possessory orders, calling upon the presidents of the various seized companies to serve as operating managers for the United States. They were directed to carry on their activities in accordance with regulations and directions of the Secretary. The next morning the President sent a message to Congress reporting his action. Twelve days later he sent a second message. Congress has taken no action.

Obeying the Secretary's orders under protest, the companies brought proceedings against him in the District Court. Their complaints charged that the seizure was not authorized by an act of Congress or by any constitutional provisions. The District Court was asked to declare the orders of the President and the Secretary invalid and to issue preliminary and permanent injunctions restraining their enforcement. Opposing the motion for preliminary injunction, the

United States asserted that a strike disrupting steel production for even a brief period would so endanger the well-being and safety of the Nation that the President had "inherent power" to do what he had done — power "supported by the Constitution, by historical precedent, and by court decisions." The Government also contended that in any event no preliminary injunction should be issued because the companies had made no showing that their available legal remedies were inadequate or that their injuries from seizure would be irreparable. Holding against the Government on all points, the District Court on April 30 issued a preliminary injunction restraining the Secretary from "continuing the seizure and possession of the plants . . . and from acting under the purported authority of Executive Order No. 10340." [T]he Court of Appeals stayed the District Court's injunction. Deeming it best that the issues raised be promptly decided by this Court, we granted certiorari on May 3 and set the cause for argument on May 12.

. . . .

II.

The President's power, if any, to issue the order must stem either from an act of Congress or from the Constitution itself. There is no statute that expressly authorizes the President to take possession of property as he did here. Nor is there any act of Congress to which our attention has been directed from which such a power can fairly be implied. Indeed, we do not understand the Government to rely on statutory authorization for this seizure. There are two statutes which do authorize the President to take both personal and real property under certain conditions. However, the Government admits that these conditions were not met and that the President's order was not rooted in either of the statutes. The Government refers to the seizure provisions of one of these statutes (§ 201(b) of the Defense Production Act) as "much too cumbersome, involved, and time-consuming for the crisis which was at hand."

Moreover, the use of the seizure technique to solve labor disputes in order to prevent work stoppages was not only unauthorized by any congressional enactment; prior to this controversy, Congress had refused to adopt that method of settling labor disputes. When the Taft-Hartley Act was under consideration in 1947, Congress rejected an amendment which would have authorized such governmental seizures in cases of emergency. Apparently it was thought that the technique of seizure, like that of compulsory arbitration, would interfere with the process of collective bargaining. Consequently, the plan Congress adopted in that Act did not provide for seizure under any circumstances. Instead, the plan sought to bring about settlements by use of the customary devices of mediation, conciliation, investigation by boards of inquiry, and public reports. In some instances temporary injunctions were authorized to provide cooling-off periods. All this failing, unions were left free to strike after a secret vote by employees as to whether they wished to accept their employers' final settlement offer.

It is clear that if the President had authority to issue the order he did, it must be found in some provision of the Constitution. And it is not claimed that express constitutional language grants this power to the President. The contention is that presidential power should be implied from the aggregate of his powers under the Constitution. Particular reliance is placed on provisions in Article II which say that "The executive Power shall be vested in a President"; that "he shall take Care that the Laws be faithfully executed"; and that he "shall be Commander in Chief of the Army and Navy of the United States."

The order cannot properly be sustained as an exercise of the President's military power as Commander in Chief of the Armed Forces. The Government attempts to do so by citing a number of cases upholding broad powers in military commanders engaged in day-to-day fighting in a theater of war. Such cases need not concern us here. Even though "theater of war" be an expanding concept, we cannot with faithfulness to our constitutional system hold that the Commander in Chief of the Armed Forces has the ultimate power as such to take possession of private property in order to keep labor disputes from stopping production. This is a job for the Nation's lawmakers, not for its military authorities.

Nor can the seizure order be sustained because of the several constitutional provisions that grant executive power to the President. In the framework of our Constitution, the President's power to see that the laws are faithfully executed refutes the idea that he is to be a lawmaker. The Constitution limits his functions in the lawmaking process to the recommending of laws he thinks wise and the vetoing of laws he thinks bad. And the Constitution is neither silent nor equivocal about who shall make laws which the President is to execute. The first section of the first article says that "All legislative Powers herein granted shall be vested in a Congress of the United States . . . ." After granting many powers to the Congress, Article I goes on to provide that Congress may "make all Laws which shall be necessary and proper for carrying into Execution the foregoing Powers, and all other Powers vested by this Constitution in the Government of the United States, or in any Department or Officer thereof."

The President's order does not direct that a congressional policy be executed in a manner prescribed by Congress — it directs that a presidential policy be executed in a manner prescribed by the President. The preamble of the order itself, like that of many statutes, sets out reasons why the President believes certain policies should be adopted, proclaims these policies as rules of conduct to be followed, and again, like a statute, authorizes a government official to promulgate additional rules and regulations consistent with the policy proclaimed and needed to carry that policy into execution. The power of Congress to adopt such public policies as those proclaimed by the order is beyond question. It can authorize the taking of private property for public use. It can make laws regulating the relationships between employers and employees, prescribing rules designed to settle labor disputes, and fixing wages and working conditions in certain fields of our economy. The Constitution does not subject this law-making power of Congress to presidential or military supervision or control.

It is said that other Presidents without congressional authority have taken possession of private business enterprises in order to settle labor disputes. But even if this be true, Congress has not thereby lost its exclusive constitutional authority to make laws necessary and proper to carry out the powers vested by the Constitution "in the Government of the United States, or in any Department or Officer thereof."

The Founders of this Nation entrusted the law making power to the Congress alone in both good and bad times. It would do no good to recall the historical events, the fears of power and the hopes for freedom that lay behind their choice. Such a review would but confirm our holding that this seizure order cannot stand.

The judgment of the District Court is affirmed.

Justice Frankfurter, concurring.

. . . .

[The Framers] rested the structure of our central government on the system of checks and balances. For them the doctrine of separation of powers was not mere theory; it was a felt necessity. Not so long ago it was fashionable to find our system of checks and balances obstructive to effective government. It was easy to ridicule that system as outmoded — too easy. The experience through which the world has passed in our own day has made vivid the realization that the Framers of our Constitution were not inexperienced doctrinaires. These long-headed statesmen had no illusion that our people enjoyed biological or psychological or sociological immunities from the hazards of concentrated power. It is absurd to see a dictator in a representative product of the sturdy democratic traditions of the Mississippi Valley. The accretion of dangerous power does not come in a day. It does come, however slowly, from the generative force of unchecked disregard of the restrictions that fence in even the most disinterested assertion of authority.

The Framers, however, did not make the judiciary the overseer of our government. They were familiar with the revisory functions entrusted to judges in a few of the States and refused to lodge such powers in this Court. Judicial power can be exercised only as to matters that were the traditional concern of the courts at Westminster, and only if they arise in ways that to the expert feel of lawyers constitute "Cases" or "Controversies." Even as to questions that were the staple of judicial business, it is not for the courts to pass upon them unless they are indispensably involved in a conventional litigation — and then, only to the extent that they are so involved. Rigorous adherence to the narrow scope of the judicial function is especially demanded in controversies that arouse appeals to the Constitution. The attitude with which this Court must approach its duty when confronted with such issues is precisely the opposite of that normally manifested by the general public. So-called constitutional questions seem to exercise a mesmeric influence over the popular mind. This eagerness to settle — preferably forever — a specific problem on the basis of the broadest possible constitutional pronouncements may not unfairly be called one of our minor national traits. An English observer of our scene has acutely described it: "At the first sound of a new argument over the United States Constitution and its interpretation the hearts of Americans leap with a fearful joy . . . ."

. . . .

The pole-star for constitutional adjudications is John Marshall's greatest judicial utterance that "it is *a constitution* we are expounding." *McCulloch v. Maryland*, 17 U.S. 316, 407 (1819). That requires both a spacious view in applying an instrument of government "made for an undefined and expanding future," *Hurtado v. California*, 110 U.S. 516, 530 (1884), and as narrow a delimitation of the constitutional issues as the circumstances permit. Not the least characteristic of great statesmanship which the Framers manifested was the extent to which they did not attempt to bind the future. It is no less incumbent upon this Court to avoid putting fetters upon the future by needless pronouncements today.

. . . .

It is in this mood and with this perspective that the issue before the Court must be approached. We must therefore put to one side consideration of what powers the President would have had if there had been no legislation whatever bearing on the authority asserted by the seizure, or if the seizure had been only for a short, explicitly temporary period, to be terminated automatically unless Congressional approval were given. These and other questions, like or unlike, are not now here. I would exceed my authority were I to say anything about them.

The question before the Court comes in this setting. Congress has frequently — at least 16 times since 1916 — specifically provided for executive seizure of production, transportation, communications, or storage facilities. In every case it has qualified this grant of power with limitations and safeguards. . . .

. . . .

. . . In formulating legislation for dealing with industrial conflicts, Congress could not more clearly and emphatically have withheld authority than it did in 1947. . . . Previous seizure legislation had subjected the powers granted to the President to restrictions of varying degrees of stringency. Instead of giving him even limited powers, Congress in 1947 deemed it wise to require the President, upon failure of attempts to reach a voluntary settlement, to report to Congress if he deemed [seizure power necessary]. . . .

. . . .

By the Labor Management Relations Act of 1947, Congress said to the President, "You may not seize. Please report to us and ask for seizure power if you think it is needed in a specific situation." This of course calls for a report on the unsuccessful efforts to reach a voluntary settlement, as a basis for discharge by Congress of its responsibility — which it has unequivocally reserved — to fashion further remedies than it provided. . . . Absence of authority in the President to deal with a crisis does not imply want of power in the Government. Conversely the fact that power exists in the Government does not vest it in the President. The need for new legislation does not enact it. Nor does it repeal or amend existing law.

. . . .

It is one thing to draw an intention of Congress from general language and to say that Congress would have explicitly written what is inferred, where Congress has not addressed itself to a specific situation. It is quite impossible, however, when Congress did specifically address itself to a problem, as Congress did to that of seizure, to find secreted in the interstices of legislation the very grant of power which Congress consciously withheld. To find authority so explicitly withheld is not merely to disregard in a particular instance the clear will of Congress. It is to disrespect the whole legislative process and the constitutional division of authority between President and Congress.

. . . .

Apart from his vast share of responsibility for the conduct of our foreign relations, the embracing function of the President is that "he shall take Care that the Laws be faithfully executed . . . ." Art. II, § 3. The nature of that authority has for me been comprehensively indicated by Justice Holmes. "The duty of the President to see that the laws be executed is a duty that does not go beyond the laws or require him to achieve more than Congress sees fit to leave within his power." *Myers v. United States,* 272 U.S. 52, 177 (1926). The powers of the President are not as particularized as are those of Congress. But unenumerated powers do not mean undefined powers. The separation of powers built into our Constitution gives essential content to undefined provisions in the frame of our government.

To be sure, the content of the three authorities of government is not to be derived from an abstract analysis. The areas are partly interacting, not wholly disjointed. The Constitution is a framework for government. Therefore the way the framework has consistently operated fairly establishes that it has operated according to its true nature. Deeply embedded traditional ways of conducting government cannot supplant the Constitution or legislation, but they give meaning to the words of a text or supply them. It is an inadmissibly narrow conception of American constitutional law to confine it to the words of the Constitution and to disregard the gloss which life has written upon them. In short, a systematic, unbroken, executive practice, long pursued to the knowledge of the Congress and never before questioned, engaged in by Presidents who have also sworn to uphold the Constitution, making as it were such exercise of power part of the structure of our government, may be treated as a gloss on "executive Power" vested in the President by [Article II, section 1].

. . . .

A scheme of government like ours no doubt at times feels the lack of power to act with complete, all-embracing, swiftly moving authority. No doubt a government with distributed authority, subject to be challenged in the courts of law, at least long enough to consider and adjudicate the challenge, labors under restrictions from which other governments are free. It has not been our tradition to envy such governments. In any event our government was designed to have such restrictions. The price was deemed not too high in view of the safeguards which these restrictions afford. I know no more impressive words on this subject than those of Justice Brandeis:

> The doctrine of the separation of powers was adopted by the Convention of 1787, not to promote efficiency but to preclude the exercise of arbitrary power. The purpose was, not to avoid friction, but, by means of the inevitable friction incident to the distribution of the governmental powers among three departments, to save the people from autocracy.

Myers v. United States, 272 U.S. at 240.

. . . .

In reaching the conclusion that conscience compels, I too derive consolation from the reflection that the President and the Congress between them will continue to safeguard the heritage which comes to them straight from George Washington.

JUSTICE DOUGLAS, concurring.

. . . The President can act more quickly than the Congress. The President with the armed services at his disposal can move with force as well as with speed. All executive power — from the reign of ancient kings to the rule of modern dictators — has the outward appearance of efficiency.

Legislative power, by contrast, is slower to exercise. There must be delay while the ponderous machinery of committees, hearings, and debates is put into motion. That takes time; and while the Congress slowly moves into action, the emergency may take its toll in wages, consumer goods, war production, the standard of living of the people, and perhaps even lives. . . .

We therefore cannot decide this case by determining which branch of government can deal most expeditiously with the present crisis. The answer must depend on the allocation of powers under the Constitution. That in turn requires an analysis of the conditions giving rise to the seizure and of the seizure itself.

. . . .

The legislative nature of the action taken by the President seems to me to be clear. When the United States takes over an industrial plant to settle a labor controversy, it is condemning property. . . .

The power of the Federal Government to condemn property is well established. *Kohl v. United States,* 91 U.S. 367 (1875). . . . But there is a duty to pay for all property taken by the Government. The command of the Fifth Amendment is that no "private property be taken for public use, without just compensation." That constitutional requirement has an important bearing on the present case.

The President has no power to raise revenues. That power is in the Congress by Article I, Section 8 of the Constitution. The President might seize and the Congress by subsequent action might ratify the seizure. But until and unless Congress acted, no condemnation would be lawful. The branch of government that has the power to pay compensation for a seizure is the only one able to authorize a seizure or make lawful one that the President had effected. That seems to me to be the necessary result of the condemnation provision in the Fifth Amendment. It squares with the theory of checks and balances expounded by Justice Black in the opinion of the Court in which I join.

If we sanctioned the present exercise of power by the President, we would be expanding Article II of the Constitution and rewriting it to suit the political conveniences of the present emergency. Article II which vests the "executive Power" in the President defines that power with particularity. . . .

. . . .

JUSTICE JACKSON, concurring in the judgment and opinion of the Court.

. . . [A]s we approach the question of presidential power, we half overcome mental hazards by recognizing them. The opinions of judges, no less than executives and publicists, often suffer the infirmity of confusing the issue of a power's validity with the cause it is invoked to promote, of confounding the permanent executive office with its temporary occupant. The tendency is strong to emphasize transient results upon policies — such as wages or stabilization — and lose sight of enduring consequences upon the balanced power structure of our Republic.

A judge, like an executive adviser, may be surprised at the poverty of really useful and unambiguous authority applicable to concrete problems of executive power as they actually present themselves. Just what our forefathers did envision, or would have envisioned had they foreseen modern conditions, must be divined from materials almost as enigmatic as the dreams Joseph was called upon to interpret for Pharaoh. A century and a half of partisan debate and scholarly speculation yields no net result but only supplies more or less apt quotations from respected sources on each side of any question. They largely cancel each other. And court decisions are indecisive because of the judicial practice of dealing with the largest questions in the most narrow way.

The actual art of governing under our Constitution does not and cannot conform to judicial definitions of the power of any of its branches based on isolated clauses or even single Articles torn from context. While the Constitution diffuses power the better to secure liberty, it also contemplates that practice will integrate the dispersed powers into a workable government. It enjoins upon its branches separateness but interdependence, autonomy but reciprocity. Presidential powers are not fixed but fluctuate, depending upon their disjunction or conjunction with those of Congress. We may well begin by a somewhat over-simplified grouping of practical situations in which a President may doubt, or others may challenge, his powers, and by distinguishing roughly the legal consequences of this factor of relativity.

1. When the President acts pursuant to an express or implied authorization of Congress, his authority is at its maximum, for it includes all that he possesses in his own right plus all that Congress can delegate. In these circumstances, and in these only, may he be said (for what it may be worth) to personify the federal sovereignty. If his act is held unconstitutional under these circumstances, it usually means that the Federal Government as an undivided whole lacks power. A seizure executed by the President pursuant to an Act of Congress would be supported by the strongest of presumptions and the widest latitude of judicial interpretation, and the burden of

persuasion would rest heavily upon any who might attack it.

2. When the President acts in absence of either a congressional grant or denial of authority, he can only rely upon his own independent powers, but there is a zone of twilight in which he and Congress may have concurrent authority, or in which its distribution is uncertain. Therefore, congressional inertia, indifference or quiescence may sometimes, at least as a practical matter, enable, if not invite, measures on independent presidential responsibility. In this area, any actual test of power is likely to depend on the imperatives of events and contemporary imponderables rather than on abstract theories of law.

3. When the President takes measures incompatible with the expressed or implied will of Congress, his power is at its lowest ebb, for then he can rely only upon his own constitutional powers minus any constitutional powers of Congress over the matter. Courts can sustain exclusive presidential control in such a case only by disabling the Congress from acting upon the subject. Presidential claim to a power at once so conclusive and preclusive must be scrutinized with caution, for what is at stake is the equilibrium established by our constitutional system.

Into which of these classifications does this executive seizure of the steel industry fit? It is eliminated from the first by admission, for it is conceded that no congressional authorization exists for this seizure. That takes away also the support of the many precedents and declarations which were made in relation, and must be confined, to this category.

Can it then be defended under flexible tests available to the second category? It seems clearly eliminated from that class because Congress has not left seizure of private property an open field but has covered it by three statutory policies inconsistent with this seizure. In cases where the purpose is to supply needs of the Government itself, two courses are provided: one, seizure of a plant which fails to comply with obligatory orders placed by the Government; another, condemnation of facilities, including temporary use under the power of eminent domain. The third is applicable where it is the general economy of the country that is to be protected rather than exclusive governmental interests. None of these were invoked. In choosing a different and inconsistent way of his own, the President cannot claim that it is necessitated or invited by failure of Congress to legislate upon the occasions, grounds and methods for seizure of industrial properties.

This leaves the current seizure to be justified only by the severe tests under the third grouping, where it can be supported only by any remainder of executive power after subtraction of such powers as Congress may have over the subject. In short, we can sustain the President only by holding that seizure of such strike-bound industries is within his domain and beyond control by Congress. Thus, this Court's first review of such seizures occurs under circumstances which leave presidential power most vulnerable to attack and in the least favorable of possible constitutional postures.

I did not suppose, and I am not persuaded, that history leaves it open to question, at least in the courts, that the executive branch, like the Federal Government as a whole, possesses only delegated powers. The purpose of the Constitution was not only to grant power, but to keep it from getting out of hand. However, because the President does not enjoy unmentioned powers does not mean that the mentioned ones should be narrowed by a niggardly construction. Some clauses could be made almost unworkable, as well as immutable, by refusal to indulge some latitude of interpretation for changing times. I have heretofore, and do now, give to the enumerated powers the scope and elasticity afforded by what seem to be reasonable, practical implications instead of the rigidity dictated by a doctrinaire textualism.

The Solicitor General seeks the power of seizure in three clauses of the Executive Article, the first reading, "The executive Power shall be vested in a President of the United States of America." Lest I be thought to exaggerate, I quote the interpretation which his brief puts upon it: "In our view, this clause constitutes a grant of all the executive powers of which the Government is capable." If that be true, it is difficult to see why the forefathers bothered to add several specific items, including some trifling ones.

The example of such unlimited executive power that must have most impressed the forefathers was the prerogative exercised by George III, and the description of its evils in the Declaration of Independence leads me to doubt that they were creating their new Executive in his image. Continental European examples were no more appealing. And if we seek instruction from our own times, we can match it only from the executive powers in those governments we disparagingly describe as totalitarian. I cannot accept the view that this clause is a grant in bulk of all conceivable executive power but regard it as an allocation to the presidential office of the generic powers thereafter stated.

The clause on which the Government next relies is that "The President shall be Commander in Chief of the Army and Navy of the United States . . . ." These cryptic words have given rise to some of the most persistent controversies in our constitutional history. Of course, they imply something more than an empty title. But just what authority goes with the name has plagued presidential advisers who would not waive or narrow it by nonassertion yet cannot say where it begins or ends. It undoubtedly puts the Nation's armed forces under presidential command. Hence, this loose appellation is sometimes advanced as support for any presidential action, internal or external, involving use of force, the idea being that it vests power to do anything, anywhere, that can be done with an army or navy.

That seems to be the logic of an argument tendered at our bar — that the President having, on his own responsibility, sent American troops abroad derives from that act "affirmative power" to seize the means of producing a supply of steel for them. . . .

I cannot foresee all that it might entail if the Court should indorse this argument. Nothing in our Constitution is plainer than that declaration of a war is entrusted only to Congress. . . .

Assuming that we are in a war *de facto*, whether it is or is not a war *de jure*, does that empower the Commander-in-Chief to seize industries he thinks necessary to supply our army? The Constitution expressly places in Congress power "to raise and *support* Armies" and "to *provide* and *maintain* a Navy." This certainly lays upon Congress primary responsibility for supplying the armed forces. . . .

There are indications that the Constitution did not contemplate that the title Commander-in-Chief *of the Army and Navy* will constitute him also Commander-in-Chief of the country, its industries and its inhabitants. He has no monopoly of "war powers," whatever they are. While Congress cannot deprive the President of the command of the army and navy, only Congress can provide him an army or navy to command. It is also empowered to make rules for the "Government and Regulation of land and naval Forces," by which it may to some unknown extent impinge upon even command functions.

That military powers of the Commander-in-Chief were not to supersede representative government of internal affairs seems obvious from the Constitution and from elementary American history. Time out of mind, and even now in many parts of the world, a military commander can seize private housing to shelter his troops. Not so, however, in the United States, for the Third Amendment says, "No Soldier shall, in time of peace be quartered in any house, without the consent of the Owner, nor in time of war, but in a manner to be prescribed by law." Thus, even in war time, his seizure of needed military housing must be authorized by Congress. It also was expressly left to Congress to "provide for calling forth the Militia to execute the Laws of the Union, suppress Insurrections and repel Invasions . . . ." [Art. I, § 8, cl. 15.] Such a limitation on the command power, written at a time when the militia rather than a standing army was contemplated as the military weapon of the Republic, underscores the Constitution's policy that Congress, not the Executive, should control utilization of the war power as an instrument of domestic policy. . . .

The third clause in which the Solicitor General finds seizure powers is that "he shall take Care that the Laws be faithfully executed." That authority must be matched against words of the Fifth Amendment that "No person shall be . . . deprived of life, liberty, or property, without due process of law." One gives a governmental authority that reaches so far as there is law, the other gives a private right that authority shall go no farther. These signify about all there is of the principle that ours is a government of laws, not of men, and that we submit ourselves to rulers only if under rules.

The Solicitor General lastly grounds support of the seizure upon nebulous, inherent powers never expressly granted but said to have accrued to the office from the customs and claims of preceding administrations. The plea is for a resulting power to deal with a crisis or an emergency according to the necessities of the case, the unarticulated assumption being that necessity knows no law.

. . . .

The vagueness and generality of the clauses that set forth presidential powers afford a plausible basis for pressures within and without an administration for presidential action beyond that supported by those whose responsibility it is to defend his actions in court. The claim of inherent and unrestricted presidential powers has long been a persuasive dialectical weapon in political controversy. . . .

The Solicitor General, acknowledging that Congress has never authorized the seizure here, says practice of prior Presidents has authorized it. He seeks color of legality from claimed executive precedents, chief of which is President Roosevelt's seizure of June 9, 1941, of the California plant of the North American Aviation Company. Its superficial similarities with the present case, upon analysis, yield to distinctions so decisive that it cannot be regarded as even a precedent, much less an authority for the present seizure.

. . . .

In view of the ease, expedition and safety with which Congress can grant and has granted large emergency powers, certainly ample to embrace this crisis, I am quite unimpressed with the argument that we should affirm possession of them without statute. Such power either has no beginning or it has no end. If it exists, it need submit to no legal restraint. I am not alarmed that it would plunge us straightway into dictatorship, but it is at least a step in that wrong direction.

As to whether there is imperative necessity for such powers, it is relevant to note the gap that exists between the President's paper powers and his real powers. The Constitution does not disclose the measure of the actual controls wielded by the modern presidential office. That instrument must be understood as an Eighteenth-Century sketch of a government hoped for, not as a blueprint of the Government that is. Vast accretions of federal power, eroded from that reserved by the States, have magnified the scope of presidential activity. Subtle shifts take place in the centers of real power that do not show on the face of the Constitution.

Executive power has the advantage of concentration in a single head in whose choice the whole Nation has a part, making him the focus of public hopes and expectations. In drama, magnitude and finality his decisions so far overshadow any others that almost alone he fills the public eye and ear. No other personality in public life can begin to compete with him in access to the public mind through modern methods of communications. By his prestige as head of state and his influence upon public opinion he exerts a leverage upon those who are supposed to check and balance his power which often cancels their effectiveness.

Moreover, rise of the party system has made a significant extraconstitutional supplement to real executive power. No appraisal of his necessities is realistic which overlooks that he heads a political system as well as a legal system. Party loyalties and interests, sometimes more binding than law, extend his effective control into branches of government other than his own and he often may win, as a political leader, what he cannot command under the Constitution. Indeed, Woodrow Wilson, commenting on the President as leader both of his party and of the Nation, observed, "If he rightly interpret the national thought and boldly insist upon it, he is irresistible. . . . His office is anything he has the sagacity and force to make it." I cannot be brought to believe that this country will suffer if the Court refuses further to aggrandize the presidential office, already so potent and so relatively immune from judicial review, at the expense of Congress.

But I have no illusion that any decision by this Court can keep power in the hands of Congress if it is not wise and timely in meeting its problems. A crisis that challenges the President equally, or perhaps primarily, challenges Congress. If not good law, there was worldly wisdom in the maxim attributed to Napoleon that "The tools belong to the man who can use them." We may say that power to legislate for emergencies belongs in the hands of Congress, but only Congress itself can prevent power from slipping through its fingers.

. . . The Executive, except for recommendation and veto, has no legislative power. The executive action we have here originates in the individual will of the President and represents an exercise of authority without law. No one, perhaps not even the President, knows the limits of the power he may seek to exert in this instance and the parties affected cannot learn the limit of their rights. We do not know today what powers over labor or property would be claimed to flow from Government possession if we should legalize it, what rights to compensation would be claimed or recognized, or on what contingency it would end. With all its defects, delays and inconveniences, men have discovered no technique for long preserving free government except that the Executive be under the law, and that the law be made by parliamentary deliberations.

Such institutions may be destined to pass away. But it is the duty of the Court to be last, not first, to give them up.

Justice Burton, concurring in both the opinion and judgment of the Court.

My position may be summarized as follows:

The validity of the President's order of seizure is at issue and ripe for decision. Its validity turns upon its relation to the constitutional division of governmental power between Congress and the President.

. . . .

For the purposes of this case the most significant feature of that Act is its omission of authority to seize an affected industry. The debate preceding its passage demonstrated the significance of that omission. Collective bargaining, rather than governmental seizure, was to be relied upon. Seizure was not to be resorted to without specific congressional authority. Congress reserved to itself the opportunity to authorize seizure to meet particular emergencies.

. . . .

Now it is contended that although the President did not follow the procedure authorized by the Taft-Hartley Act, his substituted procedure served the same purpose and must be accepted as its equivalent. Without appraising that equivalence, it is enough to point out that neither procedure carried statutory authority for the seizure of private industries in the manner now at issue. The exhaustion of both procedures fails to cloud the clarity of the congressional reservation of seizure for its own consideration.

The foregoing circumstances distinguish this emergency from one in which Congress takes no action and outlines no governmental policy. In the case before us, Congress authorized a procedure which the President declined to follow. Instead, he followed another procedure which he hoped might eliminate the need for the first. Upon its failure, he issued an executive order to seize the steel properties in the face of the reserved right of Congress to adopt or reject that course as a matter of legislative policy.

This brings us to a further crucial question. Does the President, in such a situation, have inherent constitutional power to seize private property which makes congressional action in relation thereto unnecessary? We find no such power available to him under the present circumstances. The present situation is not comparable to that of an imminent invasion or threatened attack. We do not face the issue of what might be the President's constitutional power to meet such catastrophic situations. Nor is it claimed that the current seizure is in the nature of a military command addressed by the President, as Commander-in-Chief, to a mobilized nation waging, or imminently threatened with, total war.

The controlling fact here is that Congress, within its constitutionally delegated power, has prescribed for the President specific procedures, exclusive of seizure, for his use in meeting the present type of emergency. Congress has reserved to itself the right to determine where and when to authorize the seizure of property in meeting such an emergency. Under these circumstances, the President's order of April 8 invaded the jurisdiction of Congress. It violated the essence of the principle of the separation of governmental powers. Accordingly, the injunction against its effectiveness should be sustained.

JUSTICE CLARK, concurring in the judgment of the Court.

. . . .

The limits of presidential power are obscure. However, Article II, no less than Article I, is part of "a constitution intended to endure for ages to come, and, consequently, to be adapted to the various *crises* of human affairs." *McCulloch v. Maryland*, 17 U.S. 316, 415 (1819). Some of our Presidents, such as Lincoln, "felt that measures otherwise unconstitutional might become lawful by becoming indispensable to the preservation of the Constitution through the preservation of the nation." Others, such as Theodore Roosevelt, thought the President to be capable, as a "steward" of the people, of exerting all power save that which is specifically prohibited by the Constitution or the Congress. In my view — taught me not only by the decision of Chief Justice Marshall in *Little v. Barreme*, 6 U.S. 170 (1804), but also by a score of other pronouncements of distinguished members of this bench — the Constitution does grant to the President extensive authority in times of grave and imperative national emergency. In fact, to my thinking, such a grant may well be necessary to the very existence of the Constitution itself. As Lincoln aptly said, "[is] it possible to lose the nation and yet preserve the Constitution?" . . .

I conclude that where Congress has laid down specific procedures to deal with the type of crisis confronting the President, he must follow those procedures in meeting the crisis; but that in the absence of such action by Congress, the President's independent power to act depends upon the gravity of the situation confronting the nation. . . . Congress had prescribed methods to be followed by the President in meeting the emergency at hand.

. . . .

[The Defense Production Act of 1950, the Labor-Management Relations Act also called the Taft-Hartley Act, and the Selective Service Act of 1948] furnish the guideposts for decision in this case. Prior to seizing the steel mills on April 8 the President had exhausted the mediation procedures of the Defense Production Act through the Wage Stabilization Board. Use of those procedures had failed to avert the impending crisis; however, it had resulted in a 99-day postponement of the strike. The Government argues that this accomplished more than the maximum 80-day waiting period possible under the sanctions of the Taft-Hartley Act, and therefore amounted to compliance with the substance of that Act. Even if one were to accept this somewhat hyperbolic conclusion, the hard fact remains that neither the Defense Production Act nor Taft-Hartley authorized the seizure challenged here, and the Government made no effort to comply with the procedures established by the Selective Service Act of 1948, a statute which expressly authorizes seizures when producers fail to supply necessary defense materiel.

For these reasons I concur in the judgment of the Court. As Justice Story once said: "For the executive department of the government, this court entertain[s] the most entire respect; and amidst the multiplicity of cares in that department, it may, without any violation of decorum, be presumed, that sometimes there may be an inaccurate construction of a law. It is our duty to expound the laws as we find them in the records of state; and we cannot, when called upon by the citizens of the country, refuse our opinion, however it may differ from that of very great authorities."

CHIEF JUSTICE VINSON, with whom JUSTICES REED and MINTON join, dissenting.

The President of the United States directed the Secretary of Commerce to take temporary possession of the Nation's steel mills during the existing emergency because "a work stoppage would immediately jeopardize and imperil our national defense and the defense of those joined with us in resisting aggression, and would add to the continuing danger of our soldiers, sailors and airmen engaged in combat in the field." The District Court ordered the mills returned to their private owners on the ground that the President's action was beyond his powers under the Constitution.

This Court affirms. Some members of the Court are of the view that the President is without power to act in time of crisis in the absence of express statutory authorization. Other members of the Court affirm on the basis of their reading of certain statutes. Because we cannot agree that affirmance is proper on any ground, and because of the transcending importance of the questions presented not only in this critical litigation but also to the powers the President and of future Presidents to act in time of crisis, we are compelled to register this dissent.

. . . .

Those who suggest that this is a case involving extraordinary powers should be mindful that these are extraordinary times. A world not yet recovered from the devastation of World War II has been forced to face the threat of another and more terrifying global conflict.

. . . .

. . . The whole of the "executive Power" is vested in the President. Before entering office, the President swears that he "will faithfully execute the Office of President of the United States, and will to the best of [his] Ability, preserve, protect and defend the Constitution of the United States." Art. II, § 1.

. . . .

In passing upon the grave constitutional question presented in this case, we must never forget, as Chief Justice Marshall admonished, that the Constitution is "intended to endure for ages to come, and, consequently, to be adapted to the various *crises* of human affairs," and that "[i]ts means are adequate to its ends."[1] Cases do arise presenting questions which could not have been foreseen by the Framers. In such cases, the Constitution has been treated as a living document adaptable to new situations. But we are not called upon today to expand the Constitution to meet a new situation. For, in this case, we need only look to history and time-honored principles of constitutional law — principles that have been applied consistently by all branches of the Government throughout our history. It is those who assert the invalidity of the Executive Order who seek to amend the Constitution in this case.

. . . .

A review of executive action demonstrates that our Presidents have on many occasions exhibited the leadership contemplated by the Framers when they made the President Commander in Chief, and imposed upon him the trust to "take Care that the Laws be faithfully executed." With or without explicit statutory authorization, Presidents have at such times dealt with national emergencies by acting promptly and resolutely to enforce legislative programs, at least to save those programs until Congress could act. Congress and the courts have responded to such executive initiative with consistent approval.

Our first President displayed at once the leadership contemplated by the Framers. When the national revenue laws were openly flouted in some sections of Pennsylvania, President Washington, without waiting for a call from the state government, summoned the militia and took decisive steps to secure the faithful execution of the laws.[30] When international disputes engendered by the French revolution threatened to involve this country in war, and while congressional policy remained uncertain, Washington issued his Proclamation of Neutrality. Hamilton, whose defense of the Proclamation has endured the test of time, invoked the argument that the Executive has the duty to do that which will preserve the peace until Congress acts and, in addition, pointed to the need for keeping the Nation informed of the requirements of existing laws and treaties as part of the faithful execution of the laws.

President John Adams issued a warrant for the arrest of Jonathan Robbins in order to execute the extradition provisions of a treaty. . . .

---

[1] *McCulloch v. Maryland*, 17 U.S. 316, 415, 424 (1819).

[30] 4 Annals of Congress 1411, 1413 (1794).

Jefferson's initiative in the Louisiana Purchase, the Monroe Doctrine, and Jackson's removal of Government deposits from the Bank of the United States further serve to demonstrate by deed what the Framers described by word when they vested the whole of the executive power in the President.

Without declaration of war, President Lincoln took energetic action with the outbreak of the War Between the States. He summoned troops and paid them out of the Treasury without appropriation therefor. He proclaimed a naval blockade of the Confederacy and seized ships violating that blockade. Congress, far from denying the validity of these acts, gave them express approval. The most striking action of President Lincoln was the Emancipation Proclamation, issued in aid of the successful prosecution of the War Between the States, but wholly without statutory authority.

In an action furnishing a most apt precedent for this case, President Lincoln without statutory authority directed the seizure of rail and telegraph lines leading to Washington. Many months later, Congress recognized and confirmed the power of the President to seize railroads and telegraph lines and provided criminal penalties for interference with Government operation. This Act did not confer on the President any additional powers of seizure. Congress plainly rejected the view that the President's acts had been without legal sanction until ratified by the legislature. Sponsors of the bill declared that its purpose was only to confirm the power which the President already possessed. Opponents insisted a statute authorizing seizure was unnecessary and might even be construed as limiting existing Presidential powers.

. . . .

President Hayes authorized the wide-spread use of federal troops during the Railroad Strike of 1877. President Cleveland also used the troops in the Pullman Strike of 1895 and his action is of special significance. No statute authorized this action. . . .

President Theodore Roosevelt seriously contemplated seizure of Pennsylvania coal mines if a coal shortage necessitated such action. In his autobiography, President Roosevelt expounded the "Stewardship Theory" of Presidential power, stating that "the executive is subject only to the people, and, under the Constitution, bound to serve the people affirmatively in cases where the Constitution does not explicitly forbid him to render the service." Because the contemplated seizure of the coal mines was based on this theory, then ex-President Taft criticized President Roosevelt in a passage in his book relied upon by the District Court in this case. WILLIAM HOWARD TAFT, OUR CHIEF MAGISTRATE AND HIS POWERS 139–47 (1916). In the same book, however, President Taft agreed that such powers of the President as the duty "to take Care that the Laws be faithfully executed" could not be confined to "express Congressional statutes." *Id.* at 88. *In re Neagle,* 135 U.S. 1 (1890), and *In re Debs,* 158 U.S. 564 (1895), were cited as conforming with Taft's concept of the office, as they were later to be cited with approval in his opinion as Chief Justice in *Myers v. United States,* 272 U.S. 52, 133 (1926).

In 1909, President Taft was informed that government-owned oil lands were being patented by private parties at such a rate that public oil lands would be depleted in a matter of months. Although Congress had explicitly provided that these lands were open to purchase by United States citizens, the President nevertheless ordered the lands withdrawn from sale "[i]n aid of proposed legislation." In *United States v. Midwest Oil Co.,* 236 U.S. 459 (1915), the President's action was sustained as consistent with executive practice throughout our history. . . . [T]he situation confronting President Taft was described as "an emergency; there was no time to wait for the action of Congress." . . .

. . . .

During World War I, President Wilson established a War Labor Board without awaiting specific direction by Congress. . . . [T]he Board had as its purpose the prevention of strikes and lockouts interfering with the production of goods needed to meet the emergency. Effectiveness of War Labor Board decision was accomplished by Presidental action, including seizure of industrial plants. Seizure of the Nation's railroads was also ordered by President Wilson.

Beginning with the Bank Holiday Proclamation and continuing through World War II, executive leadership and initiative were characteristic of President Franklin D. Roosevelt's administration. . . .

In 1941, President Roosevelt acted to protect Iceland from attack by Axis powers, when British forces were withdrawn, by sending our forces to occupy Iceland. Congress was informed of this action on the same day that our forces reached Iceland. The occupation of Iceland was but one of "at least 125 incidents" in our history in which Presidents, "without congressional authorization, and in the absence of a declaration of war, [have] ordered the Armed Forces to take action or maintain positions abroad."

Some six months before Pearl Harbor, a dispute at a single aviation plant at Inglewood, California, interrupted a segment of the production of military aircraft. In spite of the comparative insignificance of this work stoppage to total defense production as contrasted with the complete paralysis now threatened by a shutdown of the entire basic steel industry, and even though our armed forces were not then engaged in combat, President Roosevelt ordered the seizure of the plant "pursuant to the powers vested in [him] by the Constitution and laws of the United States, as President of the United States of America and Commander in Chief of the Army and Navy of the United States." The Attorney General (Jackson) vigorously proclaimed that the President had the moral duty to keep this Nation's defense effort a "going concern." His ringing moral justification was coupled with a legal justification equally well stated: "The Presidential proclamation rests upon the aggregate of the Presidential powers derived from the Constitution itself and from statutes enacted by the Congress . . . ."

. . . .

This is but a cursory summary of executive leadership. But it amply demonstrates that Presidents have taken prompt action to enforce the laws and protect the country whether or not Congress happened to provide in advance for the particular method of execution. At the minimum, the executive actions reviewed herein sustain the action of the President in this case. And many of the cited examples of Presidential practice go far beyond the extent of power necessary to sustain the President's order to seize the steel mills. The fact that temporary executive seizures of industrial plants to meet an emergency have not been directly tested in this Court furnishes not the slightest suggestion that such actions have been illegal. Rather, the fact that Congress and the courts have consistently recognized and given their support to such executive action indicates that such a power of seizure has been accepted throughout our history.

History bears out the genius of the Founding Fathers, who created a Government subject to law but not left subject to inertia when vigor and initiative are required.

. . . .

The diversity of views expressed in the six opinions of the majority, the lack of reference to authoritative precedent, the repeated reliance upon prior dissenting opinions, the complete disregard of the uncontroverted facts showing the gravity of the emergency and the temporary nature of the taking all serve to demonstrate how far afield one must go to affirm the order of the District Court.

The broad executive power granted by Article II to an officer on duty 365 days a year cannot, it is said, be invoked to avert disaster. Instead, the President must confine himself to sending a message to Congress recommending action. Under this messenger-boy concept of the Office, the President cannot even act to preserve legislative programs from destruction so that Congress will have something left to act upon. There is no judicial finding that the executive action was unwarranted because there was in fact no basis for the President's finding of the existence of an emergency for, under this view, the gravity of the emergency and the immediacy of the threatened disaster are considered irrelevant as a matter of law.

Seizure of plaintiffs' property is not a pleasant undertaking. Similarly unpleasant to a free country are the draft which disrupts the home and military procurement which causes economic dislocation and compels adoption of price controls, wage stabilization and allocation of materials. The President informed Congress that even a temporary Government operation of plaintiffs' properties was "thoroughly distasteful" to him, but was necessary to prevent immediate paralysis of the mobilization program. Presidents have been in the past, and any man worthy of the Office should be in the future, free to take at least interim action necessary to execute legislative programs essential to survival of the Nation. A sturdy judiciary should not be swayed by the unpleasantness or unpopularity of necessary executive action, but must independently determine for itself whether the President was acting, as required by the Constitution, to "take Care that the Laws be faithfully executed."

. . . [J]udicial, legislative and executive precedents throughout our history demonstrate that in this case the President acted in full conformity with his duties under the Constitution. Accordingly, we would reverse the order of the District Court.

A NOTE ON DIFFERENT APPROACHES TO SEPARATION OF POWERS ISSUES

The opinions in the "Steel Seizure Case" illustrate at least three different theoretical approaches to adjudicating controversies about the separation of powers. Each of the following three approaches carries the vote of at least one Justice currently on the Court.

The opinion of Justice Black illustrates the "formalist" approach. A formalist compares the political act in question with the text of the Constitution. President Truman's seizure by executive order was legislative in character. Because Article I vests all legislative power in Congress, the President exceeded his authority. A formalist methodology tends to lend legitimacy to *judicial* resolution of the dispute because, as this example illustrates, the analysis is grounded in the text of the Constitution. Formalism also serves to enforce an originalist view of the Constitution, with its design of three separated branches. In a government that includes a vast administrative bureaucracy including various "independent" agencies, however, this approach may be put to a serious test.

The opinions of Justice Jackson and Justice Frankfurter, demonstrate a second approach known as "constrained functionalism." This process-based approach examines the effect of a political act and not just its formal classification. Under this approach, the President may take actions not specifically authorized by Article II but, in doing so, he may not disregard limits imposed by congressional enactments. This approach permits the answer to questions of constitutional authority to evolve over time, as the functions and details of the government evolve over time. One disadvantage to this methodology is that constrained functionalism is unsupported by constitutional text and, thus, subjects the judiciary to criticism for enhancing its own power and creating new law.

The dissenting opinion may be seen as an example of "evolutive functionalism" (also called "constitutional adverse possession"). The dissent rationalized the validity of the executive order by citing examples of open and notorious executive exercises of power with the acquiescence (and sometimes ratification or endorsement) of Congress. Under this approach, the Court could essentially defer to the political process to resolve disputes between the two elected branches of the federal government. In theory, doing so would ultimately put the matter in the hands of the electorate as they would decide who to reward or punish at the polls. One concern with this approach is that it could eventually place powers in one branch that the plain text of the Constitution (and original understanding) placed elsewhere, undermining the notion of the Constitution as the supreme law and the Supreme Court as the expositor of that law. A second concern with this approach is that it may tend to favor evolution in one particular direction. For example, Justice Jackson warned that this approach would result in a slow, steady transfer of power to the executive, potentially leading to conditions that foster dictatorship.

Reconsider the various opinions in *Myers* and *Humphrey's Executor*. Does a majority of the Court consistently adhere to one of these three theories of separation of powers? If not, are differences in the outcomes in the cases attributable to different theoretical starting points?

Exercise 4:

Consider the following questions in connection with *Youngstown Sheet & Tube Co. v. Sawyer*:

(1) Did the President have any statutory authority for his Executive Order?

(2) What inference, if any, can reasonably be drawn from the rejection by Congress of an amendment to the Taft-Hartley Act which would have authorized the President to make seizures in the event of emergencies?

(3) What argument, if any, is there that the Constitution *expressly* grants the President authority for his Executive Order? What textual provisions are pertinent to that analysis?

(4) Justice Black noted: "It is said that other Presidents without congressional authority have taken possession of private business enterprises in order to settle labor disputes." Should that matter? Why or why not?

(5) Justice Jackson observed the shortage of judicial precedents providing "really useful and unambiguous authority applicable to concrete problems of executive power." Should the judiciary frame its opinions so as to provide broader guidance? Why or why not?

(6) Justice Jackson identified three classes of cases spanning the spectrum of the "fluctuat[ing]" Presidential powers. Into which of the three classes does the case at bar properly fall? Why? How useful is this framework for resolving future cases?

(7) Justice Jackson asserted that the clause vesting the "executive Power" in the President must be read narrowly in order to preserve the meaning of "several specific items" addressed in Article II. Is that a fair reading of the clause and/or of

Article II as a whole? Could the specific items be explained in any other way? Is Justice Jackson's construction consistent with the view of this text articulated by the Court in *Myers* and/or *Humphrey's Executor*?

(8) What textual argument, if any, is there against finding extraordinary executive authority in times of crisis? What policy argument, if any, is there against such powers?

(9) Justice Jackson asserted that the "real powers" of the President include "[v]ast accretions of federal power, eroded from that reserved by the States." Are such accretions "that do not show on the face of the Constitution" proper? Why or why not?

(10) What additional reasons, if any, did Justice Douglas provide for limiting executive power to issue the Executive Order?

(11) Did Justices Douglas and Frankfurter, in their separate opinions, open the door to future Presidents to engage in seizures?

(12) What is the "gloss" on the terms of the Constitution that Justice Frankfurter identified? Should that gloss control judicial construction of the Constitution? Why or why not? What are the criteria Justice Frankfurter implicitly applies to distinguish such gloss from routine, continuing disputes among the branches of government over the scope of their authority?

(13) The dissenters asserted that the Court could decide the case without establishing a precedent to govern "seizure of a farm, a corner grocery store or even a single industrial plant." In contrast, Justice Jackson asserted that the power of executive seizure "either had no beginning or it has no end"; Justice Douglas asserted that such a power could be misused "to prevent a wage increase, to curb trade unionists, to regiment labor" in an oppressive manner; and Justice Frankfurter asserted that "accretion of dangerous power does not come in a day." Which approach best fits the role of the judiciary?

(14) The dissenters asserted that there was a long history, dating back to the administration of President Washington, of executive action without prior legislative authorization. In contrast, Justice Jackson asserted that the only pertinent history consisted of a few examples in 1941. Do they disagree on the historical facts or only about the inferences to be drawn from the facts?

(15) None of the opinions cited any prior judicial precedent regarding the constitutionality of executive seizures in the absence of statutory authorization. What conclusion should be drawn from the absence of prior court opinions?

(16) The dissenters assert that the President acted only on a "temporary" basis, having sought approval of his actions from Congress and agreeing to abide by its determination. Justice Douglas, however, asserted that the case would be different if, after the seizure, Congress "ratif[ied] the seizure" and Justice Frankfurter asserted that the case could be distinguished from one where "the seizure had been only for a short, explicitly temporary period." What then was the holding of a majority of the Court regarding temporary seizures pending legislative approval? How did the situation presented in the case differ from a temporary seizure pending legislative approval?

(17) What are the implications of this case for other claims of "inherent" authority of the President, or authority "implied" by (but not express in) the Constitution? How should the Court respond to a claim that the President has inherent or implied authority to remove from office non-judicial officers without limitation? Are there some such officers as to whom the claimed power is stronger than with respect to other officers?

BUCKLEY v. VALEO

424 U.S. 1 (1976)

PER CURIAM.

These appeals present constitutional challenges to the key provisions of the Federal Elections Campaign Act of 1971 (Act), and related provisions of the Internal Revenue Code of 1954, all as amended in 1974.

The Court of Appeals, in sustaining the legislation in large part against constitutional challenges, viewed it as "by far the most comprehensive reform legislation [ever] passed by Congress concerning the election of the President, Vice-President, and members of Congress." The statutes at issue summarized in broad terms, contain the following provisions: (a) individual political contributions are limited to $1,000 to any single candidate per election, with an overall annual limitation of $25,000 by any one contributor; independent expenditures by individuals and groups "relative to a clearly identified candidate" are limited to $1,000 per year; campaign spending by candidates for various federal offices and spending for national conventions by political parties are subject to prescribed limits; (b) contributions and expenditures above certain threshold levels must be reported and publicly disclosed; (c) a system for public funding of Presidential campaign activities is established . . .; and (d) a Federal Election Commission is established to administer and enforce the legislation.

. . . .

In this Court, appellants argue that the Court of Appeals failed to give this legislation the critical scrutiny demanded under accepted First Amendment and equal protection principles. . . . Finally, appellants renew their attack on the Commission's composition and powers.

. . . .

Iv. THE FEDERAL ELECTION COMMISSION

The 1974 amendments to the Act create an eight-member Federal Election Commission (Commission) and vest in it primary and substantial responsibility for administering and enforcing the Act. The question that we address in this portion of the opinion is whether, in view of the manner in which a majority of its members are appointed, the Commission may under the Constitution exercise the powers conferred upon it. . . .

[The Act] makes the Commission the principal repository of the numerous reports and statements which are required by [the Act] to be filed by those engaging in the regulated political activities. Its duties under § 438(a) with respect to these reports and statements include filing and indexing, making them available for public inspection, preservation, and auditing and field investigations. It is directed to "serve as a national clearinghouse for information in respect to the administration of elections." § 438(b).

Beyond these recordkeeping, disclosure, and investigative functions, however, the Commission is given extensive rulemaking and adjudicative powers. Its duty under § 438(a)(10) is "to prescribe suitable rules and regulations to carry out the provisions of . . . chapter [14]." Under § 437d(a)(8) the Commission is empowered to make such rules "as are necessary to carry out the provisions of this Act." Section 437d(a)(9) authorizes it to "formulate general policy with respect to the administration of this Act" and enumerated sections of Title 18's Criminal Code, as to all of which provisions the Commission "has primary jurisdiction with respect to [their] civil enforcement." § 437c(b). The Commission is authorized under § 437f(a) to render advisory opinions with respect to activities possibly violating the Act, the Title 18 sections, or the campaign funding provisions of Title 26, the effect of which is that "[n]otwithstanding any other provision of law, any person with respect to whom an advisory opinion is rendered . . . who acts in good faith in accordance with the provisions and findings [thereof] shall be presumed to be in compliance with the [statutory provision] with respect to which such advisory opinion is rendered." § 437f(b). In the course of administering the provisions for Presidential campaign financing, the Commission may authorize convention expenditures which exceed the statutory limits. 26 U.S.C. § 9008(d)(3).

The Commission's enforcement power is both direct and wide ranging. It may institute a civil action for (i) injunctive or other relief against "any acts or practices which constitute or will constitute a violation of this Act," § 437g(a)(5); (ii) declaratory or injunctive relief "as may be appropriate to implement or con[s]true any provisions" of Chapter 95 of Title 26, governing administration of funds for Presidential election campaigns and national party conventions, 26 U.S.C. § 9011(b)(1); and (iii) "such injunctive relief as is appropriate to implement any provision" of Chapter 96 of Title 26, governing the payment of matching funds for Presidential primary campaigns, 26 U.S.C. § 9040(c). If after the Commission's post-disbursement audit of candidates receiving payments under Chapter 95 or 96 it finds an overpayment, it is empowered to seek repayment of all funds due the Secretary of the Treasury. 26 U.S.C. §§ 9010(b), 9040(b). In no respect do the foregoing civil actions require the concurrence of or participation by the Attorney General; conversely, the decision not to seek judicial relief in the above respects would appear to rest solely with the Commission. With respect to the referenced Title 18 sections, § 437g(a)(7) provides that if, after notice and opportunity for a hearing before it, the Commission finds an actual or threatened criminal violation, the Attorney General "upon request by the Commission . . . shall institute a civil action for relief." Finally, as "[a]dditional enforcement authority," § 456(a) authorizes the Commission, after notice and opportunity for hearing, to make "a finding that a person . . . while a candidate for Federal office, failed to file" a required report of contributions or expenditures. If that finding is made within the applicable limitations period for prosecutions, the candidate is thereby "disqualified from becoming a candidate in any future election for Federal office for a period of time beginning on the date of such finding and ending one year after the expiration of the term of the Federal office for which such person was a candidate."

The body in which this authority is reposed consists of eight members. The Secretary of the Senate and the Clerk of the House of Representatives are *ex officio* members of the Commission without the right to vote. Two members are appointed by the President *pro tempore* of the Senate "upon the recommendations of the majority leader of the Senate and the minority leader of the Senate." Two more are to be appointed by the Speaker of the House of Representatives, likewise upon the recommendations of its respective majority and minority leaders. The remaining two members are appointed by the President. Each of the six voting members of the Commission must be confirmed by the majority of both Houses of Congress, and each of the three appointing authorities is forbidden to choose both of their appointees from the same political party.

. . . .

B. The Merits

Appellants urge that since Congress has given the Commission wide-ranging rulemaking and enforcement powers with respect to the substantive provisions of the Act, Congress is precluded under the principle of separation of powers from vesting in itself the authority to appoint those who will exercise such authority. Their argument is based on the language of Art. II, § 2, cl. 2, of the Constitution . . . .

Appellants' argument is that this provision is the exclusive method by which those charged with executing the laws of the United States may be chosen. Congress, they assert, cannot have it both ways. If the Legislature wishes the Commission to exercise all of the conferred powers, then its members are in fact "Officers of the United States" and must be appointed under the Appointments Clause. But if Congress insists upon retaining the power to appoint, then the members of the Commission may not discharge those many functions of the Commission which can be performed only by "Officers of the United States," as that term must be construed within the doctrine of separation of powers.

Appellee Commission and *amici* in support of the Commission urge that the Framers of the Constitution, while mindful of the need for checks and balances among the three branches of the National Government, had no intention of denying to the Legislative Branch authority to appoint its own officers. Congress, either under the Appointments Clause or under its grants of substantive legislative authority and the Necessary and Proper Clause in Art. I, is in their view empowered to provide for the appointment to the Commission in the manner which it did because the Commission is performing "appropriate legislative functions."

. . . .

1. Separation of Powers

We do not think appellants' arguments based upon Art. II, § 2, cl. 2, of the Constitution may be so easily dismissed as did the majority of the Court of Appeals. Our inquiry of necessity touches upon the fundamental principles of the Government established by the Framers of the Constitution, and all litigants and all of the courts which have addressed themselves to the matter start on common ground in the recognition of the intent of the Framers that the powers of the three great branches of the National Government be largely separate from one another.

James Madison, writing in the Federalist No. 47, defended the work of the Framers against the charge that these three governmental powers were not *entirely* separate from one another in the proposed Constitution. He asserted that while there was some admixture, the Constitution was nonetheless true to Montesquieu's well-known maxim that the legislative, executive, and judicial departments ought to be separate and distinct:

> The reasons on which Montesquieu grounds his maxim are a further demonstration of his meaning. "When the legislative and executive powers are united in the same person or body," says he, "there can be no liberty, because apprehensions may arise lest *the same* monarch or senate should *enact* tyrannical laws to *execute* them in a tyrannical manner." Again: "Were the power of judging joined with the legislative, the life and liberty of the subject would be exposed to arbitrary control, for *the judge* would then be *the legislator*. Were it joined to the executive power, *the judge* might behave with all the violence of *an oppressor*." Some of these reasons are more fully explained in other passages; but briefly stated as they are here, they sufficiently establish the meaning which we have put on this celebrated maxim of this celebrated author.

Yet it is also clear from the provisions of the Constitution itself, and from the Federalist Papers, that the Constitution by no means contemplates total separation of each of these three essential branches of Government. The President is a participant in the lawmaking process by virtue of his authority to veto bills enacted by Congress. The Senate is a participant in the appointive process by virtue of its authority to refuse to confirm persons nominated to office by the President. The men who met in Philadelphia in the summer of 1787 were practical statesmen, experienced in politics, who viewed the principle of separation of powers as a vital check against tyranny. But they likewise saw that a hermetic sealing off of the three branches of Government from one another would preclude the establishment of a Nation capable of governing itself effectively.

. . . .

This Court has not hesitated to enforce the principle of separation of powers embodied in the Constitution when its application has proved necessary for the decisions of cases or controversies properly before it. The Court has held that executive or administrative duties of a nonjudicial nature may not be imposed on judges holding office under Art. III of the Constitution. *United States v. Ferreira*, 54 U.S. 40 (1852); *Hayburn's Case*, 2 U.S. 409 (1792). The Court has held that the President may not execute and exercise legislative authority belonging only to Congress. *Youngstown Sheet & Tube Co. v. Sawyer*. . . .

More closely in point to the facts of the present case is this Court's decision in *Springer v. Philippine Islands*, 277 U.S. 189 (1928), where the Court held that the legislature of the Philippine Islands could not provide for legislative appointment to executive agencies.

2. The Appointments Clause

The principle of separation of powers was not simply an abstract generalization in the minds of the Framers: it was woven into the document that they drafted in Philadelphia in the summer of 1787. Article I, § 1, declares: "All legislative Powers herein granted shall be vested in a Congress of the United States." Article II, § 1, vests the executive power "in a President of the United States of America," and Art. III, § 1, declares that "The judicial Power of the United States, shall be vested in one supreme Court, and in such inferior Courts as the Congress may from time to time ordain and establish." The further concern of the Framers of the Constitution with maintenance of the separation of powers is found in the so-called "Ineligibility" and "Incompatibility" Clauses contained in Art. I, § 6 . . . .

It is in the context of these cognate provisions of the document that we must examine the language of Art. II, § 2, cl. 2, which appellants contend provides the only authorization for appointment of those to whom substantial executive or administrative authority is given by statute. . . .

The Appointments Clause could, of course, be read as merely dealing with etiquette or protocol in describing "Officers of the United States," but the drafters had a less frivolous purpose in mind. This conclusion is supported by language from *United States v. Germaine*, 99 U.S. 508, 509–10 (1879):

> The Constitution for purposes of appointment very clearly divides all its officers into two classes. The primary class requires a nomination by the President and confirmation by the Senate. But foreseeing that when offices became numerous, and sudden removals necessary, this mode might be inconvenient, it was provided that, in regard to officers inferior to those specially mentioned, Congress might by law vest their appointment in the President alone, in the courts of law, or in the heads of departments. *That all persons who can be said to hold an office under the government about*

> *to be established under the Constitution were intended to be included within one or the other of these modes of appointment there can be but little doubt.*

We think that the term "Officers of the United States" as used in Art. II, defined to include "all persons who can be said to hold an office under the government" in *United States v. Germaine* is a term intended to have substantive meaning. We think its fair import is that any appointee exercising significant authority pursuant to the laws of the United States is an "Officer of the United States," and must, therefore, be appointed in the manner prescribed by § 2, cl. 2, of that Article.

If "all persons who can be said to hold an office under the government about to be established under the Constitution were intended to be included within one or the other of these modes of appointment," *United States v. Germaine,* it is difficult to see how the members of the Commission may escape inclusion. If a postmaster first class, *Myers v. United States,* 272 U.S. 52 (1926), and the clerk of a district court, *Ex parte Hennen,* 38 U.S. 225 (1839), are inferior officers of the United States within the meaning of the Appointments Clause, as they are, surely the Commissioners before us are at the very least such "inferior Officers" within the meaning of that Clause.

Although two members of the Commission are initially selected by the President, his nominations are subject to confirmation not merely by the Senate, but by the House of Representatives as well. The remaining four voting members of the Commission are appointed by the President *pro tempore* of the Senate and by the Speaker of the House. While the second part of the Clause authorizes Congress to vest the appointment of the officers described in that part in "the Courts of Law, or in the Heads of Departments," neither the Speaker of the House nor the President *pro tempore* of the Senate comes within this language.

The phrase "Heads of Departments," used as it is in conjunction with the phrase "Courts of Law," suggests that the Departments referred to are themselves in the Executive Branch or at least have some connection with that branch. While the Clause expressly authorizes Congress to vest the appointment of certain officers in the "Courts of Law," the absence of similar language to include Congress must mean that neither Congress nor its officers were included within the language "Heads of Departments" in this part of cl. 2.

Thus with respect to four of the six voting members of the Commission, neither the President, the head of any department, nor the Judiciary has any voice in their selection.

The Appointments Clause specifies the method of appointment only for "Officers of the United States" whose appointment is not "otherwise provided for" in the Constitution. But there is no provision of the Constitution remotely providing any alternative means for the selection of the members of the Commission or for anybody like them. Appellee Commission has argued, and the Court of Appeals agreed, that the Appointments Clause of Art. II should not be read to exclude the "inherent power of Congress" to appoint its own officers to perform functions necessary to that body as an institution. But there is no need to read the Appointments Clause contrary to its plain language in order to reach the result sought by the Court of Appeals. Article I, § 3, cl. 5, expressly authorizes the selection of the President *pro tempore* of the Senate, and § 2, cl. 5, of that Article provides for the selection of the Speaker of the House. Ranking nonmembers, such as the Clerk of the House of Representatives, are elected under the internal rules of each House and are designated by statute as "officers of the Congress." There is no occasion for us to decide whether any of these member officers are "Officers of the United States" whose "appointment" is otherwise provided for within the meaning of the Appointments Clause, since even if they were such officers their appointees would not be. Contrary to the fears expressed by the majority of the Court of Appeals, nothing in our holding with respect to Art. II, § 2, cl. 2, will deny to Congress "all power to appoint its own inferior officers to carry out appropriate legislative functions."

Appellee Commission and *amici* contend somewhat obliquely that because the Framers had no intention of relegating Congress to a position below that of the coequal Judicial and Executive Branches of the National Government, the Appointments Clause must somehow be read to include Congress or its officers as among those in whom the appointment power may be vested. But the debates of the Constitutional Convention, and the Federalist Papers, are replete with expressions of fear that the Legislative Branch of the National Government will aggrandize itself at the expense of the other two branches. The debates during the Convention, and the evolution of the draft version of the Constitution, seem to us to lend considerable support to our reading of the language of the Appointments Clause itself.

. . . .

. . . In the final version, the Senate is shorn of its power to appoint Ambassadors and Judges of the Supreme Court. The President is given, not the power to *appoint* public officers of the United States, but only the right to *nominate* them, and a provision is inserted by virtue of which Congress may require Senate confirmation of his nominees.

It would seem a fair surmise that a compromise had been made. But no change was made in the concept of the term "Officers of the United States," which since it had first appeared . . . had been taken by all concerned to embrace all appointed officials exercising responsibility under the public laws of the Nation.

. . . .

The position that because Congress has been given explicit and plenary authority to regulate a field of activity, it must therefore have the power to appoint those who are to administer the regulatory statute is both novel and contrary to the language of the Appointments Clause. Unless their selection is elsewhere provided for, *all* Officers of the United States are to be appointed in accordance with the Clause. Principal officers are selected by the President with the advice and consent of the Senate. Inferior officers Congress may allow to be appointed by the President alone, by the heads of departments, or by the Judiciary. No class or type of officer is excluded because of its special functions. The President appoints judicial as well as executive officers. Neither has it been disputed — and apparently it is not now disputed — that the Clause controls the appointment of the members of a typical administrative agency even though its functions, as this Court recognized in *Humphrey's Executor v. United States,* 295 U.S. 602, 624 (1935), may be "predominantly quasi-judicial and quasi-legislative" rather than executive. The Court in that case carefully emphasized that although the members of such agencies were to be independent of the Executive in their day-to-day operations, the Executive was not excluded from selecting them. *Id.* at 625–26.

. . . .

We are also told by appellees and *amici* that Congress had good reason for not vesting in a Commission composed wholly of Presidential appointees the authority to administer the Act, since the administration of the Act would undoubtedly have a bearing on any incumbent President's campaign for re-election. While one cannot dispute the basis for this sentiment as a practical matter, it would seem that those who sought to challenge incumbent Congressmen might have equally good reason to fear a Commission which was unduly responsive to members of Congress whom they were seeking to unseat. But such fears, however rational, do not by themselves warrant a distortion of the Framers' work.

Appellee Commission and *amici* finally contend, and the majority of the Court of Appeals agreed with them, that whatever shortcomings the provisions for the appointment of members of the Commission might have under Art. II, Congress had ample authority under the Necessary and Proper Clause of Art. I to effectuate this result. We do not agree. The proper inquiry when considering the Necessary and Proper Clause is not the authority of Congress to create an office or a commission, which is broad indeed, but rather its authority to provide that its own officers may make appointments to such office or commission.

So framed, the claim that Congress may provide for this manner of appointment under the Necessary and Proper Clause of Art. I stands on no better footing than the claim that it may provide for such manner of appointment because of its substantive authority to regulate federal elections. Congress could not, merely because it concluded that such a measure was "necessary and proper" to the discharge of its substantive legislative authority, pass a bill of attainder or *ex post facto* law contrary to the prohibitions contained in § 9 of Art. I. No more may it vest in itself, or in its officers, the authority to appoint officers of the United States when the Appointments Clause by clear implication prohibits it from doing so.

The trilogy of cases from this Court dealing with the constitutional authority of Congress to circumscribe the President's power to *remove* officers of the United States is entirely consistent with this conclusion. In *Myers v. United States,* 272 U.S. 52 (1926), the Court held that Congress could not by statute divest the President of the power to remove an officer in the Executive Branch whom he was initially authorized to appoint. . . .

In the later case of *Humphrey's Executor,* where it was held that Congress could circumscribe the President's power to remove members of independent regulatory agencies, the Court was careful to note that it was dealing with an agency intended to be independent of executive authority "*except in its selection.*" 295 U.S. at 625. . .

This conclusion is buttressed by the fact that Justice Sutherland, the author of the Court's opinion in *Humphrey's Executor,* likewise wrote the opinion for the Court in *Springer v. Philippine Islands,* 277 U.S. 189 (1928), in which it was said:

> Not having the power of appointment, unless expressly granted or incidental to its powers, the legislature cannot ingraft executive duties upon a legislative office, since that would be to usurp the power of appointment by indirection; though the case might be different if the additional duties were devolved upon an appointee of the executive.

Id. at 202.

3. The Commission's Powers

Thus, on the assumption that all of the powers granted in the statute may be exercised by an agency whose members *have been* appointed in accordance with the Appointments Clause, the ultimate question is which, if any, of those powers may be exercised by the present voting Commissioners, none of whom *was* appointed as provided by that Clause. . . .

Insofar as the powers confided in the Commission are essentially of an investigative and informative nature, falling in the same general category as those powers which Congress might delegate to one of its own committees, there can be no question that the Commission as presently constituted may exercise them. *McGrain v. Daugherty,* 273 U.S. 135 (1927). . . .

But when we go beyond this type of authority to the more substantial powers exercised by the Commission, we reach a different result. The Commission's enforcement power, exemplified by its discretionary power to seek judicial relief, is authority that cannot possibly be regarded as merely in aid of the legislative function of Congress. A lawsuit is the ultimate remedy for a breach of the law, and it is to the President, and not to the Congress, that the Constitution entrusts the responsibility to "take Care that the Laws be faithfully executed." Art. II, § 3.

Congress may undoubtedly under the Necessary and Proper Clause create "offices" in the generic sense and provide such method of appointment to those "offices" as it chooses. But Congress' power under that Clause is inevitably bounded by the express language of Art. II, § 2, cl. 2, and unless the method it provides comports with the latter, the holders of those offices will not be "Officers of the United States." They may, therefore, properly perform duties only in aid of those functions that Congress may carry out by itself, or in an area sufficiently removed from the administration and enforcement of the public law as to permit their being performed by persons not "Officers of the United States."

. . . .

We hold that these provisions of the Act, vesting in the Commission primary responsibility for conducting civil litigation in the courts of the United States for vindicating public rights, violate Art. II, § 2, cl. 2, of the Constitution. Such functions may be discharged only by persons who are "Officers of the United States" within the language of that section.

. . . .

. . . [T]he judgment of the Court of Appeals is affirmed in part and reversed in part. . . .

JUSTICE STEVENS took no part in the consideration or decision of these cases.

CHIEF JUSTICE BURGER, concurring in part and dissenting in part.

For reasons set forth more fully later, I dissent from those parts of the Court's holding sustaining the statutory provisions . . . .

. . . I question whether the residue leaves a workable program.

. . . .

Finally, I agree with the Court that the members of the Federal Election Commission were unconstitutionally appointed. . . .

JUSTICE WHITE, concurring in part and dissenting in part.

. . . .

The answers to the questions turn on whether the FEC is illegally constituted because its members were not selected in the manner required by Art. II, § 2, cl. 2, the Appointments Clause. It is my view that with one exception Congress could endow a properly constituted commission with the powers and duties it has given the FEC.

. . . .

It is apparent that none of the members of the FEC is selected in a manner Art. II specifies for the appointment of officers of the United States. . . .

The Appointments Clause applies only to officers of the United States whose appointment is not "otherwise provided for" in the Constitution. Senators and

Congressmen are officers of the United States, but the Constitution expressly provides the mode of their selection. The Constitution also expressly provides that each House of Congress is to appoint its own officers. But it is not contended here that FEC members are officers of either House selected pursuant to these express provisions, if for no other reason, perhaps, than that none of the Commissioners was selected in the manner specified by these provisions — none of them was finally selected by either House acting alone as Art. I authorizes.

The appointment power provided in Art. II also applies only to officers, as distinguished from employees, of the United States, but there is no claim the Commissioners are employees of the United States rather than officers. That the Commissioners are among those officers of the United States referred to in the Appointments Clause of Art. II is evident from the breadth of their assigned duties and the nature and importance of their assigned functions.

. . . .

It is thus not surprising that the FEC, in defending the legality of its members' appointments, does not deny that they are "officers of the United States" as that term is used in the Appointments Clause of Art. II. Instead, for reasons the Court outlines, its position appears to be that even if its members are officers of the United States, Congress may nevertheless appoint a majority of the FEC without participation by the President. This position that Congress may itself appoint the members of a body that is to administer a wide-ranging statute will not withstand examination in light of either the purpose and history of the Appointments Clause or of prior cases in this Court.

The language of the Appointments Clause was not mere inadvertence. The matter of the appointment of officers of the new Federal Government was repeatedly debated by the Framers, and the final formulation of the Clause arrived at only after the most careful debate and consideration of its place in the overall design of government. . . .

. . . .

Under Art. II as finally adopted, law enforcement authority was not to be lodged in elected legislative officials subject to political pressures. Neither was the Legislative Branch to have the power to appoint those who were to enforce and administer the law. Also, the appointment power denied Congress and vested in the President was not limited to purely executive officers but reached officers performing judicial functions as well as all other officers of the United States.

I thus find singularly unpersuasive the proposition that because the FEC is implementing statutory policies with respect to the conduct of elections, which policies Congress has the power to propound, its members may be appointed by Congress. . . .

Congress clearly has the power to create federal offices and to define the powers and duties of those offices, *Myers v. United States*, 272 U.S. 52, 128–29 (1926), but no case in this Court even remotely supports the power of Congress to appoint an officer of the United States aside from those officers each House is authorized by Art. I to appoint to assist in the legislative processes.

. . . .

It is said that historically Congress has used its own officers to receive and file the reports of campaign expenditures and contributions as required by law and that this Court should not interfere with this practice. . . . But the FEC may also make rules and regulations with respect to the disclosure requirements, may investigate reported violations, issue subpoenas, hold its own hearings and institute civil enforcement proceedings in its own name. Absent a request by the FEC, it would appear that the Attorney General has no role in the civil enforcement of the reporting and disclosure requirements. The FEC may also issue advisory opinions with respect to the legality of any particular activities so as to protect those persons who in good faith have conducted themselves in reliance on the FEC's opinion. These functions go far beyond mere information gathering, and there is no long history of lodging such enforcement powers in congressional appointees.

Nor do the FEC's functions stop with policing the reporting and disclosure requirements of the Act. The FEC is given express power to administer, obtain compliance with, and "to formulate general policy" with respect to 18 U.S.C. §§ 608–617, so much so that the Act expressly provides that "[t]he Commission has primary jurisdiction with respect to the civil enforcement of such provisions." Following its own proceedings the FEC may request the Attorney General to bring civil enforcement proceedings, a request which the Attorney General must honor. And good-faith conduct taken in accordance with the FEC's advisory opinions as to whether any transaction or activity would violate any of these criminal provisions "shall be presumed to be in compliance with" these sections. § 437f(b). Finally, the FEC has the central role in administering and enforcing the provisions of Title 26 contemplating the public financing of political campaigns.

It is apparent that the FEC is charged with the enforcement of the election laws in major respects. Indeed, except for the conduct of criminal proceedings, it would appear that the FEC has the entire responsibility for enforcement of the statutes at issue here. . . .

It is suggested . . . that the FEC would be willing to forgo its civil enforcement powers and that absent these functions, it is left with nothing that purely legislative officers may not do. The difficulty is that the statute invests the FEC not only with authority but with the *duties* that unquestionably make its members officers of the United States . . . .

. . . .

[The separate opinions of Marshall, Blackmun, and Rehnquist, each of whom concurred in Part IV of the Court's opinion and dissented on other matters, have been omitted.]

Exercise 5(A):

Consider the following questions in regard to *Buckley v. Valeo*:

(1) What is the test for distinguishing an "Officer of the United States" from a mere "employee" of the central government or an "Officer of Congress"?

(2) Which functions, if any, vested in the FEC could be exercised without significant constitutional problems?

(3) Which functions, if any, vested in the FEC were "executive" functions that could be exercised only by one or more "Officers of the United States"?

(4) What constitutional issues, if any, were presented by the inclusion of the *ex officio* members of the FEC?

(5) What constitutional issues, if any, were presented with respect to the presidential appointees to the FEC?

(6) What constitutional issues, if any, were presented with respect to the congressional appointees to the FEC?

(7) With respect to the issues addressed by the Court, what interpretation of the Constitution is suggested by structural considerations, textual analysis, shared original understanding, tradition, and judicial precedent?

(8) With respect to the issues addressed by the Court, what interpretation of the Constitution is suggested by practical policy and political considerations? What weight does the Court give to such matters?

(9) Throughout *Buckley v. Valeo,* did the Court fairly characterize *Myers* and *Humphrey's Executor,* two of its important precedents on removal of officers?

BOWSHER v. SYNAR

478 U.S. 714 (1986)

CHIEF JUSTICE BURGER delivered the opinion of the Court.

The question presented by these appeals is whether the assignment by Congress to the Comptroller General of the United States of certain functions under the Balanced Budget and Emergency Deficit Control Act of 1985 violates the doctrine of separation of powers.

I

A

On December 12, 1985, the President signed into law the Balanced Budget and Emergency Deficit Control Act of 1985, popularly known as the "Gramm-Rudman-Hollings Act." The purpose of the Act is to eliminate the federal budget deficit. To that end, the Act sets a "maximum deficit amount" for federal spending for each of fiscal years 1986 through 1991. The size of that maximum deficit amount progressively reduces to zero in fiscal year 1991. If in any fiscal year the federal budget deficit exceeds the maximum deficit amount by more than a specified sum, the Act requires across-the-board cuts in federal spending to reach the targeted deficit level . . . .

These "automatic" reductions are accomplished through a rather complicated procedure, spelled out in § 251, the so-called "reporting provisions" of the Act. Each year, the Directors of the Office of Management and Budget (OMB) and the Congressional Budget Office (CBO) independently estimate the amount of the federal budget deficit for the upcoming fiscal year. If that deficit exceeds the maximum targeted deficit amount for that fiscal year by more than a specified amount, the Directors of OMB and CBO independently calculate, on a program-by-program basis, the budget reductions necessary to ensure that the deficit does not exceed the maximum deficit amount. The Act then requires the Directors to report jointly their deficit estimates and budget reduction calculations to the Comptroller General.

The Comptroller General, after reviewing the Directors' reports, then reports his conclusions to the President. § 251(b). The President in turn must issue a "sequestration" order mandating the spending reductions specified by the Comptroller General. § 252. There follows a period during which Congress may by legislation reduce spending to obviate, in whole or in part, the need for the sequestration order. If such reductions are not enacted, the sequestration order becomes effective and the spending reductions included in that order are made.

[The Act contained a "fall back" provision in the event the reporting procedures were invalidated. Under this alternative procedure, the report prepared by the

Directors of the OMB and CBO would be submitted to a congressional committee, which would prepare a joint resolution to be presented to Congress for consideration under special, expedited rules that preclude amendments. If both Houses passed the resolution and the President signed it, it would serve "as the basis for a Presidential sequestration order."]

B

Within hours of the President' signing of the Act,[31] Congressman Synar, who had voted against the Act, filed a complaint seeking declaratory relief that the Act was unconstitutional. Eleven other Members later joined Congressman Synar's suit. A virtually identical lawsuit was also filed by the National Treasury Employee's Union. The Union alleged that its members had been injured as a result of the Act's automatic spending reduction provisions, which have suspended certain cost-of-living benefit increases to the Union's members.

[A three-judge District Court concluded that the parties had standing to bring the suit and, on the merits, rejected certain arguments.]

[The District Court held] that the role of the Comptroller General in the deficit reduction process violated the constitutionally imposed separation of powers. The court first explained that the Comptroller General exercises executive functions under the Act. However, the Comptroller General, while appointed by the President with the advice and consent of the Senate, is removable not by the President but only by a joint resolution of Congress or by impeachment. The District Court reasoned that this arrangement could not be sustained under this Court's decisions in *Myers v. United States*, 272 U.S. 52 (1926), and *Humphrey's Executor v. United States*, 295 U.S. 602 (1935). Under the separation of powers established by the Framers of the Constitution, the court concluded, Congress may not retain the power of removal over an officer performing executive functions. The congressional removal power created a "here-and-now subservience" of the Comptroller General to Congress. The District Court therefore held that

> since the powers conferred upon the Comptroller General as part of the automatic deficit reduction process are executive powers, which cannot constitutionally be exercised by an officer removable by Congress, those powers cannot be exercised and therefore the automatic deficit reduction process to which they are central cannot be implemented.

. . . .

[After finding that at least one member of the Union had standing, the Court proceeded to consider the merits, without considering the standing of the Union itself or Members of Congress.]

III

We noted recently that "[t]he Constitution sought to divide the delegated powers of the new Federal Government into three defined categories, Legislative, Executive, and Judicial." *INS v. Chadha*, 462 U.S. 919, 951 (1983). The declared purpose of separating and dividing the powers of the government, of course, was to "diffus[e] power to better secure liberty." *Youngstown Sheet & Tube Co. v. Sawyer*, 343 U.S. 579, 635 (1952) (Jackson, J., concurring). Justice Jackson's words echo the

---

[31] In his signing statement, the President expressed his view that the Act was constitutionally defective because of the Comptroller General's ability to exercise supervisory authority over the President.

famous warning of Montesquieu, quoted by James Madison in The Federalist No. 47, that " 'there can be no liberty where the legislative and executive powers are united in the same person, or body of magistrates' . . . ."

. . . .

The Constitution does not contemplate an active role for Congress in the supervision of officers charged with the execution of the laws it enacts. The President appoints "Officers of the United States" with the "Advice and Consent of the Senate." Art. II, § 2. Once the appointment has been made and confirmed, however, the Constitution explicitly provides for removal of Officers of the United States by Congress only upon impeachment by the House of Representatives and conviction by the Senate. An impeachment by the House and trial by the Senate can rest only on "Treason, Bribery or other high crimes and Misdemeanors." Art. II, § 4. A direct congressional role in the removal of officers charged with the execution of the laws beyond this limited one is inconsistent with separation of powers.

This was made clear in the First Congress in 1789. When Congress considered an amendment to a bill establishing the Department of Foreign Affairs, the debate centered around whether the Congress "should recognize and declare the power of the President under the Constitution to remove the Secretary of Foreign Affairs without the advice and consent of the Senate." *Myers*, 272 U.S. at 114. James Madison urged rejection of a congressional role in the removal of Executive Branch officers, other than by impeachment, saying in debate:

> Perhaps there was no argument urged with more success, or more plausibly grounded against the Constitution, under which we are now deliberating, than that founded on the mingling of the Executive and Legislative branches of the Government in one body. It has been objected, that the Senate have too much of the Executive power even, by having a control over the President in the appointment to office. Now, shall we extend this conne[ction] between the Legislative and Executive departments, which will strengthen the objection, and diminish the responsibility we have in the head of the Executive?

1 Annals of Cong. 380 (1789). Madison's position ultimately prevailed, and a congressional role in the removal process was rejected. This "Decision of 1789" provides "contemporaneous and weighty evidence" of the Constitution's meaning since many of the Members of the First Congress "had taken part in framing that instrument." *Marsh v. Chambers*, 463 U.S. 783 (1983).

This Court first directly addressed this issue in *Myers v. United States*, 272 U.S. 52 (1925). . . . Chief Justice Taft, writing for the Court, declared the statute unconstitutional on the ground that for Congress to "draw to itself, or to either branch of it, the power to remove or the right to participate in the exercise of that power . . . would be . . . to infringe the constitutional principle of the separation of governmental powers." *Id.* at 161.

A decade later, in *Humphrey's Executor v. United States*, 295 U.S. 602 (1935), relied upon heavily by appellants, a Federal Trade Commissioner who had been removed by the President sought backpay. *Humphrey's Executor* involved an issue not presented either in the *Myers* case or in this case — *i.e.*, the power of Congress to limit the President's powers of removal of a Federal Trade Commissioner. 295 U.S. at 630. . . . The Court distinguished *Myers*, reaffirming its holding that congressional participation in the removal of executive officers is unconstitutional. Justice Sutherland's opinion for the Court also underscored the crucial role of separated powers in our system:

> The fundamental necessity of maintaining each of the three general departments of government entirely free from the control or coercive influence, direct or indirect, of either of the others, has often been stressed and is hardly open to serious question. So much is implied in the very fact of the separation of the powers of these departments by the Constitution; and in the rule which recognizes their essential co-equality.

295 U.S. at 629–30. The Court reached a similar result in *Wiener v. United States,* 357 U.S. 349 (1958), concluding that, under *Humphrey's Executor,* the President did not have unrestrained removal authority over a member of the War Claims Commission.

In light of these precedents, we conclude that Congress cannot reserve for itself the power of removal of an officer charged with the execution of the laws except by impeachment. To permit the execution of the laws to be vested in an officer answerable only to Congress would, in practical terms, reserve in Congress control over the execution of the laws. As the District Court observed: "Once an officer is appointed, it is only the authority that can remove him, and not the authority that appointed him, that he must fear and, in the performance of his functions, obey." The structure of the Constitution does not permit Congress to execute the laws; it follows that Congress cannot grant to an officer under its control what it does not possess.

. . . Congress could simply remove, or threaten to remove, an officer for executing the laws in any fashion found to be unsatisfactory to Congress. This kind of congressional control over the execution of the laws . . . is unconstitutionally impermissible.

The dangers of congressional usurpation of Executive Branch functions have long been recognized. "[T]he debates of the Constitutional Convention, and the Federalist Papers, are replete with expressions of fear that the Legislative Branch of the National Government will aggrandize itself at the expense of the other two branches." *Buckley v. Valeo,* 424 U.S. 1, 129 (1976). Indeed, we also have observed only recently that "[t]he hydraulic pressure inherent within each of the separate Branches to exceed the outer limits of its power, even to accomplish desirable objectives, must be resisted." *INS v. Chadha,* 462 U.S. 919, 951 (1983). With these principles in mind, we turn to consideration of whether the Comptroller General is controlled by Congress.

IV

Appellants urge that the Comptroller General performs his duties independently and is not subservient to Congress. We agree with the District Court that this contention does not bear close scrutiny.

The critical factor lies in the provisions of the statute defining the Comptroller General's office relating to removability. Although the Comptroller General is nominated by the President from a list of three individuals recommended by the Speaker of the House of Representatives and the President *pro tempore* of the Senate, and confirmed by the Senate, he is removable only at the initiative of Congress. He may be removed not only by impeachment but also by joint resolution of Congress "at any time" resting on any of the following bases:

(i) permanent disability;

(ii) inefficiency;

(iii) neglect of duty;

(iv) malfeasance; or

(v) a felony or conduct involving moral turpitude.

31 U.S.C. § 703(e)(1)B.[7] This provision was included, as one Congressman explained in urging the passage of the Act, because Congress "felt that [the Comptroller General] should be brought under the sole control of Congress, so that Congress at any moment when it found he was inefficient and was not carrying on the duties of his office as he should and as the Congress expected, could remove him without the long, tedious process of a trial by impeachment." 61 Cong. Rec. 1081 (1921).

The removal provision was an important part of the legislative scheme, as a number of Congressman recognized. Representative Hawley commented: "[H]e is our officer, in a measure, getting information for us . . . . If he does not do his work properly, we, as practically his employers, ought to be able to discharge him from his office." 58 Cong. Rec. 7136 (1919). Representative Sisson observed that the removal provisions would give "[t]he Congress of the United States . . . absolute control of the man's destiny in office." 61 Cong. Rec. 987 (1921). The ultimate design was to "give the legislative branch of the Government control of the audit, not through the power of appointment, but through the power of removal." 58 Cong. Rec. 7211 (1919) (Rep. Temple).

Justice White contends: "The statute does not permit anyone to remove the Comptroller at will; removal is permitted only for specified cause, with the existence of cause to be determined by Congress following a hearing. Any removal under the statute would presumably be subject to post-termination judicial review to ensure that a hearing had in fact been held and that the finding of cause for removal was not arbitrary." That observation by the dissenter rests on at least two arguable premises: (a) that the enumeration of certain specified causes of removal excludes the possibility of removal for other causes, *cf. Shurtleff v. United States,* 189 U.S. 311, 315–16 (1903); and (b) that any removal would be subject to judicial review, a position that appellants were unwilling to endorse.[8]

Glossing over these difficulties, the dissent's assessment of the statute fails to recognize the breadth of the grounds for removal. The statute permits removal for "inefficiency," "neglect of duty," or "malfeasance." These terms are very broad and, as interpreted by Congress, could sustain removal of a Comptroller General for any number of actual or perceived transgressions of the legislative will. The Constitutional Convention chose to permit impeachment of executive officers only for "Treason, Bribery, or other high Crimes and Misdemeanors." It rejected language that would have permitted impeachment for "maladministration," with Madison arguing that "[s]o vague a term will be equivalent to a tenure during pleasure of the Senate." 2 MAX FARRAND, RECORDS OF THE FEDERAL CONVENTION OF 1787, p. 550 (1911).

We need not decide whether "inefficiency" or "malfeasance" are terms as broad as "maladministration" in order to reject the dissent's position that removing the Comptroller General requires "a feat of bipartisanship more difficult than that required to impeach and convict." Surely no one would seriously suggest that

---

[7] Although the President could veto such a joint resolution, the veto could be overridden by a two-thirds vote of both Houses of Congress. Thus, the Comptroller General could be removed in the face of Presidential opposition. . . .

[8] The dissent relies on *Humphrey's Executor v. United States,* 295 U.S. 602 (1935), as its only Court authority for this point, but the President did not assert that he had removed the Federal Trade Commissioner in compliance with one of the enumerated statutory causes for removal. *See id.* at 612.

judicial independence would be strengthened by allowing removal of federal judges only by a joint resolution finding "inefficiency," "neglect of duty," or "malfeasance."

Justice White, however, assures us that "[r]ealistic consideration" of the "practical result of the removal provision" reveals that the Comptroller General is unlikely to be removed by Congress. The separated powers of our Government cannot be permitted to turn on judicial assessment of whether an officer exercising executive power is on good terms with Congress. The Framers recognized that, in the long term, structural protections against abuse of power were critical to preserving liberty. In constitutional terms, the removal powers over the Comptroller General's office dictate that he will be subservient to Congress.

This much said, we must also add that the dissent is simply in error to suggest that the political realities reveal that the Comptroller General is free from influence by Congress. The Comptroller General heads the General Accounting Office (GAO), "an instrumentality of the United States Government independent of the executive departments," 31 U.S.C. § 702(a), which was created by Congress in 1921 as part of the Budget and Accounting Act of 1921, 42 Stat. 23. Congress created the office because it believed that it "needed an officer, responsible to it alone, to check upon the application of public funds in accordance with appropriations." H. MANSFIELD, THE COMPTROLLER GENERAL: A STUDY IN THE LAW AND PRACTICE OF FINANCIAL ADMINISTRATION 65 (1939).

It is clear that Congress has consistently viewed the Comptroller General as an officer of the Legislative Branch. . . .

Over the years, Comptrollers General have also viewed themselves as part of the Legislative Branch. . . .

Against this background, we see no escape from the conclusion that, because Congress has retained removal authority over the Comptroller General, he may not be entrusted with executive powers. The remaining question is whether the Comptroller General has been assigned such powers in the [Gramm-Rudman-Hollings Act].

V

The primary responsibility of the Comptroller General under the instant Act is the preparation of a "report." This report must contain detailed estimates of projected federal revenues and expenditures. The report must also specify the reductions, if any, necessary to reduce the deficit to the target for the appropriate fiscal year. The reductions must be set forth on a program-by-program basis.

In preparing the report, the Comptroller General is to have "due regard" for the estimates and reductions set forth in a joint report submitted to him by the Director of CBO and the Director of OMB, the President's fiscal and budgetary adviser. However, the Act plainly contemplates that the Comptroller General will exercise his independent judgment and evaluation with respect to those estimates. The Act also provides that the Comptroller General's report "shall explain fully any differences between the contents of such report and the report of the Directors." § 251(b)(2).

Appellants suggest that the duties assigned to the Comptroller General in the Act are essentially ministerial and mechanical so that their performance does not constitute "execution of the law" in a meaningful sense. On the contrary, we view these functions as plainly entailing execution of the law in constitutional terms. Interpreting a law enacted by Congress to implement the legislative mandate is the very essence of "execution" of the law. Under § 251, the Comptroller General must exercise judgment concerning facts that affect the application of the Act. He must also interpret the provisions of the Act to determine precisely what budgetary calculations are required. Decisions of that kind are typically made by officers charged with executing the statute.

The executive nature of the Comptroller General's functions under the Act is revealed in § 252(a)(3) which gives the Comptroller General the ultimate authority to determine the budget cuts to be made. Indeed, the Comptroller General commands the President himself to carry out, without the slightest variation (with exceptions not relevant to the constitutional issues presented), the directive of the Comptroller General as to the budget reductions . . . .

Congress of course initially determined the content of the [Act]; and undoubtedly the content of the Act determines the nature of the executive duty. However, . . . once Congress makes its choice in enacting legislation, its participation ends. Congress can thereafter control the execution of its enactment only indirectly — by passing new legislation. By placing the responsibility for execution of the [Act] in the hands of an officer who is subject to removal only by itself, Congress in effect has retained control over the execution of the Act and has intruded into the executive function. The Constitution does not permit such intrusion.

. . . .

VII

No one can doubt that Congress and the President are confronted with fiscal and economic problems of unprecedented magnitude, but "the fact that a given law or procedure is efficient, convenient, and useful in facilitating functions of government, standing alone, will not save it if it is contrary to the Constitution . . . ." *Chadha*, 462 U.S. at 944.

We conclude that the District Court correctly held that the powers vested in the Comptroller General under § 251 violate the command of the Constitution that the Congress play no direct role in the execution of the laws. Accordingly, the judgment and order of the District Court are affirmed.

Our judgment is stayed for a period not to exceed 60 days to permit Congress to implement the fallback provisions.

JUSTICE STEVENS with whom JUSTICE MARSHALL joins, concurring in the judgment.

. . . I agree with the Court that the "Gramm-Rudman-Hollings" Act contains a constitutional infirmity so severe that the flawed provision may not stand. I disagree with the Court, however, on the reasons why the Constitution prohibits the Comptroller General from exercising the powers assigned to him by § 251(b) and § 251(c)(2) of the Act. . . . [T]he Comptroller General must be characterized as an agent of Congress because of his longstanding statutory responsibilities; that the powers assigned to him under the Gramm-Rudman-Hollings Act require him to make policy that will bind the Nation; and that, when Congress, or a component or an agent of Congress, seeks to make policy that will bind the Nation, it must follow the procedures mandated by Article I of the Constitution — through passage by both houses and presentment to the President. . . .

I

The fact that Congress retained for itself the power to remove the Comptroller General is important evidence supporting the conclusion that he is a member of the Legislative Branch of the Government. Unlike the Court, however, I am not persuaded that the congressional removal power is either a necessary, or a sufficient, basis for concluding that his statutory assignment is invalid.

. . . .

The notion that the removal power at issue here automatically creates some kind of "here-and-now subservience" of the Comptroller General to Congress is belied by history. There is no evidence that Congress has ever removed, or threatened to remove, the Comptroller General for reasons of policy. Moreover, the President has long possessed a comparable power to remove members of the Federal Trade Commission, yet it is universally accepted that they are independent of, rather than subservient to, the President in performing their official duties. Thus, the statute that the Court construed in *Humphrey's Executor v. United States,* 295 U.S. 602 (1935), provided: "Any commissioner may be removed by the President for inefficiency, neglect of duty, or malfeasance in office." In upholding the congressional limitations on the President's power of removal, the Court stressed the independence of the Commission from the President. There was no suggestion that the retained Presidential removal powers — similar to those at issue here — created a subservience to the President.

. . . .

II

In assessing the role of the Comptroller General, it is appropriate to consider his already existing statutory responsibilities. Those responsibilities leave little doubt that one of the identifying characteristics of the Comptroller General is his statutorily required relationship to the Legislative Branch.

In the statutory section that identifies the Comptroller General's responsibilities for investigating the use of public money, four of the five enumerated duties specifically describe an obligation owed to Congress. . . .

. . . .

The Comptroller General's current statutory responsibilities on behalf of Congress are fully consistent with the historic conception on the Comptroller General's office. . . . On at least three occasions since 1921, moreover, in considering the structure of Government, Congress has defined the Comptroller General as being a part of the Legislative Branch. . . .

. . . The Comptroller General is statutorily required to audit the Internal Revenue Service and the Bureau of Alcohol, Tobacco, and Firearms (and provide congressional committees with information respecting the audits). . . .

. . . [T]he Comptroller General retains certain obligations with respect to the Executive Branch.[9] Obligations to two branches are not, however, impermissible and the presence of such dual obligations does not prevent the characterization of the official with the dual obligations as part of one branch. It is at least clear that, in most, if not all, of his statutory responsibilities, the Comptroller General is properly characterized as an agent of the Congress.

III

Everyone agrees that the powers assigned to the Comptroller General by § 251(b) and § 251(c)(2) of the Gramm-Rudman-Hollings Act are extremely impor-

[9] The Comptroller General, of course, is also appointed by the President. So too, however, are the Librarian of Congress, the Architect of the Capitol, and the Public Printer.

tant. . . . His duties are anything but ministerial — he is not merely a clerk wearing a "green eyeshade" as he undertakes these tasks. Rather, he is vested with the kind of responsibilities that Congress has elected to discharge itself under the fallback provision that will become effective if and when § 251(b) and § 251(c)(2) are held invalid. . . .

. . . .

IV

. . . .

The Gramm-Rudman-Hollings Act assigns to the Comptroller General the duty to make policy decisions that have the force of law. . . .

Article I of the Constitution specifies the procedures that Congress must follow when it makes policy that binds the Nation: its legislation must be approved by both Houses and presented to the President. . . .

. . . .

As a result, to decide this case there is no need to consider the Decision of 1789, the President's removal power, or the abstract nature of "executive power." Once it is clear that the Comptroller General, whose statutory duties define him as an agent of Congress, has been assigned the task of making policy determinations that will bind the Nation, the question is simply one of congressional process. There can be no doubt that the Comptroller General's statutory duties under Gramm-Rudman-Hollings do not follow the constitutionally prescribed procedures for congressional lawmaking.

. . . It is for this reason that I believe § 251(b) and § 251(c)(2) of the Act are unconstitutional.

. . . .

JUSTICE WHITE, dissenting.

The Court, acting in the name of separation of powers, takes upon itself to strike down the Gramm-Rudman-Hollings Act, one of the most novel and far-reaching legislative responses to a national crisis since the New Deal. . . . Like the Court, I will not purport to speak to the wisdom of the policies incorporated in the legislation the Court invalidates; that is a matter for the Congress and the Executive, *both* of which expressed their assent to the statute barely half a year ago. I will, however, address the wisdom of the Court's willingness to interpose its distressingly formalistic view of separation of powers as a bar to the attainment of governmental objectives through the means chosen by the Congress and the President in the legislative process established by the Constitution. . . . As I will explain, the Court's decision rests on a feature of the legislative scheme that is of minimal practical significance and that presents no substantial threat to the basic scheme of separation of powers. . . .

I

The Court's argument is straightforward: the Act vests the Comptroller General with "executive" powers, that is, powers to "[i]nterpre[t] a law enacted by Congress [in order] to implement the legislative mandate;" such powers may not be vested by Congress in itself or its agents, *see Buckley v. Valeo*, 424 U.S. 1, 120–141 (1976), for the system of Government established by the Constitution for the most part limits Congress to a legislative rather than executive or judicial role; the Comptroller General is an agent of Congress by virtue of a provision in the Budget and

Accounting Act of 1921 granting Congress the power to remove the Comptroller for cause through joint resolution; therefore the Comptroller General may not constitutionally exercise the executive power granted him in the Gramm-Rudman-Hollings Act, and the Act's automatic budget-reduction mechanism, which is premised on the Comptroller's exercise of those powers, must be struck down.

Before examining the merits of the Court's argument, I wish to emphasize what it is that the Court quite pointedly does *not* hold: namely, that "executive" powers of the sort granted the Comptroller by the Act may only be exercised by officers removable at will by the President. The Court's apparent unwillingness to accept this argument, which has been tendered in this Court by the Solicitor General, is fully consistent with the Court's longstanding recognition that it is within the power of Congress under the "Necessary and Proper" Clause to vest authority that falls within the Court's definition of executive power in officers who are not subject to removal at will by the President and are therefore not under the President's direct control. . . .

The Court's recognition of the legitimacy of legislation vesting "executive" authority in officers independent of the President does not imply derogation of the President's own constitutional authority — indeed, duty — to "take Care that the Laws be faithfully executed," Art. II, § 3, for any such duty is necessarily limited to a great extent by the content of the laws enacted by the Congress. . . . [T]here are undoubtedly executive functions that, regardless of the enactments of Congress, must be performed by officers subject to removal at will by the President. Whether a particular function falls within this class or within the far larger class that may be relegated to independent officers "will depend upon the character of the office." *Humphrey's Executor v. United States,* 295 U.S. 602, 631 (1935). In determining whether a limitation on the President's power to remove an officer performing executive functions constitutes a violation of the constitutional scheme of separation of powers, a court must "focu[s] on the extent to which [such a limitation] prevents the Executive Branch from accomplishing its constitutionally assigned functions." *Nixon v. Administrator of General Services,* 433 U.S. 425, 443 (1977). "Only where the potential for disruption is present must we then determine whether that impact is justified by an overriding need to promote objectives within the constitutional authority of Congress." *Id.* This inquiry is, to be sure, not one that will beget easy answers; it provides nothing approaching a bright-line rule or set of rules. Such an inquiry, however, is necessitated by the recognition that "formalistic and unbending rules" in the area of separation of powers may "unduly constrict Congress' ability to take needed and innovative action pursuant to its Article I powers."

It is evident (and nothing in the Court's opinion is to the contrary) that the powers exercised by the Comptroller General under the Gramm-Rudman-Hollings Act are not such that vesting them in an officer not subject to removal at will by the President would itself improperly interfere with Presidential powers. Determining the level of spending by the Federal Government is not by nature a function central either to the exercise of the President's enumerated powers or to his general duty to ensure the execution of the laws; rather, appropriating funds is a peculiarly legislative function, and one expressly committed to Congress by Art. I, § 9. . . . In enacting Gramm-Rudman-Hollings, Congress has chosen to exercise this legislative power to establish the level of federal spending by providing a detailed set of criteria for reducing expenditures below the level of appropriations in the event that certain conditions are met. Delegating the execution of this legislation — that is, the power to apply the Act's criteria and make the required calculations — to an officer independent of the President's will does not deprive the President of any power that he would otherwise have or that is essential to the performance of the duties of his office. Rather, the result of such a delegation, from the standpoint of the President, is no different from the result of more traditional forms of appropriation: under either system, the level of funds available to the Executive Branch to carry out its duties is not within the President's discretionary control. To be sure, if the budget-cutting mechanism required the responsible officer to exercise a great deal of policymaking discretion, one might argue that having created such broad discretion Congress had some obligation based upon Art. II to vest it in the Chief Executive or his agents. In Gramm-Rudman-Hollings, however, Congress has done no such thing; instead, it has created a precise and articulated set of criteria designed to minimize the degree of policy choice exercised by the officer executing the statute and to ensure that the relative spending priorities established by Congress in the appropriations it passes into law remain unaltered. Given that the exercise of policy choice by the officer executing the statute would be inimical to Congress' goal in enacting "automatic" budget-cutting measures, it is eminently reasonable and proper for Congress to vest the budget-cutting authority in an officer who is to the greatest degree possible nonpartisan and independent of the President and his political agenda and who therefore may be relied upon not to allow his calculations to be colored by political considerations. Such a delegation deprives the President of no authority that is rightfully his.

II

If, as the Court seems to agree, the assignment of "executive" powers under Gramm-Rudman-Hollings to an officer not removable at will by the President would not in itself represent a violation of the constitutional scheme of separated powers, the question remains whether, as the Court concludes, the fact that the officer to whom Congress has delegated the authority to implement the Act is removable by a joint resolution of Congress should require invalidation of the Act. . . . I have no quarrel with the proposition that the powers exercised by the Comptroller under the Act may be characterized as "executive" in that they involve the interpretation and carrying out of the Act's mandate. I can also accept the general proposition that although Congress has considerable authority in designating the officers who are to execute legislation, the constitutional scheme of separated powers does prevent Congress from reserving an executive role for itself or for its "agents." I cannot accept, however, that the exercise of authority by an officer removable for cause by a joint resolution of Congress is analogous to the impermissible execution of the law by Congress itself, nor would I hold that the congressional role in the removal process renders the Comptroller an "agent" of the Congress, incapable of receiving "executive" power.

. . . Because the Comptroller is not an appointee of Congress but an officer of the United States appointed by the President with the advice and consent of the Senate, *Buckley* neither requires that he be characterized as an agent of the Congress nor in any other way calls into question his capacity to exercise "executive" authority. *See* 424 U.S. at 128 n.165.

. . . .

The deficiencies in the Court's reasoning are apparent. First, the Court badly mischaracterizes the removal provision when it suggests that it allows Congress to remove the Comptroller for "executing the laws in any fashion found to be unsatisfactory;" in fact, Congress may remove the Comptroller only for one or more of five specified reasons . . . .

Second, and more to the point, the Court overlooks or deliberately ignores . . . [the provision that] Congress may remove the Comptroller only through a joint resolution, which by definition must be passed by both Houses and signed by the President. *See United States v. California*, 332 U.S. 19, 28 (1947). In other words, a removal of the Comptroller under the statute *satisfies the requirements of bicameralism and presentment*. . . .

. . . .

. . . [T]he question is whether there is a genuine threat of "encroachment or aggrandizement of one branch at the expense of the other." *Buckley v. Valeo*, 424 U.S. at 122. Common sense indicates that the existence of the removal provision poses no such threat to the principle of separation of powers.

The statute does not permit anyone to remove the Comptroller at will; removal is permitted only for specified cause, with the existence of cause to be determined by Congress following a hearing. Any removal under the statute would presumably be subject to post-termination judicial review to ensure that a hearing had in fact been held and that the finding of cause for removal was not arbitrary. These procedural and substantive limitations on the removal power militate strongly against the characterization of the Comptroller as a mere agent of Congress by virtue of the removal authority. Indeed, similarly qualified grants of removal power are generally deemed to protect the officers to whom they apply and to establish their independence from the domination of the possessor of the removal power. *See Humphrey's Executor*, 295 U.S. at 625–26, 629–30. Removal authority limited in such a manner is more properly viewed as motivating adherence to a substantive standard established by law than as inducing subservience to the particular institution that enforces that standard. . . .

More importantly, the substantial role played by the President in the process of removal through joint resolution reduces to utter insignificance the possibility that the threat of removal will induce subservience to Congress. . . . The requirement of Presidential approval obviates the possibility that the Comptroller will perceive himself as so completely at the mercy of Congress that he will function as its tool. If the Comptroller's conduct in office is not so unsatisfactory to the President as to convince the latter that removal is required under the statutory standard, Congress will have no independent power to coerce the Comptroller unless it can muster a two-thirds majority in both Houses — a feat of bipartisanship more difficult than required to impeach and convict. . . .

The practical result of the removal provision is not to render the Comptroller unduly dependent upon or subservient to Congress, but to render him one of the most independent officers in the entire federal establishment. Those who have studied the office agree that the procedural and substantive limits on the power of Congress and the President to remove the Comptroller make dislodging him against his will practically impossible. . . .

Realistic consideration of the nature of the Comptroller General's relation to Congress thus reveals that the threat to separation of powers conjured up by the majority is wholly chimerical. The power over removal retained by the Congress is not a power that is exercised outside the legislative process as established by the Constitution, nor does it appear likely that it is a power that adds significantly to the influence Congress may exert over executive officers through other, undoubtedly constitutional exercises of legislative power. . . .

The majority's contrary conclusion rests on the rigid dogma that, outside of the impeachment process, any "direct congressional role in the removal of officers charged with the execution of the laws . . . is inconsistent with separation of powers." Reliance on such an unyielding principle to strike down a statute posing no real danger of aggrandizement of congressional power is extremely misguided and insensitive to our constitutional role. . . .

JUSTICE BLACKMUN, dissenting.

. . . [I]t seems to me that an attempt by Congress to participate *directly* in the removal of an executive officer — other than through the constitutionally prescribed procedure of impeachment — might well violate the principle of separation of powers by assuming for Congress part of the President's constitutional responsibility to carry out the laws.

In my view, however, that important and difficult question need not be decided in this litigation . . . . Any incompatability, I feel, should be cured by refusing to allow congressional removal — if it is ever attempted — and not by striking down the central provisions of the Deficit Control Act. . . .

Exercise 5(B):

Consider the following questions in regard to *Bowsher v. Synar*:

(1) Does this case follow *Buckley v. Valeo* in distinguishing among an "Officer of the United States," a mere "employee" of the central government, and an "Officer of Congress"? If not, does it suggest an alternative test?

(2) Which functions, if any, vested in the Comptroller General could be exercised without significant constitutional problems?

(3) Which functions, if any, vested in the Comptroller General were "executive" functions that could be exercised only by one or more "Officers of the United States"?

(4) With respect to the constitutional addressed by the Court, what interpretation of the Constitution is suggested by structural considerations, textual analysis, shared original understanding, tradition, and judicial precedent?

(5) With respect to the issues presented in *Bowsher v. Synar,* what interpretation of the Constitution is suggested by practical policy and political considerations? What weight does the Court give to such matters?

(6) In *Bowsher,* the Act called for the Comptroller General to review the independent calculations of OMB and CBO to formulate his own conclusion which he then reported to the President. If, instead, the calculations of OMB and CBO were reported directly to the President to provide information with which the President could prepare a "sequestration" order, would the process have been constitutional? Why or why not? Would it have made a difference if, before the Presidential sequestration order became effective, there was a period during which Congress could legislate to reduce spending so as to obviate, in whole or in part, the need for the sequestration order? Why or why not?

(7) Assume that Congress followed the approach of Question 6 and provided that any Presidential sequestration order would not become effective for thirty days after notice of the order was communicated to Congress. Assume further that the Act provided that the two houses of Congress, by majority vote within the thirty day period, could disallow the application of the sequestration order to any specific agency or program. Would that process have been constitutional? Why or why not?

(8) The first suit challenging the constitutionality of the Gramm-Rudman-Hollings Act was filed by Congressman Synar (which eleven other members of Congress then joined). If that was the only suit filed, how should the Court have ruled? Why?

(9) With regard to the role of the Comptroller General under the Act, the Supreme Court considered whether there was any textual support for a constitutional role for Congress in the removal of officers outside of the impeachment process. Is there any less textual support for congressional removal than there is for Presidential removal?

(10) Throughout *Bowsher v. Synar*, did the Court fairly characterize *Myers* and *Humphrey's Executor*, two of its important precedents on removal of officers?

(11) The Court observed that the Budget and Accounting Act of 1921 (on the DVD-ROM) created the office of "Comptroller General" and provided criteria for his removal from office. Section 303 of that statute specified that the officer, who would be nominated by the President and confirmed by the Senate, would serve a single term of 15 years. At the time it was enacted, would this statute have been understood to limit the President's power to remove the officer during the 15 year term? Why or why not? Assuming the statute was so understood, did Congress have authority, in 1921, to provide this officer with tenure in office that would limit Presidential removal? Why or why not?

(12) In dissent, Justice White asserted that the *Bowsher* Court recognized "the legitimacy of legislation vesting 'executive' authority in officers independent of the President." Did the Court do so? If so, did the Court reserve some portion of that power for the President, consistent with Justice White's suggestion that there "are undoubtedly executive functions that, regardless of the enactments of Congress, must be performed by officers subject to removal at will by the President"? What are the characteristics of such functions that distinguish them from functions that can be vested by Congress in officers who are not subject to removal at will by the President?

(13) In dissent, Justice White asserted that the core executive functions (addressed in the immediately preceding question) were not at issue in the case and that the functions vested in the Comptroller General were not such as "would in itself improperly interfere with Presidential powers." Does the majority reject the test as well as the conclusion? That is, does the majority of the Court suggest that it is simply the wrong question to ask: "Whether placing the duties at issue in an officer not removable at will by the President improperly interferes with the President's duties?" Or do they agree with that question but reach a different answer?

(14) In dissent, Justice White accused the majority of the *Bowsher* Court of adhering to "rigid dogma" and a "distressingly formalistic view of separation of powers." Which approach — that of the majority or Justice White in dissent — produces the most appropriate role for the judiciary?

In the course of their work, Professors Calabresi and Yoo address the various historical episodes referenced in this chapter, including:

- President Truman's seizure of the steel mills, *see* STEVEN G. CALABRESI AND CHRISTOPHER S. YOO, THE UNITARY EXECUTIVE: PRESIDENTIAL POWER FROM WASHINGTON TO BUSH 315–16 (2008); and
- President Reagan's opposition to the role assigned to the Comptroller General, *see id.* at 379.

CHAPTER 3

MODERN CASES ON APPOINTMENT AND REMOVAL

Chapter 1 of this Volume introduced the judicial precedents addressing conflicts between the Executive and Legislative branches of the central government in the context of the appointment and removal of officers. Chapter 2 of this Volume illustrated conflicts between the Executive and Legislative branches in broader contexts, as well as introducing judicial precedents that limit the power of Congress to circumvent constitutional provisions on the appointment and removal of officers. Those materials provide the foundation for evaluation of more recent cases posing questions about the power of Congress to limit the President's power to appoint and remove officers.

MORRISON v. OLSON

487 U.S. 654 (1988)

CHIEF JUSTICE REHNQUIST delivered the opinion of the Court.

This case presents us with a challenge to the independent counsel provisions of the Ethics in Government Act of 1978. We hold today that these provisions of the Act do not violate the Appointments Clause of the Constitution, Art. II, § 2, cl. 2, or the limitations of Article III, nor do they impermissibly interfere with the President's authority under Article II in violation of the constitutional principle of separation of powers.

I

Briefly stated, Title VI of the Ethics in Government Act (Title VI or the Act), 28 U.S.C. §§ 591–599, allows for the appointment of an "independent counsel" to investigate and, if appropriate, prosecute certain high-ranking Government officials for violations of federal criminal laws. The Act requires the Attorney General, upon receipt of information that he determines is "sufficient to constitute grounds to investigate whether any person [covered by the Act] may have violated any Federal criminal law," to conduct a preliminary investigation of the matter. When the Attorney General has completed this investigation, or 90 days has elapsed, he is required to report to a special court (the Special Division) created by the Act "for the purpose of appointing independent counsels." 28 U.S.C. § 49. If the Attorney General determines that "there are no reasonable grounds to believe that further investigation is warranted," then he must notify the Special Division of this result. In such a case, "the division of the court shall have no power to appoint an independent counsel." § 592(b)(1). If, however, the Attorney General has determined that there are "reasonable grounds to believe that further investigation or prosecution is warranted," then he "shall apply to the division of the court for the appointment of an independent counsel." The Attorney General's application to the court "shall contain sufficient information to assist the [court] in selecting an independent counsel and in defining that independent counsel's prosecutorial jurisdiction." § 592(d). Upon receiving this application, the Special Division "shall appoint an appropriate independent counsel and shall define that independent counsel's prosecutorial jurisdiction." § 593(b).

With respect to all matters within the independent counsel's jurisdiction, the Act grants the counsel "full power and independent authority to exercise all investigative and prosecutorial functions and powers of the Department of Justice, the Attorney General, and any other officer or employee of the Department of Justice." § 594(a). The functions of the independent counsel include conducting grand jury proceedings and other investigations, participating in civil and criminal court proceedings and litigation, and appealing any decision in any case in which the counsel participates in an official capacity. §§ 594(a)(1)–(3). Under § 594(a)(9), the counsel's powers include "initiating and conducting prosecutions in any court of competent jurisdiction, framing and signing indictments, filing informations, and handling all aspects of any case, in the name of the United States." . . . The Act also states that an independent counsel "shall, except where not possible, comply with the written or other established policies of the Department of Justice respecting enforcement of the criminal laws." § 594(f). In addition, whenever a matter has been referred to an independent counsel under the Act, the Attorney General and the Justice Department are required to suspend all investigations and proceedings regarding the matter. § 597(a). An independent counsel has "full authority to dismiss matters within [his or her] prosecutorial jurisdiction without conducting an investigation or at any subsequent time before prosecution, if to do so would be consistent" with Department of Justice policy. § 594(g).

Two statutory provisions govern the length of an independent counsel's tenure in office. The first defines the procedure for removing an independent counsel. Section 596(a)(1) provides:

> An independent counsel appointed under this chapter may be removed from office, other than by impeachment and conviction, only by the personal action of the Attorney General and only for good cause, physical disability, mental incapacity, or any other condition that substantially impairs the performance of such independent counsel's duties.

. . . .

The other provision governing the tenure of the independent counsel defines the procedures for "terminating" the counsel's office. Under § 596(b)(1), the office of an independent counsel terminates when he or she notifies the Attorney General that he or she has completed or substantially completed any investigations or prosecutions undertaken pursuant to the Act. In addition, the Special Division, acting either on its own or on the suggestion of the Attorney General, may terminate the office of an independent counsel at any time if it finds that "the investigation of all matters within the prosecutorial jurisdiction of such independent counsel . . . have been completed or so substantially completed that it would be appropriate for the Department of Justice to complete such investigations and prosecutions." § 596(b)(2).

Finally, the Act provides for congressional oversight of the activities of independent counsel. An independent counsel may from time to time send Congress statements or reports on his or her activities. § 595(a)(2). The "appropriate committees of the Congress" are given oversight jurisdiction in regard to the official conduct of an independent counsel, and the counsel is required by the Act to cooperate with Congress in the exercise of this jurisdiction. § 595(a)(1). The counsel is required to inform the House of Representatives of "substantial and credible information which [the counsel] receives . . . that may constitute grounds for an impeachment." § 595(c). In addition, the Act gives certain congressional committee members the power to "request in writing that the Attorney General apply for the appointment of an independent counsel." § 592(g)(1). The Attorney General is required to respond to this request within a specified time but is not required to accede to the request. § 592(g)(2).

The proceedings in this case provide an example of how the Act works in practice. In 1982, two Subcommittees of the House of Representatives issued subpoenas directing the Environmental Protection Agency (EPA) to produce certain documents relating to the efforts of the EPA and the Land and Natural Resources Division of the Justice Department to enforce the "Superfund Law." At that time, appellee Olson was the Assistant Attorney General for the Office of Legal Counsel (OLC) . . . . Acting on the advice of the Justice Department, the President ordered the Administrator of EPA to invoke executive privilege to withhold certain of the documents on the ground that they contained "enforcement sensitive information." The Administrator obeyed this order and withheld the documents. In response, the House voted to hold the Administrator in contempt, after which the Administrator and the United States together filed a lawsuit against the House. The conflict abated in March 1983, when the administration agreed to give the House Subcommittees limited access to the documents.

The following year, the House Judiciary Committee began an investigation into the Justice Department's role in the controversy over the EPA documents. During this investigation, appellee Olson testified before a House Subcommittee on March 10, 1983. Both before and after that testimony, the Department complied with several Committee requests to produce certain documents. Other documents were at first withheld, although these documents were eventually disclosed by the Department after the Committee learned of their existence. In 1985, the majority members of the Judiciary Committee published a lengthy report on the Committee's investigation. The report not only criticized various [DOJ] officials . . . for their role in the EPA executive privilege dispute, but it also suggested that appellee Olson had given false and misleading testimony to the Subcommittee on March 10, 1983 . . . thus obstructing the Committee's investigation. The Chairman of the Judiciary Committee forwarded a copy of the report to the Attorney General with a request, pursuant to 28 U.S.C. § 592(c), that he seek the appointment of an independent counsel to investigate the allegations against Olson . . . .

The Attorney General directed the Public Integrity Section of the Criminal Division to conduct a preliminary investigation. The Section's report concluded that the appointment of an independent counsel was warranted to investigate the Committee's allegations . . . . [T]he Attorney General chose to apply to the Special Division for the appointment of an independent counsel solely with respect to appellee Olson. The Attorney General accordingly requested appointment of an independent counsel to investigate whether Olson's March 10, 1983, testimony "regarding the completeness of [OLC's] response to the Judiciary Committee's request for OLC documents, and regarding his knowledge of EPA's willingness to turn over certain disputed documents to Congress, violated . . . federal criminal law." The Attorney General also requested that the independent counsel have authority to investigate "any other matter related to that allegation."

On April 23, 1986, the Special Division appointed . . . [an] independent counsel to investigate "whether the testimony of . . . Olson and his revision of such testimony on March 10, 1983, violated . . . federal law." The court also ordered that the independent counsel

> shall have jurisdiction to investigate any other allegation of evidence of violation of any Federal criminal law by Theodore Olson developed during investigations, by the Independent Counsel, referred to above, and connected with or arising out of that investigation, and Independent Counsel shall have jurisdiction to prosecute for any such violation.

. . . .

In January 1987, appellant asked the Attorney General pursuant to § 594(e) to refer to her as "related matters" the Committee's allegations against appellees Schmults and Dinkins. The Attorney General refused to refer the matters, concluding that his decision not to request the appointment of an independent counsel in regard to those matters was final under § 592(b)(1). Appellant then asked the Special Division to order that the matters be referred to her under § 594(e). On April 2, 1987, the Division ruled that the Attorney General's decision not to seek appointment of an independent counsel with respect to Schmults and Dinkins was final and unreviewable under § 592(b)(1), and that therefore the court had no authority to make the requested referral. The court ruled, however, that its original grant of jurisdiction to appellant was broad enough to permit inquiry into whether Olson may have conspired with others, including Schmults and Dinkins, to obstruct the Committee's investigation.

Following this ruling, in May and June 1987, appellant caused a grand jury to issue and serve subpoenas *ad testificandum* and *duces tecum* on appellees. All three appellees moved to quash the subpoenas, claiming, among other things, that the independent counsel provisions of the Act were unconstitutional and that appellant accordingly had no authority to proceed. On July 20, 1987, the District Court upheld the constitutionality of the Act and denied the motions to quash. The court subsequently ordered that appellees be held in contempt . . . for continuing to refuse to comply with the subpoenas. The court stayed the effect of its contempt orders pending expedited appeal.

A divided Court of Appeals reversed. . . . Appellant then sought review by this Court, and we noted probable jurisdiction. We now reverse.

. . . .

III

. . . .

The parties do not dispute that "[t]he Constitution for purposes of appointment . . . divides all its officers into two classes." *United States v. Germaine*, 99 U.S. 508, 509 (1879). As we stated in *Buckley v. Valeo*, 424 U.S. 1, 132 (1976): "[P]rincipal officers are selected by the President with the advice and consent of the Senate. Inferior officers Congress may allow to be appointed by the President alone, by the heads of departments, or by the Judiciary." The initial question is, accordingly, whether appellant is an "inferior" or a "principal" officer. If she is the latter . . . then the Act is in violation of the Appointments Clause.

The line between "inferior" and "principal" officers is one that is far from clear, and the Framers provided little guidance into where it should be drawn. *See, e.g.*, 2 JOSEPH STORY, COMMENTARIES ON THE CONSTITUTION § 1536, pp. 397–98 (3d ed. 1858) ("In the practical course of the government there does not seem to have been any exact line drawn, who are and who are not to be deemed *inferior* officers, in the sense of the constitution, whose appointment does not necessarily require the concurrence of the senate"). We need not attempt here to decide exactly where the line falls between the two types of officers, because in our view appellant clearly falls on the "inferior officer" side of that line. Several factors lead to this conclusion.

First, appellant is subject to removal by a higher Executive Branch official. Although appellant may not be "subordinate" to the Attorney General (and the President) insofar as she possesses a degree of independent discretion to exercise the powers delegated to her under the Act, the fact that she can be removed by the Attorney General indicates that she is to some degree "inferior" in rank and authority. Second, appellant is empowered by the Act to perform only certain, limited duties. An independent counsel's role is restricted primarily to investigation and, if appropriate, prosecution for certain federal crimes. Admittedly, the Act delegates to appellant "full power and independent authority to exercise all investigative and prosecutorial functions and powers of the Department of Justice," § 594(a), but this grant of authority does not include any authority to formulate policy for the Government or the Executive Branch, nor does it give appellant any administrative duties outside of those necessary to operate her office. The Act specifically provides that in policy matters appellant is to comply to the extent possible with the policies of the Department. § 594(f).

Third, appellant's office is limited in jurisdiction. Not only is the Act itself restricted in applicability to certain federal officials suspected of certain serious federal crimes, but an independent counsel can only act within the scope of the jurisdiction that has been granted by the Special Division pursuant to a request by the Attorney General. Finally, appellant's office is limited in tenure. There is concededly no time limit on the appointment of a particular counsel. Nonetheless, the office of independent counsel is "temporary" in the sense that an independent counsel is appointed essentially to accomplish a single task, and when that task is over the office is terminated, either by the counsel herself or by action of the Special Division. Unlike other prosecutors, appellant has no ongoing responsibilities that extend beyond the accomplishment of the mission that she was appointed for and authorized by the Special Division to undertake. In our view, these factors relating to the "ideas of tenure, duration . . . and duties" of the independent counsel, *Germaine*, 99 U.S. at 511, are sufficient to establish that appellant is an "inferior" officer in the constitutional sense.

. . . .

This does not, however, end our inquiry under the Appointments Clause. Appellees argue that even if appellant is an "inferior" officer, the Clause does not empower Congress to place the power to appoint such an officer outside the Executive Branch. . . . On its face, the language of [the] "excepting clause" [of the Appointments Clause] admits of no limitation on interbranch appointments. Indeed, the inclusion of "as they think proper" seems clearly to give Congress significant discretion to determine whether it is "proper" to vest the appointment of, for example, executive officials in the "courts of Law." We recognized as much in one of our few decisions in this area, *Ex parte Siebold*, where we stated:

> It is no doubt usual and proper to vest the appointment of inferior officers in that department of the government, executive or judicial, or in that particular executive department to which the duties of such officers appertain. But there is no absolute requirement to this effect in the Constitution; and, if there were, it would be difficult in many cases to determine to which department an office properly belonged. . . .
>
> But as the Constitution stands, the selection of the appointing power, as between the functionaries named, is a matter resting in the discretion of Congress. And, looking at the subject in a practical light, it is perhaps better that it should rest there, than that the country should be harassed by the endless controversies to which a more specific direction on this subject might have given rise.

100 U.S. 371, 397–98.

. . . .

We also note that the history of the Clause provides no support for appellees' position. Throughout most of the process of drafting the Constitution, the Convention concentrated on the problem of who should have the authority to appoint judges. At the suggestion of James Madison, the Convention adopted a proposal that the Senate should have this authority, 1 MAX FARRAND, RECORDS OF THE FEDERAL CONVENTION OF 1787, pp. 232–233 (1966), and several attempts to transfer the appointment power to the President were rejected. *See* 2 *id.* at 42–44. The August 6, 1787, draft of the Constitution reported by the Committee of Detail retained Senate appointment of Supreme Court Judges, provided also for Senate appointment of ambassadors, and vested in the President the authority to "appoint officers in all cases not otherwise provided for by this Constitution." *Id.* at 183, 185. This scheme was maintained until September 4, when the Committee of Eleven reported its suggestions to the Convention. This Committee suggested that the Constitution be amended to state that the President "shall nominate and by and with the advice and consent of the Senate shall appoint ambassadors, and other public Ministers, Judges of the Supreme Court, and all other Officers of the [United States], whose appointments are not otherwise herein provided for." *Id.* at 498–99. After the addition of "Consuls" to the list, the Committee's proposal was adopted, *id.* at 539, and was subsequently reported to the Convention by the Committee of Style. *See id.* at 599. It was at this point, on September 15, that Gouverneur Morris moved to add the Excepting Clause to Art. II, § 2. *Id.* at 627. The one comment made on this motion was by Madison, who felt that the Clause did not go far enough in that it did not allow Congress to vest appointment powers in "Superior Officers below Heads of Departments." The first vote on Morris' motion ended in a tie. It was then put forward a second time, with the urging that "some such provision [was] too necessary, to be omitted." This time the proposal was adopted. *Id.* at 627–28. As this discussion shows, there was little or no debate on the question whether the Clause empowers Congress to provide for interbranch appointments, and there is nothing to suggest that the Framers intended to prevent Congress from having that power.

. . . We have recognized that courts may appoint private attorneys to act as prosecutor for judicial contempt judgments. [W]e approved court appointment of United States commissioners, who exercised certain limited prosecutorial powers. In *Siebold*, as well, we indicated that judicial appointment of federal marshals, who are "executive officer[s]," would not be inappropriate. Lower courts have also upheld interim judicial appointments of United States Attorneys and Congress itself has vested the power to make these interim appointments in the district courts. Congress, of course, was concerned when it created the office of independent counsel with the conflicts of interest that could arise in situations when the Executive Branch is called upon to investigate its own high-ranking officers. If it were to remove the appointing authority from the Executive Branch, the most logical place to put it was in the Judicial Branch. In the light of the Act's provision making the judges of the Special Division ineligible to participate in any matters relating to an independent counsel they have appointed, 28 U.S.C. § 49(f), we do not think that appointment of the independent counsel by the court runs afoul of the constitutional limitation on "incongruous" interbranch appointments.

IV

Appellees next contend that the powers vested in the Special Division by the Act conflict with Article III of the Constitution. We have long recognized that by the express provision of Article III, the judicial power of the United States is limited to "Cases" and "Controversies." As a general rule, we have broadly stated that "executive or administrative duties of a nonjudicial nature may not be imposed on judges holding office under Art. III of the Constitution." *Buckley*, 424 U.S. at 123. The purpose of this limitation is to help ensure the independence of the Judicial

Branch and to prevent the Judiciary from encroaching into areas reserved for the other branches. . . .

. . . [T]he Act vests in the Special Division the power to choose who will serve as independent counsel and the power to define his or her jurisdiction. § 593(b). Clearly, once it is accepted that the Appointments Clause gives Congress the power to vest the appointment of officials such as the independent counsel in the "courts of Law," there can be no Article III objection to the Special Division's exercise of that power, as the power itself derives from the Appointments Clause, a source of authority for judicial action that is independent of Article III. Appellees contend, however, that the Division's Appointments Clause powers do not encompass the power to define the independent counsel's jurisdiction. We disagree. In our view, Congress' power under the Clause to vest the "Appointment" of inferior officers in the courts may, in certain circumstances, allow Congress to give the courts some discretion in defining the nature and scope of the appointed official's authority. Particularly when, as here, Congress creates a temporary "office" the nature and duties of which will by necessity vary with the factual circumstances giving rise to the need for an appointment in the first place, it may vest the power to define the scope of the office in the court as an incident to the appointment of the officer pursuant to the Appointments Clause. This said, we do not think that Congress may give the Division unlimited discretion to determine the independent counsel's jurisdiction. In order for the Division's definition of the counsel's jurisdiction to be truly "incidental" to its power to appoint, the jurisdiction that the court decides upon must be demonstrably related to the factual circumstances that gave rise to the Attorney General's investigation and request for the appointment of the independent counsel in the particular case.

. . . .

Leaving aside for the moment the Division's power to terminate an independent counsel, we do not think that Article III absolutely prevents Congress from vesting these other miscellaneous powers in the Special Division pursuant to the Act. As we observed above, one purpose of the broad prohibition upon the courts' exercise of "executive or administrative duties of a nonjudicial nature," is to maintain the separation between the Judiciary and the other branches of the Federal Government by ensuring that judges do not encroach upon executive or legislative authority or undertake tasks that are more properly accomplished by those branches. In this case, the miscellaneous powers described above do not impermissibly trespass upon the authority of the Executive Branch. Some of these allegedly "supervisory" powers conferred on the court are passive: the Division merely "receives" reports from the counsel or the Attorney General, it is not entitled to act on them or to specifically approve or disapprove of their contents. Other provisions of the Act do require the court to exercise some judgment and discretion, but the powers granted by these provisions are themselves essentially ministerial. The Act simply does not give the Division the power to "supervise" the independent counsel in the exercise of his or her investigative or prosecutorial authority. And, the functions that the Special Division is empowered to perform are not inherently "Executive"; indeed, they are directly analogous to functions that federal judges perform in other contexts, such as deciding whether to allow disclosure of matters occurring before a grand jury, deciding to extend a grand jury investigation, or awarding attorney's fees.

We are more doubtful about the Special Division's power to terminate the office of the independent counsel pursuant to § 596(b)(2). . . . [T]he power to terminate, especially when exercised by the Division on its own motion, is "administrative" to the extent that it requires the Special Division to monitor the progress of proceedings of the independent counsel and come to a decision as to whether the counsel's job is "completed." It also is not a power that could be considered typically "judicial," as it has few analogues among the court's more traditional powers. Nonetheless, we do not . . . view this provision as a significant judicial encroachment upon executive power or upon the prosecutorial discretion of the independent counsel.

. . . .

The termination provisions of the Act do not give the Special Division anything approaching the power to remove the counsel while an investigation or court proceeding is still underway — this power is vested solely in the Attorney General. As we see it, "termination" may occur only when the duties of the counsel are truly "completed" or "so substantially completed" that there remains no need for any continuing action by the independent counsel. It is basically a device for removing from the public payroll an independent counsel who has served his or her purpose, but is unwilling to acknowledge the fact. . . . [This] power to terminate does not pose a sufficient threat of judicial intrusion into matters that are more properly within the Executive's authority to require that the Act be invalidated as inconsistent with Article III.

Nor do we believe, as appellees contend, that the Special Division's exercise of the various powers specifically granted to it under the Act poses any threat to the "impartial and independent federal adjudication of claims within the judicial power of the United States." We reach this conclusion for two reasons. First, the Act as it currently stands gives the Special Division itself no power to review any of the actions of the independent counsel or any of the actions of the Attorney General with regard to the counsel. Accordingly, there is no risk of partisan or biased adjudication of claims regarding the independent counsel by that court. Second, the Act prevents members of the Special Division from participating in "any judicial proceeding concerning a matter which involves such independent counsel while such independent counsel is serving in that office or which involves the exercise of such independent counsel's official duties, regardless of whether such independent counsel is still serving in that office." 28 U.S.C. § 49(f). We think both the special court and its judges are sufficiently isolated by these statutory provisions from the review of the activities of the independent counsel so as to avoid any taint of the independence of the Judiciary such as would render the Act invalid under Article III.

. . . .

V

We now turn to consider whether the Act is invalid under the constitutional principle of separation of powers. Two related issues must be addressed: The first is whether the provision of the Act restricting the Attorney General's power to remove the independent counsel to only those instances in which he can show "good cause," taken by itself, impermissibly interferes with the President's exercise of his constitutionally appointed functions. The second is whether, taken as a whole, the Act violates the separation of powers by reducing the President's ability to control the prosecutorial powers wielded by the independent counsel.

A

Two Terms ago we had occasion to consider whether it was consistent with the separation of powers for Congress to pass a statute that authorized a Government official who is removable only by Congress to participate in what we found to be "executive powers." *Bowsher v. Synar,* 478 U.S. 714, 730 (1986). . . .

Unlike both *Bowsher* and *Myers,* this case does not involve an attempt by Congress itself to gain a role in the removal of executive officials other than its established powers of impeachment and conviction. The Act instead puts the removal power squarely in the hands of the Executive Branch; an independent counsel may be removed from office, "only by the personal action of the Attorney General, and only for good cause." § 596(a)(1). There is no requirement of congressional approval of the Attorney General's removal decision, though the decision is subject to judicial review. § 596(a)(3). In our view, the removal provisions of the Act make this case more analogous to *Humphrey's Executor v. United States,* 295 U.S. 602 (1935), and *Wiener v. United States,* 357 U.S. 349 (1958), than to *Myers* or *Bowsher.*

In *Humphrey's Executor,* the issue was whether a statute restricting the President's power to remove the Commissioners of the Federal Trade Commission (FTC) only for "inefficiency, neglect of duty, or malfeasance in office" was consistent with the Constitution. 295 U.S. at 619. We stated that whether Congress can "condition the [President's power of removal] by fixing a definite term and precluding a removal except for cause, will depend upon the character of the office." *Id.* at 631. Contrary to the implication of some *dicta* in *Myers,* the President's power to remove Government officials simply was not "all-inclusive in respect of civil officers with the exception of the judiciary provided for by the Constitution." 295 U.S. at 629. At least in regard to "quasi-legislative" and "quasi-judicial" agencies such as the FTC, "[t]he authority of Congress, in creating [such] agencies, to require them to act in discharge of their duties independently of executive control . . . includes, as an appropriate incident, power to fix the period during which they shall continue in office, and to forbid their removal except for cause in the meantime." *Id.* In *Humphrey's Executor,* we found it "plain" that the Constitution did not give the President "illimitable power of removal" over the officers of independent agencies. *Id.* Were the President to have the power to remove FTC Commissioners at will, the "coercive influence" of the removal power would "threate[n] the independence of [the] commission." *Id.* at 630.

Similarly, in *Wiener* we considered whether the President had unfettered discretion to remove a member of the War Claims Commission, which had been established by Congress in the War Claims Act of 1948. The Commission's function was to receive and adjudicate certain claims for compensation from those who had suffered personal injury or property damage at the hands of the enemy during World War II. Commissioners were appointed by the President, with the advice and consent of the Senate, but the statute made no provision for the removal of officers, perhaps because the Commission itself was to have a limited existence. As in *Humphrey's Executor,* however, the Commissioners were entrusted by Congress with adjudicatory powers that were to be exercised free from executive control. In this context, "Congress did not wish to have hang over the Commission the Damocles' sword of removal by the President for no reason other than that he preferred to have on that Commission men of his own choosing." 357 U.S. at 356. Accordingly, we rejected the President's attempt to remove a Commissioner "merely because he wanted his own appointees on [the] Commission," stating that "no such power is given to the President directly by the Constitution, and none is impliedly conferred upon him by statute." *Id.*

Appellees contend that *Humphrey's Executor* and *Wiener* are distinguishable from this case because they did not involve officials who performed a "core executive function." They argue that our decision in *Humphrey's Executor* rests on a distinction between "purely executive" officials and officials who exercise "quasi-legislative" and "quasi-judicial" powers. In their view, when a "purely executive" official is involved, the governing precedent is *Myers,* not *Humphrey's Executor.* And, under *Myers,* the President must have absolute discretion to discharge "purely" executive officials at will. *See Myers,* 272 U.S. at 132–34.

We undoubtedly did rely on the terms "quasi-legislative" and "quasi-judicial" to distinguish the officials involved in *Humphrey's Executor* and *Wiener* from those in *Myers,* but our present considered view is that the determination of whether the Constitution allows Congress to impose a "good cause"-type restriction on the President's power to remove an official cannot be made to turn on whether or not that official is classified as "purely executive." The analysis contained in our removal cases is designed not to define rigid categories of those officials who may or may not be removed at will by the President, but to ensure that Congress does not interfere with the President's exercise of the "executive power" and his constitutionally appointed duty to "take care that the laws be faithfully executed" under Article II. *Myers* was undoubtedly correct in its holding, and in its broader suggestion that there are some "purely executive" officials who must be removable by the President at will if he is to be able to accomplish his constitutional role. *See* 272 U.S. at 132–34. But as the Court noted in *Wiener:*

> The assumption was short-lived that the *Myers* case recognized the President's inherent constitutional power to remove officials no matter what the relation of the executive to the discharge of their duties and no matter what restrictions Congress may have imposed regarding the nature of their tenure.

357 U.S. at 352.

At the other end of the spectrum from *Myers,* the characterization of the agencies in *Humphrey's Executor* and *Wiener* as "quasi-legislative" or "quasi-judicial" in large part reflected our judgment that it was not essential to the President's proper execution of his Article II powers that these agencies be headed up by individuals who were removable at will. We do not mean to suggest that an analysis of the functions served by the officials at issue is irrelevant. But the real question is whether the removal restrictions are of such a nature that they impede the President's ability to perform his constitutional duty, and the functions of the officials in question must be analyzed in that light.

Considering for the moment the "good cause" removal provision in isolation from the other parts of the Act at issue in this case, we cannot say that the imposition of a "good cause" standard for removal by itself unduly trammels on executive authority. There is no real dispute that the functions performed by the independent counsel are "executive" in the sense that they are law enforcement functions that typically have been undertaken by officials within the Executive Branch. As we noted above, however, the independent counsel is an inferior officer under the Appointments Clause, with limited jurisdiction and tenure and lacking policymaking or significant administrative authority. Although the counsel exercises no small amount of discretion and judgment in deciding how to carry out his or her duties under the Act, we simply do not see how the President's need to control the exercise of that discretion is so central to the functioning of the Executive Branch as to require as a matter of constitutional law that the counsel be terminable at will by the President.

B

The final question to be addressed is whether the Act, taken as a whole, violates the principle of separation of powers by unduly interfering with the role of the Executive Branch. Time and again we have reaffirmed the importance in our constitutional scheme of the separation of governmental powers into the three coordinate branches. [T]he system of separated powers and checks and balances established in the Constitution was regarded by the Framers as "a self-executing safeguard against the encroachment or aggrandizement of one branch at the expense of the other." We have not hesitated to invalidate provisions of law which violate this principle. On the other hand, we have never held that the Constitution requires that the three branches of Government "operate with absolute independence.". . .

We observe first that this case does not involve an attempt by Congress to increase its own powers at the expense of the Executive Branch. *Cf. CFTC v. Schor,* 478 U.S. 833, 856 (1986). . . . Indeed, with the exception of the power of impeachment — which applies to all officers of the United States — Congress retained for itself no powers of control or supervision over an independent counsel. The Act does empower certain Members of Congress to request the Attorney General to apply for the appointment of an independent counsel, but the Attorney General has no duty to comply with the request, although he must respond within a certain time limit. Other than that, Congress' role under the Act is limited to receiving reports or other information and oversight of the independent counsel's activities, functions that we have recognized generally as being incidental to the legislative function of Congress.

Similarly, we do not think that the Act works any *judicial* usurpation of properly executive functions. As should be apparent from our discussion of the Appointments Clause above, the power to appoint inferior officers such as independent counsel is not in itself an "executive" function in the constitutional sense, at least when Congress has exercised its power to vest the appointment of an inferior office in the "courts of Law." We note nonetheless that under the Act the Special Division has no power to appoint an independent counsel *sua sponte;* it may only do so upon the specific request of the Attorney General, and the courts are specifically prevented from reviewing the Attorney General's decision not to seek appointment. In addition, once the court has appointed a counsel and defined his or her jurisdiction, it has no power to supervise or control the activities of the counsel. As we pointed out in our discussion of the Special Division in relation to Article III, the various powers delegated by the statute to the Division are not supervisory or administrative, nor are they functions that the Constitution requires be performed by officials within the Executive Branch. The Act does give a federal court the power to review the Attorney General's decision to remove an independent counsel, but in our view this is a function that is well within the traditional power of the Judiciary.

Finally, we do not think that the Act "impermissibly undermine[s]" the powers of the Executive Branch, *Schor,* 478 U.S. at 856, or "disrupts the proper balance between the coordinate branches [by] prevent[ing] the Executive Branch from accomplishing its constitutionally assigned functions," *Nixon v. Administrator of General Services,* 433 U.S. 425, 443 (1977). It is undeniable that the Act reduces the amount of control or supervision that the Attorney General and, through him, the President exercises over the investigation and prosecution of a certain class of alleged criminal activity. The Attorney General is not allowed to appoint the individual of his choice; he does not determine the counsel's jurisdiction; and his power to remove a counsel is limited. Nonetheless, the Act does give the Attorney

General several means of supervising or controlling the prosecutorial powers that may be wielded by an independent counsel. Most importantly, the Attorney General retains the power to remove the counsel for "good cause," a power that we have already concluded provides the Executive with substantial ability to ensure that the laws are "faithfully executed" by an independent counsel. No independent counsel may be appointed without a specific request by the Attorney General, and the Attorney General's decision not to request appointment if he finds "no reasonable grounds to believe that further investigation is warranted" is committed to his unreviewable discretion. The Act thus gives the Executive a degree of control over the power to initiate an investigation by the independent counsel. In addition, the jurisdiction of the independent counsel is defined with reference to the facts submitted by the Attorney General, and once a counsel is appointed, the Act requires that the counsel abide by Justice Department policy unless it is not "possible" to do so. Notwithstanding the fact that the counsel is to some degree "independent" and free from executive supervision to a greater extent than other federal prosecutors, in our view these features of the Act give the Executive Branch sufficient control over the independent counsel to ensure that the President is able to perform his constitutionally assigned duties.

VI

In sum, we conclude today that it does not violate the Appointments Clause for Congress to vest the appointment of independent counsel in the Special Division; that the powers exercised by the Special Division under the Act do not violate Article III; and that the Act does not violate the separation-of-powers principle by impermissibly interfering with the functions of the Executive Branch. The decision of the Court of Appeals is therefore Reversed.

JUSTICE KENNEDY took no part in the consideration or decision of this case.

JUSTICE SCALIA, dissenting.

. . . .

[T]his suit is about . . . [p]ower. The allocation of power among Congress, the President, and the courts in such fashion as to preserve the equilibrium the Constitution sought to establish — so that "a gradual concentration of the several powers in the same department," FEDERALIST NO. 51 (J. Madison), can effectively be resisted. Frequently an issue of this sort will come before the Court clad, so to speak, in sheep's clothing: the potential of the asserted principle to effect important change in the equilibrium of power is not immediately evident, and must be discerned by a careful and perceptive analysis. But this wolf comes as a wolf.

I

. . . .

As a practical matter, it would be surprising if the Attorney General had any choice (assuming this statute is constitutional) but to seek appointment of an independent counsel to pursue the charges against the principal object of the congressional request, Mr. Olson. Merely the political consequences (to him and the President) of seeming to break the law by refusing to do so would have been substantial. How could it not be, the public would ask, that a 3,000-page indictment drawn by our representatives over 2 1/2 years does not even establish "reasonable grounds to believe" that further investigation or prosecution is warranted with respect to at least the principal alleged culprit? But the Act establishes more than just practical compulsion. Although the Court's opinion asserts that the Attorney

General had "no duty to comply with the [congressional] request," that is not entirely accurate. He had a duty to comply unless he could conclude that there were "no reasonable grounds to believe," not that prosecution was warranted, but merely that "further investigation " was warranted, 28 U.S.C. § 592(b)(1), after a 90-day investigation in which he was prohibited from using such routine investigative techniques as grand juries, plea bargaining, grants of immunity, or even subpoenas, *see* § 592(a)(2). The Court also makes much of the fact that "the courts are specifically prevented from reviewing the Attorney General's decision not to seek appointment." Yes, but Congress is not prevented from reviewing it. The context of this statute is acrid with the smell of threatened impeachment. Where, as here, a request for appointment of an independent counsel has come from the Judiciary Committee of either House of Congress, the Attorney General must, if he decides not to seek appointment, explain to that Committee why. *See also* 28 U.S.C. § 595(c) (independent counsel must report to the House of Representatives information "that may constitute grounds for an impeachment").

Thus, by the application of this statute in the present case, Congress has effectively compelled a criminal investigation of a high-level appointee of the President in connection with his actions arising out of a bitter power dispute between the President and the Legislative Branch. Mr. Olson may or may not be guilty of a crime; we do not know. But we do know that the investigation of him has been commenced, not necessarily because the President or his authorized subordinates believe it is in the interest of the United States, in the sense that it warrants the diversion of resources from other efforts, and is worth the cost in money and in possible damage to other governmental interests; and not even, leaving aside those normally considered factors, because the President or his authorized subordinates necessarily believe that an investigation is likely to unearth a violation worth prosecuting; but only because the Attorney General cannot affirm, as Congress demands, that there are no reasonable grounds to believe that further investigation is warranted. The decisions regarding the scope of that further investigation, its duration, and, finally, whether or not prosecution should ensue, are likewise beyond the control of the President and his subordinates.

II

If to describe this case is not to decide it, the concept of a government of separate and coordinate powers no longer has meaning. The Court devotes most of its attention to such relatively technical details as the Appointments Clause and the removal power, addressing briefly and only at the end of its opinion the separation of powers. As my prologue suggests, I think that has it backwards. Our opinions are full of the recognition that it is the principle of separation of powers, and the inseparable corollary that each department's "defense must . . . be made commensurate to the danger of attack," FEDERALIST NO. 51 (J. Madison), which gives comprehensible content to the Appointments Clause, and determines the appropriate scope of the removal power. Thus, while I will subsequently discuss why our appointments and removal jurisprudence does not support today's holding, I begin with a consideration of the fountainhead of that jurisprudence, the separation and equilibration of powers.

First, however, I think it well to call to mind an important and unusual premise that underlies our deliberations, a premise not expressly contradicted by the Court's opinion, but in my view not faithfully observed. It is rare in a case dealing, as this one does, with the constitutionality of a statute passed by the Congress of the United States, not to find anywhere in the Court's opinion the usual, almost formulary caution that we owe great deference to Congress' view that what it has done is constitutional, *see, e.g., Columbia Broadcasting System, Inc. v. Democratic National Committee,* 412 U.S. 94, 102 (1973), and that we will decline to apply the statute only if the presumption of constitutionality can be overcome, *see id.* at 103. That caution is not recited by the Court in the present case because it does not apply. Where a private citizen challenges action of the Government on grounds unrelated to separation of powers, harmonious functioning of the system demands that we ordinarily give some deference, or a presumption of validity, to the actions of the political branches in what is agreed, between themselves at least, to be within their respective spheres. But where the issue pertains to separation of powers, and the political branches are (as here) in disagreement, neither can be presumed correct. The reason is stated concisely by Madison: "The several departments being perfectly co-ordinate by the terms of their common commission, neither of them, it is evident, can pretend to an exclusive or superior right of settling the boundaries between their respective powers . . . ." FEDERALIST NO. 49. The playing field for the present case, in other words, is a level one. As one of the interested and coordinate parties to the underlying constitutional dispute, Congress, no more than the President, is entitled to the benefit of the doubt.

To repeat, Article II, § 1, cl. 1, of the Constitution provides: "The executive Power shall be vested in a President of the United States." As I described at the outset of this opinion, this does not mean some of the executive power, but all of the executive power. It seems to me, therefore, that the decision of the Court of Appeals invalidating the present statute must be upheld on fundamental separation-of-powers principles if the following two questions are answered affirmatively: (1) Is the conduct of a criminal prosecution (and of an investigation to decide whether to prosecute) the exercise of purely executive power? (2) Does the statute deprive the President of the United States of exclusive control over the exercise of that power? . . . [T]he Court appears to concede an affirmative answer to both questions, but seeks to avoid the inevitable conclusion that since the statute vests some purely executive power in a person who is not the President of the United States it is void.

The Court concedes that "[t]here is no real dispute that the functions performed by the independent counsel are 'executive'," though it qualifies that concession by adding "in the sense that they are law enforcement functions that typically have been undertaken by officials within the Executive Branch." The qualifier adds nothing but atmosphere. In what other sense can one identify "the executive Power" that is supposed to be vested in the President (unless it includes everything the Executive Branch is given to do) except by reference to what has always and everywhere — if conducted by government at all — been conducted never by the legislature, never by the courts, and always by the executive? There is no possible doubt that the independent counsel's functions fit this description. She is vested with the "full power and independent authority to exercise all investigative and prosecutorial functions and powers of the Department of Justice [and] the Attorney General." 28 U.S.C. § 594(a). Governmental investigation and prosecution of crimes is a quintessentially executive function. *See Buckley v. Valeo,* 424 U.S. 1, 138 (1976); *United States v. Nixon,* 418 U.S. 683, 693 (1974).

As for the second question, whether the statute before us deprives the President of exclusive control over that quintessentially executive activity: The Court does not, and could not possibly, assert that it does not. . . . As we recognized in *Humphrey's Executor v. United States,* 295 U.S. 602 (1935) — indeed, what *Humphrey's Executor* was all about — limiting removal power to "good cause" is an impediment to, not an effective grant of, Presidential control. We said that limitation was necessary with respect to members of the [FTC], which we found to be "an agency of the legislative and judicial departments," and "wholly disconnected from the executive department," *id.* at 630, because "it is quite evident that one who holds his office only during the pleasure of another, cannot be depended upon to maintain an attitude of independence against the latter's will." *Id.* at 629. What we in *Humphrey's Executor* found to be a means of eliminating Presidential control, the Court today considers the "most importan[t]" means of assuring Presidential control. Congress, of course, operated under no such illusion when it enacted this statute, describing the "good cause" limitation as "protecting the independent counsel's ability to act independently of the President's direct control" since it permits removal only for "misconduct." H.R. Conf. Rep. 100-452, p. 37 (1987).

Moving on to the presumably "less important" controls that the President retains, the Court notes that no independent counsel may be appointed without a specific request from the Attorney General. As I have discussed above, the condition that renders such a request mandatory (inability to find "no reasonable grounds to believe" that further investigation is warranted) is so insubstantial that the Attorney General's discretion is severely confined. And once the referral is made, it is for the Special Division to determine the scope and duration of the investigation. *See* 28 U.S.C. § 593(b). And in any event, the limited power over referral is irrelevant to the question whether, once appointed, the independent counsel exercises executive power free from the President's control. . . . [T]he balancing of various legal, practical, and political considerations, none of which is absolute, is the very essence of prosecutorial discretion. To take this away is to remove the core of the prosecutorial function, and not merely "some" Presidential control.

As I have said, however, it is ultimately irrelevant how much the statute reduces Presidential control. The case is over when the Court acknowledges, as it must, that "[i]t is undeniable that the Act reduces the amount of control or supervision that the Attorney General and, through him, the President exercises over the investigation and prosecution of a certain class of alleged criminal activity." It effects a revolution in our constitutional jurisprudence for the Court, once it has determined that (1) purely executive functions are at issue here, and (2) those functions have been given to a person whose actions are not fully within the supervision and control of the President, nonetheless to proceed further to sit in judgment of whether "the President's need to control the exercise of [the independent counsel's] discretion is so central to the functioning of the Executive Branch" as to require complete control, whether the conferral of his powers upon someone else "sufficiently deprives the President of control over the independent counsel to interfere impermissibly with [his] constitutional obligation to ensure the faithful execution of the laws," and whether "the Act give[s] the Executive Branch sufficient control over the independent counsel to ensure that the President is able to perform his constitutionally assigned duties." It is not for us to determine, and we have never presumed to determine, how much of the purely executive powers of government must be within the full control of the President. The Constitution prescribes that they *all* are.

. . . .

. . . A system of separate and coordinate powers necessarily involves an acceptance of exclusive power that can theoretically be abused. As we reiterate this very day, "[i]t is a truism that constitutional protections have costs." *Coy v. Iowa*, 487 U.S. 1012, 1020 (1988). While the separation of powers may prevent us from righting every wrong, it does so in order to ensure that we do not lose liberty. The checks against any branch's abuse of its exclusive powers are twofold: First, retaliation by one of the other branch's use of *its* exclusive powers: Congress, for example, can impeach the executive who willfully fails to enforce the laws; the executive can decline to prosecute under unconstitutional statutes, *cf. United States v. Lovett*, 328 U.S. 303 (1946); and the courts can dismiss malicious prosecutions. Second, and ultimately, there is the political check that the people will replace those in the political branches (the branches more "dangerous to the political rights of the Constitution," FEDERALIST NO. 78) who are guilty of abuse. Political pressures produced special prosecutors — for Teapot Dome and for Watergate, for example — long before this statute created the independent counsel.

The Court has, nonetheless, replaced the clear constitutional prescription that the executive power belongs to the President with a "balancing test." What are the standards to determine how the balance is to be struck, that is, how much removal of Presidential power is too much? Many countries of the world get along with an executive that is much weaker than ours — in fact, entirely dependent upon the continued support of the legislature. Once we depart from the text of the Constitution, just where short of that do we stop? The most amazing feature of the Court's opinion is that it does not even purport to give an answer. It simply announces, with no analysis, that the ability to control the decision whether to investigate and prosecute the President's closest advisers, and indeed the President himself, is not "so central to the functioning of the Executive Branch" as to be constitutionally required to be within the President's control. Apparently that is so because we say it is so. Having abandoned as the basis for our decision-making the text of Article II that "the executive Power" must be vested in the President, the Court does not even attempt to craft a *substitute* criterion — a "justiciable standard," *see, e.g., Baker v. Carr*, 369 U.S. 186, 210 (1962). . . .

. . . .

Besides weakening the Presidency by reducing the zeal of his staff, it must also be obvious that the institution of the independent counsel enfeebles him more directly in his constant confrontations with Congress, by eroding his public support. Nothing is so politically effective as the ability to charge that one's opponent and his associates are not merely wrongheaded, naive, ineffective, but, in all probability, "crooks." And nothing so effectively gives an appearance of validity to such charges as a Justice Department investigation and, even better, prosecution. The present statute provides ample means for that sort of attack, assuring that massive and lengthy investigations will occur, not merely when the Justice Department in the application of its usual standards believes they are called for, but whenever it cannot be said that there are "no reasonable grounds to believe" they are called for. The statute's highly visible procedures assure, moreover, that unlike most investigations these will be widely known and prominently displayed. . . .

In sum, this statute does deprive the President of substantial control over the prosecutory functions performed by the independent counsel, and it does substantially affect the balance of powers. That the Court could possibly conclude otherwise demonstrates both the wisdom of our former constitutional system, in which the degree of reduced control and political impairment were irrelevant, since all purely executive power had to be in the President; and the folly of the new system of standardless judicial allocation of powers we adopt today.

III

As I indicated earlier, the basic separation-of-powers principles I have discussed are what give life and content to our jurisprudence concerning the President's power to appoint and remove officers. The same result of unconstitutionality is therefore plainly indicated by our case law in these areas.

. . . .

Because appellant (who all parties and the Court agree is an officer of the United States) was not appointed by the President with the advice and consent of the Senate, but rather by the Special Division of the United States Court of Appeals, her appointment is constitutional only if (1) she is an "inferior" officer within the meaning of the above Clause, and (2) Congress may vest her appointment in a court of law.

As to the first of these inquiries, the Court does not attempt to "decide exactly" what establishes the line between principal and "inferior" officers, but is confident that, whatever the line may be, appellant "clearly falls on the 'inferior officer' side" of it. The Court gives three reasons: *First,* she "is subject to removal by a higher Executive Branch official," namely, the Attorney General. *Second,* she is "empowered by the Act to perform only certain, limited duties." *Third,* her office is "limited in jurisdiction" and "limited in tenure."

The first of these lends no support to the view that appellant is an inferior officer. Appellant is removable only for "good cause" or physical or mental incapacity. 28 U.S.C. § 596(a)(1). By contrast, most (if not all) *principal* officers in the Executive Branch may be removed by the President *at will.* I fail to see how the fact that appellant is more difficult to remove than most principal officers helps to establish that she is an inferior officer. And I do not see how it could possibly make any difference to her superior or inferior status that the President's limited power to remove her must be exercised through the Attorney General. If she were removable at will by the Attorney General, then she would be subordinate to him and thus properly designated as inferior; but the Court essentially admits that she is not subordinate. If it were common usage to refer to someone as "inferior" who is subject to removal for cause by another, then one would say that the President is "inferior" to Congress.

The second reason offered by the Court — that appellant performs only certain, limited duties — may be relevant to whether she is an inferior officer, but it mischaracterizes the extent of her powers. As the Court states: "Admittedly, the Act delegates to appellant [the] 'full power and independent authority to exercise all investigative and prosecutorial functions and powers of the Department of Justice.'" Moreover, in addition to this general grant of power she is given a broad range of specifically enumerated powers, including a power not even the Attorney General possesses: to "contes[t] in court . . . any claim of privilege or attempt to withhold evidence on grounds of national security." § 594(a)(6). . . .

The final set of reasons given by the Court for why the independent counsel clearly is an inferior officer emphasizes the limited nature of her jurisdiction and tenure. Taking the latter first, I find nothing unusually limited about the independent counsel's tenure. To the contrary, unlike most high-ranking Executive Branch officials, she continues to serve until she (or the Special Division) decides that her work is substantially completed. *See* §§ 596(b)(1), (b)(2). This particular independent prosecutor has already served more than two years, which is at least as long as many Cabinet officials. As to the scope of her jurisdiction, there can be no doubt that is small (though far from unimportant). But within it she exercises more than the full power of the Attorney General. . . .

More fundamentally, however, it is not clear from the Court's opinion why the factors it discusses — even if applied correctly to the facts of this case — are determinative of the question of inferior officer status. The apparent source of these factors is a statement in *United States v. Germaine,* 99 U.S. 508 (1879) (discussing *United States v. Hartwell,* 73 U.S. 385, 393 (1868)), that "the term [officer] embraces the ideas of tenure, duration, emolument, and duties." Besides the fact that this was dictum, it was dictum in a case where the distinguishing characteristics of inferior officers versus superior officers were in no way relevant, but rather only the distinguishing characteristics of an "officer of the United States" (to which the criminal statute at issue applied) as opposed to a mere employee. Rather than erect a theory of who is an inferior officer on the foundation of such an irrelevancy, I think it preferable to look to the text of the Constitution and the division of power that it establishes. These demonstrate, I think, that the independent counsel is not an inferior officer because she is not *subordinate* to any officer in the Executive Branch (indeed, not even to the President). Dictionaries in use at the time of the Constitutional Convention gave the word "inferiour" two meanings which it still bears today: (1) "[l]ower in place, . . . station, . . . rank of life, . . . value or excellency," and (2) "[s]ubordinate." SAMUEL JOHNSON, DICTIONARY OF THE ENGLISH LANGUAGE (6th ed. 1785). In a document dealing with the structure (the constitution) of a government, one would naturally expect the word to bear the latter meaning — indeed, in such a context it would be unpardonably careless to use the word unless a relationship of subordination was intended. . . .

That "inferior" means "subordinate" is also consistent with what little we know about the evolution of the Appointments Clause. As originally reported to the Committee on Style, the Appointments Clause provided no "exception" from the standard manner of appointment (President with the advice and consent of the Senate) for inferior officers. 2 MAX FARRAND, RECORDS OF THE FEDERAL CONVENTION OF 1787, pp. 498–499, 599 (rev. ed. 1966). . . .

. . . .

To be sure, it is not a *sufficient* condition for "inferior" officer status that one be subordinate to a principal officer. Even an officer who is subordinate to a department head can be a principal officer. That is clear from the brief exchange following Gouverneur Morris' suggestion of the addition of the exceptions clause for inferior officers. Madison responded: "It does not go far enough if it be necessary at all — Superior Officers below Heads of Departments ought in some cases to have the appointment of the lesser offices." 2 MAX FARRAND, RECORDS OF THE FEDERAL CONVENTION of 1787, p. 627 (rev. ed. 1966). But it is surely a *necessary* condition for inferior officer status that the officer be subordinate to another officer.

The independent counsel is not even subordinate to the President. The Court essentially admits as much, noting that "appellant may not be 'subordinate' to the Attorney General (and the President) insofar as she possesses a degree of independent discretion to exercise the powers delegated to her under the Act." In fact, there is no doubt about it. As noted earlier, the Act specifically grants her the "full power and independent authority to exercise all investigative and prosecutorial functions of the Department of Justice," 28 U.S.C. § 594(a), and makes her removable only for "good cause," a limitation specifically intended to ensure that she be *independent* of, not *subordinate* to, the President and the Attorney General. *See* H.R. Conf. Rep. No. 100-452, p. 37 (1987).

Because appellant is not subordinate to another officer, she is not an "inferior" officer and her appointment other than by the President with the advice and consent of the Senate is unconstitutional.

IV

. . . .

There is, of course, no provision in the Constitution stating who may remove executive officers, except the provisions for removal by impeachment. Before the present decision it was established, however, (1) that the President's power to remove principal officers who exercise purely executive powers could not be restricted, *see Myers v. United States,* 272 U.S. 52, 127, (1926), and (2) that his power to remove inferior officers who exercise purely executive powers, and whose appointment Congress had removed from the usual procedure of Presidential appointment with Senate consent, could be restricted, at least where the appointment had been made by an officer of the Executive Branch, *see id.; United States v. Perkins,* 116 U.S. 483, 485 (1886).

The Court could have resolved the removal power issue in this case by simply relying upon its erroneous conclusion that the independent counsel was an inferior officer, and then extending our holding that the removal of inferior officers appointed by the Executive can be restricted, to a new holding that even the removal of inferior officers appointed by the courts can be restricted. That would in my view be a considerable and unjustified extension, giving the Executive full discretion in *neither* the selection *nor* the removal of a purely executive officer. . . .

Since our 1935 decision in *Humphrey's Executor v. United States* — which was considered by many at the time the product of an activist, anti-New Deal Court bent on reducing the power of President Franklin Roosevelt — it has been established that the line of permissible restriction upon removal of principal officers lies at the point at which the powers exercised by those officers are no longer purely executive. Thus, removal restrictions have been generally regarded as lawful for so-called "independent regulatory agencies," such as the Federal Trade Commission, the Interstate Commerce Commission, and the Consumer Product Safety Commission, which engage substantially in what has been called the "quasi-legislative activity" of rulemaking, and for members of Article I courts, such as the Court of Military Appeals, who engage in the "quasi-judicial" function of adjudication. It has often been observed, correctly in my view, that the line between "purely executive" functions and "quasi-legislative" or "quasi-judicial" functions is not a clear one or even a rational one. But at least it permitted the identification of certain officers, and certain agencies, whose functions were entirely within the control of the President. Congress had to be aware of that restriction in its legislation. Today, however, *Humphrey's Executor* is swept into the dustbin of repudiated constitutional principles. "[O]ur present considered view," the Court says, "is that the determination of whether the Constitution allows Congress to impose a 'good cause'-type restriction on the President's power to remove an official cannot be made to turn on whether or not that official is classified as 'purely executive.' " What *Humphrey's Executor* (and presumably *Myers*) really means, we are now told, is not that there are any "rigid categories of those officials who may or may not be removed at will by the President," but simply that Congress cannot "interfere with the President's exercise of the 'executive power' and his constitutionally appointed duty to 'take care that the laws be faithfully executed.' "

One can hardly grieve for the shoddy treatment given today to *Humphrey's Executor,* which, after all, accorded the same indignity (with much less justification) to Chief Justice Taft's opinion 10 years earlier in *Myers v. United States* — gutting, in six quick pages devoid of textual or historical precedent for the novel principle it set forth, a carefully researched and reasoned 70-page opinion. . . . But one must grieve for the Constitution. *Humphrey's Executor* at least had the decency formally to observe the constitutional principle that the President had to be the repository of all executive power, *see* 295 U.S. at 627–28, which, as *Myers* carefully explained, necessarily means that he must be able to discharge those who do not perform executive functions according to his liking. . . . As far as I can discern from the Court's opinion, it is now open season upon the President's removal power for all executive officers, with not even the superficially principled restriction of *Humphrey's Executor* as cover. The Court essentially says to the President: "Trust us. We will make sure that you are able to accomplish your constitutional role." I think the Constitution gives the President — and the people — more protection than that.

V

The purpose of the separation and equilibration of powers in general, and of the unitary Executive in particular, was not merely to assure effective government but to preserve individual freedom. Those who hold or have held offices covered by the Ethics in Government Act are entitled to that protection as much as the rest of us, and I conclude my discussion by considering the effect of the Act upon the fairness of the process they receive.

Only someone who has worked in the field of law enforcement can fully appreciate the vast power and the immense discretion that are placed in the hands of a prosecutor with respect to the objects of his investigation. Justice Robert Jackson, when he was Attorney General under President Franklin Roosevelt, described it in a memorable speech to United States Attorneys, as follows:

> . . . .
>
> If the prosecutor is obliged to choose his case, it follows that he can choose his defendants. Therein is the most dangerous power of the prosecutor: that he will pick people that he thinks he should get, rather than cases that need to be prosecuted. With the law books filled with a great assortment of crimes, a prosecutor stands a fair chance of finding at least a technical violation of some act on the part of almost anyone. In such a case, it is not a question of discovering the commission of a crime and then looking for the man who has committed it, it is a question of picking the man and then searching the law books, or putting investigators to work, to pin some offense on him. It is in this realm — in which the prosecutor picks some person whom he dislikes or desires to embarrass, or selects some group of unpopular persons and then looks for an offense, that the greatest danger of abuse of prosecuting power lies. It is here that law enforcement becomes personal, and the real crime becomes that of being unpopular with the predominant or governing group, being attached to the wrong political views, or being personally obnoxious to or in the way of the prosecutor himself.

Robert Jackson, The Federal Prosecutor, Address Delivered at the Second Annual Conference of United States Attorneys, April 1, 1940.

Under our system of government, the primary check against prosecutorial abuse is a political one. The prosecutors who exercise this awesome discretion are selected and can be removed by a President, whom the people have trusted enough to elect. Moreover, when crimes are not investigated and prosecuted fairly, nonselectively, with a reasonable sense of proportion, the President pays the cost in political damage to his administration. If federal prosecutors "pick people that [they] thin[k] [they] should get, rather than cases that need to be prosecuted," if they amass many more resources against a particular prominent individual, or against a particular class of political protesters, or against members of a particular political party, than the gravity of the alleged offenses or the record of successful prosecutions seems to warrant, the unfairness will come home to roost in the Oval Office. I leave it to the reader to recall the examples of this in recent years. That result, of course, was precisely what the Founders had in mind when they provided that all executive powers would be exercised by a *single* Chief Executive. As Hamilton put it, "[t]he ingredients which constitute safety in the republican sense are a due dependence on the people, and a due responsibility." FEDERALIST NO. 70. The President is directly dependent on the people, and since there is only *one* President, *he* is responsible. The people know whom to blame, whereas "one of the weightiest objections to a plurality in the executive . . . is that it tends to conceal faults and destroy responsibility." *Id.*

. . . Judges, after all, have life tenure, and appointing a surefire enthusiastic prosecutor could hardly be considered an impeachable offense. So if there is anything wrong with the selection, there is effectively no one to blame. The independent counsel thus selected proceeds to assemble a staff. As I observed earlier, in the nature of things this has to be done by finding lawyers who are willing to lay aside their current careers for an indeterminate amount of time, to take on a job that has no prospect of permanence and little prospect for promotion. One thing is certain, however: it involves investigating and perhaps prosecuting a particular individual. Can one imagine a less equitable manner of fulfilling the executive responsibility to investigate and prosecute? What would be the reaction if, in an area not covered by this statute, the Justice Department posted a public notice inviting applicants to assist in an investigation and possible prosecution of a certain prominent person? Does this not invite what Justice Jackson described as "picking the man and then searching the law books, or putting investigators to work, to pin some offense on him"? To be sure, the investigation must relate to the area of criminal offense specified by the life-tenured judges. But that has often been (and nothing prevents it from being) very broad — and should the independent counsel or his or her staff come up with something beyond that scope, nothing prevents him or her from asking the judges to expand his or her authority or, if that does not work, referring it to the Attorney General, whereupon the whole process would recommence and, if there was "reasonable basis to believe" that further investigation was warranted, that new offense would be referred to the Special Division, which would in all likelihood assign it to the same independent counsel. It seems to me not conducive to fairness. But even if it were entirely evident that unfairness was in fact the result — the judges hostile to the administration, the independent counsel an old foe of the President, the staff refugees from the recently defeated administration — *there would be no one accountable to the public to whom the blame could be assigned.*

I do not mean to suggest that anything of this sort (other than the inevitable self-selection of the prosecutory staff) occurred in the present case. I know and have the highest regard for the judges on the Special Division, and the independent counsel herself is a woman of accomplishment, impartiality, and integrity. But the fairness of a process must be adjudged on the basis of what it permits to happen, not what it produced in a particular case. It is true, of course, that a similar list of horribles could be attributed to an ordinary Justice Department prosecution — a vindictive prosecutor, an antagonistic staff, etc. But the difference is the difference that the Founders envisioned when they established a single Chief Executive accountable to the people: the blame can be assigned to someone who can be punished.

The above described possibilities of irresponsible conduct must, as I say, be considered in judging the constitutional acceptability of this process. But they will rarely occur, and in the average case the threat to fairness is quite different. As described in the brief filed on behalf of three ex-Attorneys General from each of the last three administrations:

> The problem is less spectacular but much more worrisome. It is that the institutional environment of the Independent Counsel — specifically, her isolation from the Executive Branch and the internal checks and balances it supplies — is designed to heighten, not to check, all of the occupational hazards of the dedicated prosecutor; the danger of too narrow a focus, of the loss of perspective, of preoccupation with the pursuit of one alleged suspect to the exclusion of other interests.

Brief for Edward H. Levi, Griffin B. Bell, and William French Smith as *Amici Curiae* 11.

It is, in other words, an additional advantage of the unitary Executive that it can achieve a more uniform application of the law. Perhaps that is not always achieved, but the mechanism to achieve it is there. The mini-Executive that is the independent counsel, however, operating in an area where so little is law and so much is discretion, is intentionally cut off from the unifying influence of the Justice Department, and from the perspective that multiple responsibilities provide. . . .

The notion that every violation of law should be prosecuted, including — indeed, *especially* — every violation by those in high places, is an attractive one, and it would be risky to argue in an election campaign that that is not an absolutely overriding value. . . . The reality is, however, that it is not an absolutely overriding value, and it was with the hope that we would be able to acknowledge and apply such realities that the Constitution spared us, by life tenure, the necessity of election campaigns. I cannot imagine that there are not many thoughtful men and women in Congress who realize that the benefits of this legislation are far outweighed by its harmful effect upon our system of government, and even upon the nature of justice received by those men and women who agree to serve in the Executive Branch. But it is difficult to vote not to enact, and even more difficult to vote to repeal, a statute called, appropriately enough, the Ethics in Government Act. If Congress is controlled by the party other than the one to which the President belongs, it has little incentive to repeal it; if it is controlled by the same party, it dare not. By its shortsighted action today, I fear the Court has permanently encumbered the Republic with an institution that will do it great harm.

Worse than what it has done, however, is the manner in which it has done it. A government of laws means a government of rules. Today's decision on the basic issue of fragmentation of executive power is ungoverned by rule, and hence ungoverned by law. It extends into the very heart of our most significant constitutional function the "totality of the circumstances" mode of analysis that this Court has in recent years become fond of. Taking all things into account, we conclude that the power taken away from the President here is not really too much. The next time executive power is assigned to someone other than the President we may conclude, taking all things into account, that it is too much. That opinion, like this one, will not be confined by any rule. We will describe, as we have today (though I hope more accurately) the effects of the provision in question, and will authoritatively announce: "The President's need to control the exercise of the [subject officer's] discretion is so central to the functioning of the Executive Branch as to require complete control." This is not analysis; it is ad hoc judgment. And it fails to explain why it is not true that — as the text of the Constitution seems to require, as the Founders seemed to expect, and as our past cases have uniformly assumed — all purely executive power must be under the control of the President.

The ad hoc approach to constitutional adjudication has real attraction, even apart from its work-saving potential. It is guaranteed to produce a result, in every case, that will make a majority of the Court happy with the law. The law is, by definition, precisely what the majority thinks, taking all things into account, it ought to be. I prefer to rely upon the judgment of the wise men who constructed our system, and of the people who approved it, and of two centuries of history that have shown it to be sound. Like it or not, that judgment says, quite plainly, that "[t]he executive Power shall be vested in a President of the United States."

Exercise 6:

Consider the following questions in connection with *Morrison v. Olson:*

(1) Under the independent counsel provisions of the Ethics in Government Act, does the Attorney General have greater power to remove an Independent Counsel ("IC") than Congress has to remove the Comptroller General? An IC removed by the Attorney General may seek reinstatement in a judicial proceeding. Would a Comptroller General removed by Congress have a similar opportunity to seek reinstatement?

(2) With respect to the majority's analysis under the Appointments Clause, what four factors did the Court find indicated that the IC was only an inferior officer? Assuming those four factors specify the appropriate test, when you apply them to the IC do you reach the same result as the Court?

(3) With respect to the majority's analysis under the Appointments Clause, do you agree with the permissibility of "interbranch appointments"? Why or why not? If such appointments were prohibited, would any text of the Appointments Clause be rendered superfluous? Could Congress authorize the Attorney General to appoint clerks for all the Article III courts? Could Congress authorize the U.S. Supreme Court to appoint the Solicitor General?

(4) With respect to the majority's analysis under the Appointments Clause, what are the context and the scope of any earlier precedent for judicial appointment of attorneys to act as prosecutors? In the specific context addressed in precedent, what would be the alternatives to such judicial appointments?

(5) With respect to the majority's analysis of whether the duties vested in the Special Division are in conflict with Article III, the Court found that the power to remove the IC did not constitute "a significant judicial encroachment upon executive power or upon the prosecutorial discretion of the independent counsel." Do you agree? Was the Court's conclusion consistent with *Bowsher v. Synar*?

(6) With respect to the majority's analysis of whether the statutory removal provisions were consistent with separation of powers principles, on what basis, if any, are *Bowsher v. Synar* and *Myers v. United States* distinguishable?

(7) In the majority's analysis of whether the statutory removal provisions were consistent with separation of powers principles, was the Court's distinction between *Myers v. United States* and *Humphrey's Executor v. United States* faithful to those decisions or a recharacterization of the precedents?

(8) Under the *Morrison* analysis, would Congress have been required to surrender a role for the Senate in the confirmation of inferior officers in order to obtain civil service protection (*i.e.*, removal only for cause) for those officers?

(9) Under the *Morrison* analysis, could Congress provide that all United States Attorneys — the chief federal prosecutor for each federal district — would be subject to removal only for cause for the first five years following appointment?

Could Congress provide similar protection for any or all of the following officers: the Solicitor General, the Administrator of the Environmental Protection Agency, and the Secretary of Commerce?

(10) In dissent, Justice Scalia asserted that the first sentence of Article II vested in the President "all" executive power. Was Justice Scalia adopting an interpretation of that text consistent with *Myers v. United States* and/or *Youngstown Sheet & Tube Co. v. Sawyer*?

(11) In dissent, Justice Scalia asserted that prosecution is a "quintessentially executive activity." Do you agree? Is there a basis to distinguish the authority to investigate and prosecute placed in the hands of the IC from that placed in the hands of the FTC and/or the FEC?

(12) In dissent, Justice Scalia asserted that the majority "replaced the clear constitutional prescription that the executive power belongs to the President with a 'balancing test.' " Is that a fair characterization of the majority's position? Why or why not?

(13) In dissent, Justice Scalia asserted that the majority's analysis provides no criteria to guide future decisions of which officers not subject to removal by the President at will may be vested with executive powers. Is that a fair criticism of the majority's approach?

(14) In dissent, Justice Scalia asserted that the IC provisions will "reduce the zeal" of the President's staff and erode the President's "public support," thereby weakening the President in head-to-head confrontations with Congress. Does the history of IC investigations and prosecutions, before and after *Morrison*, support those observations?

(15) In dissent, Justice Scalia reviewed the four criteria considered by the majority in determining whether the IC is a principal or inferior officer. Did he succeed in demonstrating that the majority misapplied their own criteria? What alternative test did Justice Scalia advance?

(16) What manner of argument did Justice Scalia assert to support his alternative test for distinguishing principal from inferior officers?

(17) In dissent, Justice Scalia summarized the Court's precedents in *Myers v. United States* and *United States v. Perkins* (discussed in *Myers*). Did he fairly state the doctrine as it existed prior to *Morrison*?

(18) In dissent, Justice Scalia addressed the historical setting of *Humphrey's Executor v. United States*. Does that context help explain the Court's departure from its then-less-than-decade-old precedent in *Myers*? Were there any other significant doctrinal shifts at the same time?

A Postscript to *Morrison v. Olson*

Congress permitted the Independent Counsel Act to lapse in 1999. Some scholars have characterized that development as follows:

> Democrats and Republicans alike came to agree that the law was both unconstitutional and unwise. Indeed, the eventual bipartisan consensus against the use of independent counsels underscores the extent to which the presidential support for the unitary executive is less a reflection of partisan politics, as some have claimed, and more the result of fundamental questions about the allocation of power within the federal government.

STEVEN S. CALABRESI & CHRISTOPHER S. YOO, THE UNITARY EXECUTIVE: PRESIDENTIAL POWER FROM WASHINGTON TO BUSH 11 (2008). For a case study of the impeachment of President Clinton and the demise of the Independent Counsel Act, see *id.* at 400–04.

EDMOND v. UNITED STATES

520 U.S. 651 (1997)

JUSTICE SCALIA delivered the Opinion of the Court.

We must determine in this case whether Congress has authorized the Secretary of Transportation to appoint civilian members of the Coast Guard Court of Criminal Appeals, and if so, whether this authorization is constitutional under the Appointments Clause of Article II.

I.

The Coast Guard Court of Criminal Appeals (formerly known as the Coast Guard Court of Military Review) is an intermediate court within the military justice system. . . . [It] hears appeals from decisions of courts-martial, and its decisions are subject to review by the United States Court of Appeals for the Armed Forces . . . .

Appellate military judges who are assigned to a Court of Criminal Appeals must be members of the bar, but may be commissioned officers or civilians. . . .

In *Weiss v. United States,* 510 U.S. 163 (1994), we considered whether the assignment of commissioned military officers to serve as military judges without reappointment under the Appointments Clause was constitutional. We held that military trial and appellate judges are officers of the United States and must be appointed pursuant to the Appointments Clause. We upheld the judicial assignments at issue in *Weiss* because each of the military judges had been previously appointed by the President as a commissioned military officer, and was serving on active duty under that commission at the time he was assigned to a military court. We noted, however, that "allowing civilians to be assigned to Courts of Military Review, without being appointed pursuant to the Appointments Clause, obviously presents quite a different question."

In anticipation of our decision in *Weiss* . . . the Secretary of Transportation issued a memorandum "adopting" the General Counsel's assignments to the Coast Guard Court of Military Review "as judicial appointments of my own." . . .

. . . .

II.

Petitioners argue that the Secretary's civilian appointments to the Coast Guard Court of Criminal Appeals are invalid for two reasons: first, the Secretary lacks authority under 49 U.S.C. § 323(a) to appoint members of the court; second, judges of military Courts of Criminal Appeals are principal, not inferior, officers within the meaning of the Appointments Clause, and must therefore be appointed by the President with the advice and consent of the Senate. We consider these contentions in turn.

[The Court construed 49 U.S.C. § 323(a) as statutory authorization for the Secretary to make the challenged appointments.]

III.

. . . .

As we recognized in *Buckley v. Valeo,* 424 U.S. 1 (1976), the Appointments Clause of Article II is more than a matter of "etiquette or protocol"; it is among the significant structural safeguards of the constitutional scheme. By vesting the President with the exclusive power to select the principal (noninferior) officers of the United States, the Appointments Clause prevents congressional encroachment upon the Executive and Judicial Branches. This disposition was also designed to assure a higher quality of appointments: The Framers anticipated that the President would be less vulnerable to interest-group pressure and personal favoritism than would a collective body. "The sole and undivided responsibility of one man will naturally beget a livelier sense of duty, and a more exact regard to reputation." THE FEDERALIST NO. 76 (A. Hamilton). The President's power to select principal officers of the United States was not left unguarded, however, as Article II further requires the "Advice and Consent of the Senate." This serves both to curb Executive abuses of the appointment power and "to promote a judicious choice of [persons] for filling the offices of the union," THE FEDERALIST NO. 76. By requiring the joint participation of the President and the Senate, the Appointments Clause was designed to ensure public accountability for both the making of a bad appointment and the rejection of a good one. [Alexander] Hamilton observed:

> The blame of a bad nomination would fall upon the president singly and absolutely. The censure of rejecting a good one would lie entirely at the door of the senate; aggravated by the consideration of their having counteracted the good intentions of the executive. If an ill appointment should be made, the executive for nominating, and the senate for approving, would participate, though in different degrees, in the opprobrium and disgrace.

THE FEDERALIST NO. 77 (A. Hamilton).

The prescribed manner of appointment for principal officers is also the default manner of appointment for inferior officers. "[B]ut," the Appointments Clause continues, "the Congress may by Law vest the Appointment of such inferior Officers, as they think proper, in the President alone, in the Courts of Law, or in the Heads of Departments." This provision, sometimes referred to as the "Excepting Clause," was added to the proposed Constitution on the last day of the Grand Convention, with little discussion. *See* 2 MAX FARRAND, RECORDS OF THE FEDERAL CONVENTION OF 1787, pp. 627–28 (1911). As one of our early opinions suggests, its obvious purpose is administrative convenience — but that convenience was deemed to outweigh the benefit of the more cumbersome procedure only with respect to the appointment of "inferior Officers." . . .

Our cases have not set forth an exclusive criterion for distinguishing between principal and inferior officers for Appointments Clause purposes. Among the offices that we have found to be inferior are that of a district court clerk, an election supervisor, a vice consul charged temporarily with the duties of the consul, and a "United States commissioner" in district court proceedings. Most recently, in *Morrison v. Olson,* 487 U.S. 654 (1988), we held that the independent counsel created by provisions of the Ethics in Government Act of 1978 was an inferior officer. In reaching that conclusion, we relied on several factors: that the independent counsel was subject to removal by a higher officer (the Attorney General), that she performed only limited duties, that her jurisdiction was narrow, and that her tenure was limited.

Petitioners are quite correct that the last two of these conclusions do not hold with regard to the office of military judge at issue here. It is not "limited in tenure," as that phrase was used in *Morrison* to describe "appoint[ment] essentially to accomplish a single task [at the end of which] the office is terminated."

Nor are military judges "limited in jurisdiction," as used in *Morrison* to refer to the fact that an independent counsel may investigate and prosecute only those individuals, and for only those crimes, that are within the scope of jurisdiction granted by the special three judge appointing panel. However, *Morrison* did not purport to set forth a definitive test for whether an office is "inferior" under the Appointments Clause. To the contrary, it explicitly stated: "We need not attempt here to decide exactly where the line falls between the two types of officers, because in our view [the independent counsel] clearly falls on the 'inferior officer' side of that line."

To support principal-officer status, petitioners emphasize the importance of the responsibilities that the Court of Criminal Appeals judges bear. They review those court-martial proceedings that result in the most serious sentences, including those "in which the sentence, as approved, extends to death, dismissal . . . dishonorable or bad-conduct discharge, or confinement for one year or more." They must ensure that the court-martial's finding of guilt and its sentence are "correct in law and fact" which includes resolution of constitutional challenges. And finally, unlike most appellate judges, Court of Criminal Appeals judges are not required to defer to the trial court's factual findings . . . . We do not dispute that military appellate judges are charged with exercising significant authority on behalf of the United States. This, however, is also true of offices that we have held were "inferior" within the meaning of the Appointments Clause. The exercise of "significant authority pursuant to the laws of the United States" marks, not the line between principal and inferior officer for Appointments Clause purposes, but rather, as we said in *Buckley,* the line between officer and nonofficer.

Generally speaking, the term "inferior officer" connotes a relationship with some higher ranking officer or officers below the President: Whether one is an "inferior" officer depends on whether he has a superior. It is not enough that other officers may be identified who formally maintain a higher rank, or possess responsibilities of greater magnitude. . . . Rather, in the context of a Clause designed to preserve political accountability relative to important Government assignments, we think it evident that "inferior officers" are officers whose work is directed and supervised at some level by others who were appointed by Presidential nomination with the advice and consent of the Senate.

This understanding of the Appointments Clause conforms with the views of the first Congress. On July 27, 1789, Congress established the first Executive department, the Department of Foreign Affairs. In doing so, it expressly designated the Secretary of the Department as a "principal officer," and his subordinate, the Chief Clerk of the Department, as an "inferior officer" . . . .

Congress used similar language in establishing the Department of War, repeatedly referring to the Secretary of that department as a "principal officer," and the Chief Clerk, who would be "employed" within the Department as the Secretary "shall deem proper," as an "inferior officer."

Supervision of the work of Court of Criminal Appeals judges is divided between the Judge Advocate General ["JAG"] (who in the Coast Guard is subordinate to the Secretary of Transportation) and the Court of Appeals for the Armed Forces. The [JAG] exercises administrative oversight over the Court of Criminal Appeals. . . . It is conceded by the parties that the [JAG] may also remove a Court of Criminal

Appeals judge from his judicial assignment without cause. The power to remove officers, we have recognized, is a powerful tool for control.

The [JAG]'s control over Court of Criminal Appeals judges is, to be sure, not complete. He may not attempt to influence (by threat of removal or otherwise) the outcome of individual proceedings and has no power to reverse decisions of the court. This latter power does reside, however, in another Executive Branch entity, the Court of Appeals for the Armed Forces.[1] . . . The scope of review is narrower than that exercised by the Court of Criminal Appeals . . . . This limitation upon review does not in our opinion render the judges of the Court of Criminal Appeals principal officers. What is significant is that the judges of the Court of Criminal Appeals have no power to render a final decision on behalf of the United States unless permitted to do so by other Executive officers.

Finally, petitioners argue that *Freytag v. Commissioner*, 501 U.S. 868 (1991), which held that special trial judges charged with assisting Tax Court judges were inferior officers and could be appointed by the Chief Judge of the Tax Court, suggests that Court of Criminal Appeals judges are principal officers. Petitioners contend that Court of Criminal Appeals judges more closely resemble Tax Court judges — who we implied (according to petitioners) were principal officers — than they do special trial judges. We note initially that *Freytag* does not hold that Tax Court judges are principal officers; only the appointment of special trial judges was at issue in that case. Moreover, there are two significant distinctions between Tax Court judges and Court of Criminal Appeals judges. First, there is no Executive Branch tribunal comparable to the Court of Criminal Appeals for the Armed Forces that reviews the work of the Tax Court; its decisions are appealable only to courts of the Third Branch. And second, there is no officer comparable to a [JAG] who supervises the work of the Tax Court, with power to determine its procedural rules, to remove any judge without cause, and to order any decision submitted for review. *Freytag* does not control our decision here.

. . . .

We conclude that 49 U.S.C. § 323(a) authorizes the Secretary of Transportation to appoint judges of the Coast Guard Court of Criminal Appeals; and that such appointment is in conformity with the Appointments Clause of the Constitution. . . .

Accordingly, we affirm the judgment of the Court of Appeals for the Armed Forces with respect to each petitioner.

JUSTICE SOUTER, concurring in part and concurring in the judgment.

I join in Parts I and II of the Court's opinion and agree with the reasoning in Part III insofar as it describes an important, and even necessary, reason for holding judges of the Coast Guard Court of Criminal Appeals to be inferior officers within the meaning of the Appointments Clause. . . .

Because the term "inferior officer" implies an official superior, one who has no superior is not an inferior officer. This unexceptional maxim will in some instances be dispositive of status; it might, for example, lead to the conclusion that United States district judges cannot be inferior officers, since the power of appellate review does not extend to them personally, but is limited to their judgments. *See In re Sealed Case*, 838 F.2d 476, 483 (D.C. Cir.), *rev'd sub nom. Morrison v. Olson*, 487 U.S. 654 (1988) (suggesting that "lower federal judges . . . are principal officers"

---

[1] . . . [T]he Court of Appeals for the Armed Forces "is established under Article I of the Constitution," and "is located for administrative purposes only in the Department of Defense." . . .

because they are "not subject to personal supervision").

It does not follow, however, that if one is subject to some supervision and control, one is an inferior officer. Having a superior officer is necessary for inferior officer status, but not sufficient to establish it. Accordingly, in *Morrison*, the Court's determination that the independent counsel was "to some degree 'inferior' " to the Attorney General did not end the enquiry. The Court went on to weigh the duties, jurisdiction, and tenure associated with the office before concluding that the independent counsel was an inferior officer. Thus, under *Morrison*, the Solicitor General of the United States, for example, may well be a principal officer, despite his statutory "inferiority" to the Attorney General. The mere existence of a "superior" is not dispositive.

. . . .

. . . I would not try to derive a single rule of sufficiency. What is needed, instead, is a detailed look at the powers and duties of these judges to see whether reasons favoring their inferior officer status within the constitutional scheme weigh more heavily than those to the contrary. . . . I therefore join not only in the Court's conclusion that the necessary supervisory condition for inferior officer status is satisfied here, but in the Court's ultimate holding that the judges of the Coast Guard Court of Criminal Appeals are inferior officers within the meaning of the Appointments Clause.

Exercise 7:

Consider the following questions in connection with *Edmond v. United States*:

(1) What distinguishes "officers" of the United States from mere "employees"? Is *Edmond* consistent with prior precedent on that point?

(2) According to *Edmond*, what distinguishes "principal officers" from "inferior officers"? Is *Edmond* consistent with prior precedent on that point?

(3) What interpretative methods and sources does the Court draw upon to answer those questions?

(4) What are the constitutionally permissible means of appointment of judges to the U.S. District Courts and U.S. Courts of Appeals?

(5) If your instructor assigned *Volume 1*, consider whether sitting Justices of the U.S. Supreme Court needed a second commission to resume holding Circuit Courts upon passage of the federal Judiciary Act of 1802. These officers had been nominated by the President, confirmed by the Senate, and commissioned to serve on the Supreme Court. Could Congress expand their duties to include serving on separate courts? Or, was Circuit Judge a distinct office requiring a separate appointment and commission?

Review Questions

1. *The Status of Special Counsel*

With the 1999 expiration of the Independent Counsel Act at issue in *Morrison v. Olson*, the Department of Justice returned to the practice of appointing a "Special Counsel" to investigate and prosecute allegations against certain powerful members of the Administration. Following the Attorney General's recusal in the matter, the Deputy Attorney General appointed Patrick Fitzgerald to investigate allegations that the identity of Valerie Plame and her relationship to the CIA had been "leaked" to the press.

Although Department of Justice regulations defined the authority of a Special Counsel, the appointment of Fitzgerald was explicitly exempted from those limitations. Fitzgerald was delegated "all the authority of the Attorney General with respect to the Department's investigation into the unauthorized disclosure of a CIA employee's identity" and "direct[ed]" to act "independent of supervision or control of any officer of the Department [of Justice]." Acting pursuant to that authority, Fitzgerald successfully prosecuted "Scooter" Libby for perjury. *United States v. Libby,* 429 F. Supp. 2d 27 (D.D.C. 2006). The defense maintained that Fitzgerald was a principal officer because (1) he had no superior officer within the Executive Branch other than the President and (2) he had been expressly granted "plenary" authority — even greater authority than an Independent Counsel — including the authority to disregard established Department policy. Fitzgerald, however, was neither appointed by the President nor subject to Senate confirmation, so if he was a principal officer, the appointment was not in conformity with the Constitution. On June 8, 2007, that argument was supported by a brief *amici curiae* filed by a dozen law professors spanning the political spectrum.

In the context of a determination whether Libby should begin to serve his prison sentence pending appeal, the district court determined that despite the absence of either a statute or regulation defining the scope of Fitzgerald's authority (and a factual record regarding his authority it described as "sparse"), the challenge to Fitzgerald's appointment did not raise a "close question" because, it concluded, the Deputy Attorney General could remove Fitzgerald and Fitzgerald was not expressly authorized to disregard Department policy. The U.S. Court of Appeals for the District of Columbia Circuit affirmed. An appeal of the sentence itself, following a partial commutation, was filed. The challenge to the appointment was a substantial issue in Libby's appeal (despite the commutation of his prison sentence). The appeal was not prosecuted to resolution on the merits. Assume that the matter were to reach the Supreme Court. How should the Court rule?

2. *The Public Company Accounting Oversight Board*

In response to a series of scandals in which corporate insiders manipulated the value of publicly-traded stock with various accounting gimmicks (*e.g.,* Enron and Worldcom), Congress enacted the Sarbanes-Oxley Act of 1992, Pub. L. No. 107-204, 116 Stat. 745. One feature of that Act was the creation of the Public Company Accounting Oversight Board. *See id.* § 101, 116 Stat. at 750 (codified as 15 U.S.C. § 7211). Congress provided that the members of the Board were to be appointed by the Securities and Exchange Commission to serve a term of five years. *See id.* at § 101(e), 116 Stat. at 752 (codified as 15 U.S.C. § 7211(e)). Members of the Board are subject to removal by the Securities and Exchange Commission "for good cause shown." *Id.* Suit was filed alleging that the Board was unconstitutional, asserting that its members were not appointed by the President nor removable by him and that the Board was funded from fees levied on publicly-traded companies rather than by congressional appropriations. Assuming that the plaintiff properly interpreted the Act in those respects, does the Act go too far in isolating the Board from accountability to *both* the President and Congress?

Regardless of how one answers that "functionalist inquiry," does the manner of appointment of Board members satisfy the Appointments Clause? In *Freytag v. Commissioner of Internal Revenue,* 501 U.S. 868 (1991) (discussed in *Edmond v. United States*), the Court stated:

> The court for more than a century has held that the term "Departmen[t]" refers only to " 'a part or division of the executive government, as the

> Department of State, or of the Treasury,' " expressly "creat[ed]" and "giv[en] . . . the name of a department" by Congress. *United States v. Germaine,* 99 U.S. 508, 510–11 (1879).

Id. at 886. The Court explained the importance of reading the term in that restrictive manner: "Confining the term 'heads of Departments' in the Appointments Clause to executive divisions like the Cabinet-level departments constrains the distribution of the appointment power." *Id.* In *Freytag,* the Court upheld the appointment of an inferior officer by holding that the Tax Court was a "Court[] of Law" within the meaning of the Appointments Clause. *Id.* at 888–91. Should the Securities and Exchange Commission be considered a "Court[] of Law"? If not, are the members of the Board properly appointed even if characterized as inferior officers? Does the answer to that question depend upon how the Board implements the Act? *See Free Enterprise Fund v. Public Company Accounting Oversight Board,* No. 06-0217, 2007 U.S. Dist. LEXIS 24310 (D.D.C. Mar. 21, 2007) (granting the Board summary judgment because plaintiffs failed to demonstrate that "no set of circumstances exist[ed] under which the Act would be valid"). Concluding that members of the Board were inferior officers and that the Commissioners of the Securities and Exchange Commission constituted the "head" of a "department," a divided panel of the U.S. Court of Appeals for the District of Columbia Circuit affirmed. *See Free Enterprise Fund v. Public Company Accounting Oversight Board,* No. 07-5127, 2008 U.S. App. LEXIS 18029 (D.C. Cir. Aug. 22, 2008). If the U.S. Supreme Court considers the case, how should it rule?

3. *Dismissal of United States Attorneys*

On December 7, 2006, President George W. Bush removed from office eight United States Attorneys. Congress initiated investigations as to the reason for the firings. The surrounding controversy placed significant political pressure on Attorney General Alberto Gonzales, who resigned from office in September 2007. At one point in the controversy, General Gonzales stated that United States Attorneys "serve at the pleasure of the President" and described the situation as "an overblown personnel matter."

The removals were hardly unprecedented. Shortly after taking office, President William J. Clinton replaced *all* United States Attorneys regardless of any tenure remaining in their five-year terms.

Although there may be significant political cost and policy concerns associated with the removal of United States Attorneys, what protection from removal may Congress constitutionally extend to the chief federal prosecutor in each of the districts?

Congress has required that Presidential nominees for U.S Attorney be subject to Senate confirmation. Prior to March 2006, when there was a vacancy in the position of U.S. Attorney it would be filled on an interim basis in one of three ways. *First,* the senior civil servant in the office of the U.S. Attorney for the relevant District could become an Acting U.S. Attorney. *Second,* the Attorney General could make an interim appointment to the position for a maximum of 120 days. *Third,* for vacancies that persisted beyond 120 days, the U.S. District Court could appoint an interim U.S. Attorney for the District.

In March 2006 the 120-day limit on service by interim appointments by the Attorney General was repealed. Democratic Members of Congress charged that the Administration would circumvent the Senate confirmation process by leaving the interim U.S. Attorneys in place indefinitely. As a result, in June 2007, President Bush signed into law a bill restoring the 120-day limitation.

Assume that as the terms of office of U.S. Attorneys were to expire, a Senate hostile to the Administration refused to act on any nominations to fill the vacancies. The result would be that the chief federal prosecutor in each District would be either a civil servant or an appointee of the District Court. In either case, there would be scores of prosecutors neither appointed by the President or the Attorney General. Would such wholesale transfer of the power to appoint federal prosecutors comport with the Constitution?

CHAPTER 4

LEGISLATIVE POWER — SEPARATION OF POWERS LIMITATIONS

Volume III introduces issues relating to the substantive parameters of federal legislative powers. In contrast, this Chapter examines limits on the process through which Congress may act. Some such limits are noted in this Volume (*e.g.*, *Buckley v. Valeo* and *Bowsher v. Synar*) and in Volume I (*e.g.*, *Miller v. French*). Those matters are not repeated in this Chapter. A few additional cases will serve to illustrate other important limitations grounded in separation of powers concerns.

MISTRETTA v. UNITED STATES

488 U.S. 361 (1989)

JUSTICE BLACKMUN delivered the Opinion of the Court.

[W]e granted certiorari . . . in order to consider the constitutionality of the Sentencing Guidelines promulgated by the United States Sentencing Commission. The Commission is a body created under the Sentencing Reform Act of 1984, 18 U.S.C. § 3551 *et seq.* . . .

I

A. *Background*

. . . .

Historically, federal sentencing . . . never has been thought to be assigned by the Constitution to the exclusive jurisdiction of any one of the three Branches of Government. Congress, of course, has the power to fix the sentence for a federal crime . . . and the scope of judicial discretion with respect to a sentence is subject to congressional control. . . . Congress early abandoned fixed-sentence rigidity, however, and put in place a system of ranges within which the sentencer could choose the precise punishment. . . . Congress delegated almost unfettered discretion to the sentencing judge to determine what the sentence should be within the customarily wide range so selected. This broad discretion was further enhanced by the power later granted the judge to suspend the sentence and by the resulting growth of an elaborate probation system. Also, with the advent of parole, Congress moved toward a "three-way sharing" of sentencing responsibility by granting corrections personnel in the Executive Branch the discretion to release a prisoner before the expiration of the sentence imposed by the judge. Thus, under the indeterminate-sentence system, Congress defined the maximum, the judge imposed a sentence within the statutory range (which he usually could replace with probation), and the Executive Branch's parole official eventually determined the actual duration of imprisonment. . . .

Serious disparities in sentences, however, were common. . . .

. . . Congress had wrestled with the problem for more than a decade when, in 1984, it enacted the sweeping reforms that are at issue here.

Helpful in our consideration and analysis of the statute is the Senate Report on the 1984 legislation . . . . It observed that the indeterminate-sentencing system had two unjustifi[ed] and "shameful" consequences. . . . The first was the great variation among sentences imposed by different judges upon similarly situated offenders. The second was the uncertainty as to the time the offender would spend in prison. Each was a serious impediment to an evenhanded and effective operation of the criminal justice system. . . .

. . . .

B. *The Act*

The Act, as adopted, revises the old sentencing process in several ways:

1. It rejects imprisonment as a means of promoting rehabilitation . . . .

2. It consolidates the power that had been exercised by the sentencing judge and the Parole Commission to decide what punishment an offender should suffer. This is done by creating the United States Sentencing Commission, directing that Commission to devise guidelines to be used for sentencing, and prospectively abolishing the Parole Commission. . . .

3. It makes all sentences basically determinate. . . .

4. It makes the Sentencing Commission's guidelines binding on the courts, although it preserves for the judge the discretion to depart from the guideline applicable to a particular case if the judge finds an aggravating or mitigating factor present that the Commission did not adequately consider when formulating the guidelines. . . . The Act also requires the court to state its reasons for the sentence imposed and to give "the specific reason" for imposing a sentence different from that described in the guideline. . . .

5. It authorizes limited appellate review of the sentence. . . .

. . . .

C. *The Sentencing Commission*

The Commission is established "as an independent commission in the judicial branch of the United States." 28 U.S.C. § 991(a). It has seven voting members (one of whom is the Chairman) appointed by the President "by and with the advice and consent of the Senate." "At least three of the members shall be Federal judges selected after considering a list of six judges recommended to the President by the Judicial Conference of the United States." *Id.* No more than four members of the Commission shall be members of the same political party. The Attorney General, or his designee, is an *ex officio* non-voting member. The Chairman and other members of the Commission are subject to removal by the President "only for neglect of duty or malfeasance in office or for other good cause shown." *Id.* . . . [A] voting member serves for six years and may not serve more than two full terms. *Id.* § 992(a), (b).

D. *The Responsibilities of the Commission*

In addition to the duty the Commission has to promulgate determinitive-sentence guidelines, it is under an obligation periodically to "review and revise" the guidelines. *Id.* § 994(o). It is to "consult with authorities on, and individual and institutional representatives of, various aspects of the Federal criminal justice system." *Id.* It must report to Congress "any amendments to the guidelines." *Id.* § 994(p). It is to make recommendations to Congress whether the grades of maximum penalties should be modified. *Id.* § 994(r). It must submit to Congress at least annually an analysis of the operation of the guidelines. *Id.* § 994(w). It is to issue "general policy statements" regarding their application. *Id.* § 994(a)(2). And it has the power to "establish general policies . . . as are necessary to carry out the purposes" of the legislation, *id.* § 995(a)(1); to "monitor the performance of probation officers" with respect to the guidelines, *id.* § 994(a)(9); to "devise and conduct periodic training programs of instruction in sentencing techniques for judicial and probation personnel" and others, *id.* § 994(a)(18); and to "perform such other functions as are required to permit Federal courts to meet their responsibilities" as to sentencing, *id.* § 995(a)(22).

. . . .

II. *This Litigation*

On December 10, 1987, John M. Mistretta (petitioner) and another were indicted in the U.S. District Court for the Western District of Missouri on three counts centering in a cocaine sale. . . . Mistretta moved to have the promulgated Guidelines ruled unconstitutional on the grounds that the Sentencing Commission was constituted in violation of the established doctrine of separation of powers, and that Congress delegated excessive authority to the Commission to structure the Guidelines. . . .

The District Court rejected petitioner's delegation argument on the ground that, despite the language of the statute, the Sentencing Commission "should be judicially characterized as having Executive Branch status," 682 F. Supp. at 1035, and that the Guidelines are similar to substantive rules promulgated by other agencies. *Id.* at 1034–35. The court also rejected petitioner's claim that the Act is unconstitutional because it requires Article III federal judges to serve on the Commission. *Id.* at 1035.

. . . Petitioner was sentenced under the Guidelines to 18 months' imprisonment, to be followed by a 3-year term of supervised release. . . . The court also imposed a $1,000 fine and a $50 special assessment. . . .

. . . Because of the "imperative public importance" of the issue . . . and because of the disarray among the Federal District Courts, we granted [petitions for expedited review].

III. *Delegation of Power*

Petitioner argues that in delegating the power to promulgate sentencing guidelines for every federal criminal offense to an independent Sentencing Commission, Congress has granted the Commission excessive legislative discretion in violation of the constitutionally based nondelegation doctrine. We do not agree.

The nondelegation doctrine is rooted in the principle of separation of powers that underlies our tripartite system of Government. The Constitution provides that "[a]ll legislative Powers herein granted shall be vested in a Congress of the United States," U.S. Const., Art. I, § 1, and we long have insisted that "the integrity and maintenance of the system of government ordained by the Constitution" mandate that Congress generally cannot delegate its legislative power to another Branch. *Field v. Clark*, 143 U.S. 649, 692 (1892). We also have recognized, however, that the separation-of-powers principle, and the nondelegation doctrine in particular, do not prevent Congress from obtaining the assistance of its coordinate Branches. In a passage now enshrined in our jurisprudence, Chief Justice Taft, writing for the Court, explained our approach to such cooperative ventures: "In determining what [Congress] may do in seeking assistance from another branch, the extent and character of that assistance must be fixed according to common sense and the inherent necessities of the government co-ordination." *J.W. Hampton Jr., & Co. v. United States*, 276 U.S. 394, 406, Treas. Dec. 42706 (1928). So long as Congress "shall lay down by legislative act an intelligible principle to which the person or body authorized to [exercise the delegated authority] is directed to conform, such legislative action is not a forbidden delegation of legislative power." *Id.* at 409.

Applying this "intelligible principle" test to congressional delegations, our jurisprudence has been driven by a practical understanding that in our increasingly complex society, replete with ever changing and more technical problems, Congress simply cannot do its job absent an ability to delegate power under broad general directives. . . .

Until 1935, this Court never struck down a challenged statute on delegation grounds. . . . After invalidating in 1935 two statutes as excessive delegations, *see A.L.A. Schechter Poultry Corp. v. United States,* 295 U.S. 495 (1935), and *Panama Refining Co. v. Ryan,* 293 U.S. 388 (1935), we have upheld, again without deviation, Congress' ability to delegate power under broad standards.[1] *See, e.g., Lichter v. United States,* 334 U.S. 742, 785–86 (1948) (upholding delegation of authority to determine excessive profits); *American Power & Light Co. v. SEC,* 329 U.S. 90, 105 (1946) (upholding delegation of authority to Securities and Exchange Commission to prevent unfair or inequitable distribution of voting power among security holders); *Yakus v. United States,* 321 U.S. 414, 426 (1944) (upholding delegation to Price Administrator to fix commodity prices that would be fair and equitable, and would effectuate purposes of Emergency Price Control Act of 1942); *FPC v. Hope Natural Gas Co.,* 320 U.S. 591, 600 (1944) (upholding delegation to Federal Power Commission to determine just and reasonable rates); *National Broadcasting Co. v. United States,* 319 U.S. 190, 225–26 (1943) (upholding delegation to Federal Communication Commission to regulate broadcast licensing "as public interest, convenience, or necessity" require).

In light of our approval of these broad delegations, we harbor no doubt that Congress' delegation of authority to the Sentencing Commission is sufficiently specific and detailed to meet constitutional requirements. Congress charged the Commission with three specific goals: to "assure the meeting of the purposes of sentencing as set forth" in the Act; to "provide certainty and fairness in meeting the purposes of sentencing, avoiding unwarranted sentencing disparities among defendants with similar records . . . while maintaining sufficient flexibility to permit individualized sentences," where appropriate; and to "reflect, to the extent practicable, advancement in knowledge of human behavior as it relates to the criminal justice process." 28 U.S.C. § 991(b)(1). Congress further specified four "purposes" of sentencing that the Commission must pursue in carrying out its mandate: "to reflect the seriousness of the offense, to promote respect for the law, and provide just punishment for the offense"; "to afford adequate deterrence to criminal conduct"; "to protect the public from further crimes of the defendant"; and "to provide the defendant with needed . . . correctional treatment." 18 U.S.C. § 3553(a)(2).

In addition, Congress prescribed the specific tool — the guidelines system — for

[1] In *Schecter* and *Panama Refining* the Court concluded that Congress had failed to articulate any policy or standard that would serve to confine the discretion of the authorities to whom Congress had delegated power. No delegation of the kind at issue in those cases is present here.

The Act does not make crimes of acts never before criminalized, *see Fahey v. Mallonee,* 332 U.S. 245, 249 (1947) (analyzing *Panama Refining*), or delegate regulatory power to private individuals, *see Yakus v. United States,* 321 U.S. 414, 424 (1944) (analyzing *Schechter*). In recent years, our application of the nondelegation doctrine principally has been limited to the interpretation of statutory texts, and, more particularly, to giving narrow constructions to statutory delegations that might otherwise be thought to be unconstitutional. *See, e.g., Industrial Union Dep't v. American Petroleum Institute,* 448 U.S. 607, 646 (1980); *National Cable Television Ass'n v. United States,* 415 U.S. 336, 342 (1974).

the Commission to use in regulating sentencing. More particularly, Congress directed the Commission to develop a system of "sentencing ranges" applicable "for each category of offense involving each category of defendant." 28 U.S.C. § 994(b). Congress instructed the Commission that these sentencing ranges must be consistent with the pertinent provisions of Title 18 of the United States Code and could not include sentences in excess of the statutory maxima. Congress also required that for sentences of imprisonment, "the maximum of the range established for such a term shall not exceed the minimum of that range by more than the greater of 25 percent or 6 months, except that, if the minimum term of the range is 30 years or more, the maximum may be life imprisonment." *Id.* § 994(b)(2). Moreover, Congress directed the Commission to use current average sentences "as a starting point" for its structuring of the sentencing ranges. *Id.* § 994(m).

To guide the Commission in its formulation of offense categories, Congress directed it to consider seven factors . . . . Congress set forth 11 factors for the Commission to consider in establishing categories of defendants. . . . Congress also prohibited the Commission from considering the "race, sex, national origin, creed, and socioeconomic status of offenders," *id.* § 994(d), and instructed that the guidelines should reflect the "general inappropriateness" of considering certain other factors, such as current unemployment, that might serve as proxies for forbidden factors, *id.* § 994(e).

In addition to these overarching constraints, Congress provided even more detailed guidance to the Commission about categories of offenses and offender characteristics. . . .

We cannot dispute petitioner's contention that the Commission enjoys significant discretion in formulating guidelines. The Commission does have discretionary authority to determine the relative severity of federal crimes and to assess the relative weight of the offender characteristics that Congress listed for the Commission to consider. . . . The Commission also has significant discretion to determine which crimes have been punished too leniently, and which too severely. . . .[11]

But our cases do not at all suggest that delegations of this type may not carry with them the need to exercise judgment on matter of policy. In *Yakus v. United States,* 321 U.S. 414 (1944), the Court upheld a delegation to the Price Administrator to fix commodity prices that "in his judgment will be generally fair and equitable and will effectuate the purposes of this Act" to stabilize prices and avert speculation. *See id.* at 420. In *National Broadcasting Co. v. United States,* 319 U.S. 190 (1943), we upheld a delegation to the Federal Communications Commission granting it the authority to promulgate regulations in accordance with its view of the "public interest." . . .

. . . The Act sets forth more than merely an "intelligible principle" or minimal standards. . . .

Developing proportionate penalties for hundreds of different crimes by a virtually limitless array of offenders is precisely the sort of intricate, labor-intensive task for which delegation to an expert body is especially appropriate. . . .

---

[11] . . . We assume, without deciding, that the Commission was assigned the power to effectuate the death penalty provisions of the Criminal Code. That the Commission may have this authority (but has not exercised it) does not affect our analysis. . . . [T]he Commission could include the death penalty within the guidelines only if that punishment was authorized in the first instance by Congress and only if such inclusion comported with the substantial guidance Congress gave the Commission in fulfilling its assignments. . . .

"Congress is not confined to that method of executing its policy which involves the least possible delegation of discretion to administrative officers." *Yakus v. United States,* 321 U.S. at 435-26. . . .

Iv. *Separation of Powers*

. . . .

The Court consistently has given voice to, and has reaffirmed, the central judgment of the Framers of the Constitution that, within our political scheme, the separation of governmental powers into three coordinate Branches is essential to the preservation of liberty. *See, e.g., Morrison v. Olson,* 487 U.S. 654, 685–96 (1988); *Bowsher v. Synar,* 478 U.S. 714, 725 (1986). Madison, in writing about the principle of separated powers, said: "No political truth is certainly of greater intrinsic value or is stamped with the authority of more enlightened patrons of liberty." THE FEDERALIST No. 47, p. 324 (J. Cooke ed. 1961).

In applying the principle of separated powers in our jurisdiction, we have sought to give life to Madison's view of the appropriate relationship among the three coequal Branches. . . . [T]he Framers did not require — and indeed rejected — the notion that the three Branches must be entirely separate and distinct. *See, e.g., Nixon v. Administrator of General Services,* 433 U.S. 425, 443 (1977) (rejecting as archaic complete division of authority among the three Branches); *United States v. Nixon,* 418 U.S. 683 (1974) (affirming Madison's flexible approach to separation of powers). . . . Madison recognized that our constitutional system imposes upon the Branches a degree of overlapping responsibility, a duty of interdependence as well as independence the absence of which "would preclude the establishment of a Nation capable of governing itself effectively." *Buckley v. Valeo,* 424 U.S. 1 (1976). In a passage now commonplace in our cases, Justice Jackson summarized the pragmatic, flexible view of differentiated governmental power to which we are heir: "While the Constitution diffuses power the better to secure liberty, it also contemplates that practice will integrate the dispersed powers into a workable government. It enjoins upon its branches separateness but interdependence, autonomy but reciprocity." *Youngstown Sheet & Tube Co. v. Sawyer,* 343 U.S. 579, 635 (1952) (Jackson, J., concurring).

In adopting this flexible understanding of separation of powers, we simply have recognized Madison's teaching that the greatest security against tyranny — the accumulation of excess authority in a single Branch — lies not in a hermetic division among the Branches, but in a carefully crafted system of checked and balanced power within each Branch. "[T]he greatest security," wrote Madison, "against a gradual concentration of the several powers in the same department, consists in giving to those who administer each department, the necessary constitutional means, and personal motives, to resist encroachments of the others." THE FEDERALIST No. 51, p. 349 (J. Cooke ed. 1961). Accordingly, as we have noted many times, the Framers "built into the tripartite Federal Government . . . a self-executing safeguard against the encroachment or aggrandizement of one branch at the expense of the other." *Buckley v. Valeo,* 424 U.S. at 122. *See also INS v. Chadha,* 462 U.S. 919, 951 (1983).

It is this concern of encroachment and aggrandizement that has animated our separation-of-powers jurisprudence and aroused our vigilance against the "hydraulic pressure inherent within each of the separate Branches to exceed the outer limits of its power." *Id.* Accordingly, we have not hesitated to strike down provisions of law that either accrete to a single Branch powers more appropriately diffused among separate Branches or that undermine the authority and independence of one or another coordinate Branch. For example, just as the Framers recognized the particular danger of the Legislative Branch's accreting to itself judicial or executive power, so too have we invalidated attempts by Congress to exercise the responsibilities of other Branches or to reassign powers vested by the Constitution in either the Judicial Branch or the Executive Branch. *Bowsher v. Synar,* 478 U.S. 714 (1986) (Congress may not exercise removal power over officer performing executive functions); *INS v. Chadha,* 462 U.S. 919 (Congress may not control execution of laws except through Art. I procedures); *Northern Pipeline Construction Co. v. Marathon Pipe Line Co.,* 458 U.S. 50 (1982) (Congress may not confer Art. III power on Art. I judge). By the same token, we have upheld statutory provisions that to some degree commingle the functions of the Branches, but that pose no danger of either aggrandizement or encroachment. *Morrison v. Olson,* 487 U.S. 654 (1988) (upholding judicial appointment of independent counsel) . . . .

. . . In cases specifically involving the Judicial Branch, we have expressed our vigilance against two dangers: first, that the Judicial Branch neither be assigned nor allowed "tasks that are more properly accomplished by [other] branches," *Morrison v. Olson,* 487 U.S. at 680–81, and, second, that no provision of law "impermissibly threatens the institutional integrity of the Judicial Branch." *CFTC v. Schor,* 478 U.S. 833, 851 (1986).

Mistretta argues that the Act suffers from each of these constitutional infirmities. He argues that Congress, in constituting the Commission as it did, effected an unconstitutional accumulation of power within the Judicial Branch while at the same time undermining the Judiciary's independence and integrity. . . .

. . . [P]etitioner asserts, Congress unconstitutionally eroded the integrity and independence of the Judiciary by requiring Article III judges to sit on the Commission, by requiring that those judges share their rulemaking authority with nonjudges, and by subjecting the Commission's members to appointment and removal by the President. . . .

. . . .

A. *Location of the Commission*

The Sentencing Commission unquestionably is a peculiar institution within the framework of our Government. Although placed by the Act in the Judicial Branch, it is not a court and does not exercise judicial power. Rather, the Commission is an "independent" body . . . entrusted by Congress with the primary task of promulgating sentencing guidelines. . . .

According to express provision of Article III, the judicial power of the United States is limited to "Cases" and "Controversies." . . . In implementing this limited grant of power, we have refused to issue advisory opinions or to resolve disputes that are not justiciable. *See, e.g., Flast v. Cohen,* 392 U.S. 83 (1968); *United States v. Ferreira,* 54 U.S. 40 (1852). These doctrines help to ensure the independence of the Judicial Branch by precluding debilitating entanglements between the Judiciary and the two political Branches, and prevent the Judiciary from encroaching into areas reserved for the other Branches by extending judicial power to matters beyond those disputes "traditionally thought to be capable of resolution through the judicial process." . . . As a general principle, we stated as recently as last Term that "executive or administrative duties of a nonjudicial nature may not be imposed on judges holding office under Art. III of the Constitution." *Morrison v. Olson,* 487 U.S. at 677 (quoting *Buckley v. Valeo,* 424

U.S. at 123 (citing *United States v. Ferreira* and *Hayburn's Case,* 2 U.S. 409 (1792))).

Nonetheless, we have recognized significant exceptions to this general rule and have approved the assumption of some nonadjudicatory activities by the Judicial Branch. . . .

. . . None of our cases indicate that rulemaking *per se* is a function that may not be performed by an entity within the Judicial Branch, either because rulemaking is inherently nonjudicial or because it is a function exclusively committed to the Executive Branch.[14] On the contrary, we specifically have held that Congress, in some circumstances, may confer rulemaking authority on the Judicial Branch. In *Sibbach v. Wilson & Co.,* 312 U.S. 1 (1941), we upheld a challenge to certain rules promulgated under the Rules Enabling Act of 1934, which conferred upon the Judiciary the power to promulgate federal rules of civil procedure. *See* 28 U.S.C. § 2072. We observed: "Congress has undoubted power to regulate the practice and procedure of federal courts, and may exercise that power by delegating to this or other federal courts authority to make rules not inconsistent with the statutes or constitution of the United States." 312 U.S. at 9–10 (footnote omitted). This passage in *Sibbach* simply echoed what had been our view since *Wayman v. Southard,* 23 U.S. 1, 43 (1825), decided more than a century earlier, where Chief Justice Marshall wrote for the Court that rulemaking power pertaining to the Judicial Branch may be "conferred on the judicial department." . . . *See also Hanna v. Plumer,* 380 U.S. 460 (1965). Pursuant to this power to delegate rulemaking authority to the Judicial Branch, Congress expressly has authorized this Court to establish rules for the conduct of its own business and to prescribe rules of procedure for lower federal courts in . . . civil cases, and in criminal cases, and to revise the Federal Rules of Evidence. . . .

. . . [W]e specifically have upheld not only Congress' power to confer on the Judicial Branch the rulemaking authority contemplated in the various enabling Acts, but also to vest in judicial councils authority to "make 'all necessary orders for the effective and expeditious administration of the business of the courts.'" . . . [B]y established practice we have recognized Congress' power to create the Judicial Conference of the United States, the Rules Advisory Committees that it oversees, and the Administrative Office of the United States Courts whose myriad responsibilities include the administration of the entire probation service. These entities, some of which are comprised of judges, others of judges and nonjudges, still others of nonjudges only, do not exercise judicial power in the constitutional sense of deciding cases and controversies, but they share the common purpose of providing for the fair and efficient fulfillment of responsibilities that are properly the province of the Judiciary. . . . [W]e have never held, and have clearly disavowed in practice, that the Constitution prohibits Congress from assigning to courts or auxiliary bodies within the Judicial Branch administrative or rulemaking duties that, in the words of Chief Justice Marshall, are "necessary and proper . . . for carrying into execution the judgments which the judicial department has power

---

[14] Our recent cases cast no doubt on the continuing vitality of the view that rulemaking is not a function exclusively committed to the Executive Branch. . . . On the contrary, rulemaking power originates in the Legislative branch and becomes an executive function only when delegated by the Legislature to the Executive Branch.

More generally, it hardly can be argued in this case that Congress has impaired the functioning of the Executive Branch. . . . Moreover, since Congress has empowered the President to appoint and remove Commission members, the President's relationship to the Commission is functionally no different from what it would have been had Congress not located the Commission in the Judicial Branch. . . .

to pronounce." *Wayman v. Southard*, 23 U.S. at 22.[16] . . .

In light of this precedent and practice, we can discern no separation-of-powers impediment to the placement of the Sentencing Commission within the Judicial Branch. . . .

Given the consistent responsibility of federal judges to pronounce sentence within the statutory range established by Congress, we find that the role of the Commission in promulgating guidelines for the exercise of the judicial function bears considerable similarity to the role of this Court in establishing rules of procedure under the various enabling Acts. . . . Just as the rules of procedure bind judges and courts in the proper management of the cases before them, so the Guidelines bind judges and courts in the exercise of their uncontested responsibility to pass sentence in criminal cases. . . .

. . . .

We agree with petitioner that the nature of the Commission's rulemaking power is not strictly analogous to this Court's rulemaking power under the enabling Acts. . . . [W]e recognize that the task of promulgating rules regulating practice and pleading before federal courts does not involve the degree of political judgment integral to the Commission's formulation of sentencing guidelines. . . . [T]he degree of political judgment about crime and criminality exercised by the Commission and the scope of the substantive effects of its work does to some extent set its rulemaking powers apart from prior judicial rulemaking. . . .

We do not believe, however, that the significantly political nature of the Commission's work renders unconstitutional its placement within the Judicial Branch. Our separation-of-powers analysis does not turn on the labeling of an activity as "substantive" as opposed to "procedural," or "political" as opposed to "judicial." *See Bowsher v. Synar*, 478 U.S. at 749. . . .

. . . Whatever constitutional problems might arise if the powers of the Commission were vested in a court, the Commission is not a court, does not exercise judicial power, and is not controlled by or accountable to members of the Judicial Branch. The Commission, on which members of the Judiciary may be a minority, is an independent agency in every relevant sense. In contrast to a court's exercising judicial power, the Commission is fully accountable to Congress, which can revoke or amend any or all of the Guidelines as it sees fit either within the 180-day waiting period . . . or at any time. In contrast to a court, its rulemaking is subject to the notice and comment requirements of the Administrative Procedure Act, 28 U.S.C. § 994(x). . . .

. . . [A]lthough the Commission wields rulemaking power and not the adjudicatory power exercised by individual judges when passing sentence, the placement of the Sentencing Commission in the Judicial Branch has not increased the Branch's authority. . . . [B]ecause the Guidelines have the effect of promoting sentencing within a narrower range than was previously applied, the power of the Judicial Branch is, if anything, somewhat diminished by the Act. . . .

. . . .

. . . Given their limited reach, the special role of the Judicial Branch in the field of sentencing, and the fact that the Guidelines are promulgated by an independent agency and not a court, it follows that as a matter of "practical consequences" the location of the Sentencing Commission within the Judicial Branch simply leaves

---

[16] . . . In the interest of effectuating their judgments, federal courts also possess inherent authority to initiate a contempt proceeding and to appoint a private attorney to prosecute the contempt. . . .

with the Judiciary what long has belonged to it.

. . . .

B. *Composition of the Commission*

. . . .

. . . Petitioner urges us to strike down the Act on the ground that its requirement of judicial participation on the Commission unconstitutionally conscripts individual federal judges for political service and thereby undermines the essential impartiality of the Judicial Branch. We find Congress' requirement of judicial service somewhat troublesome, but we do not believe that the Act impermissibly interferes with the functioning of the Judiciary.

The text of the Constitution contains no prohibition against the service of active federal judges on independent commissions such as that established by the Act. The Constitution does include an Incompatibility Clause applicable to national legislators. . . . U.S. Const., Art. I, § 6, cl. 2. No comparable restriction applies to judges, and we find it at least inferentially meaningful that at the Constitutional Convention two prohibitions against plural officeholding by members of the Judiciary were proposed, but did not reach the floor of the Convention for a vote.

Our inferential reading that the Constitution does not prohibit Article III judges from undertaking extrajudicial duties finds support in the historical practice of the Founders after ratification. . . . The first Chief Justice, John Jay, served simultaneously as Chief Justice and as Ambassador to England . . . . Oliver Ellsworth served simultaneously as Chief Justice and as Minister to France. While he was Chief Justice, John Marshall served briefly as Secretary of State and was a member of the Sinking Fund Commission with responsibility for refunding the Revolutionary War debt.

All these appointments were made by the President with the "Advice and Consent" of the Senate. Thus, at a minimum, both the Executive and Legislative Branches acquiesced in the assumption of extrajudicial duties by judges. . . . This contemporaneous practice by the Founders themselves is significant evidence that the constitutional principle of separation of powers does not absolutely prohibit extrajudicial service. . . .

Subsequent history, moreover, reveals a frequent and continuing, albeit controversial, practice of extrajudicial service. In 1877, five Justices served on the Election Commission that resolved the hotly contested Presidential Election of 1876 . . . . Justices Nelson, Fuller, Brewer, Hughes, Day, Roberts, and Van Devanter served on various arbitral commissions. Justice Roberts was a member of the commission organized to investigate the attack on Pearl Harbor. Justice Jackson was one of the prosecutors at the Nuremberg trials; and Chief Justice Warren presided over the commission investigating the assassination of President Kennedy. Such service has been no less a practice among lower court federal judges. While these extrajudicial activities spawned spirited discussion and frequent criticism, and although some of the judges who undertook these duties sometimes did so with reservation and may have looked back on their service with regret, "traditional ways of conducting government . . . give meaning" to the Constitution. *Youngstown Sheet & Tube Co. v. Sawyer,* 343 U.S. at 610 (Frankfurter, J., concurring). . . .

Furthermore, although we have not specifically addressed the constitutionality of extrajudicial service, two of our precedents reflect at least an early understanding by this Court that the Constitution does not preclude judges from assuming extrajudicial duties in their individual capacities. In *Hayburn's Case,* 2 U.S. 409 (1792), the Court considered a request for a writ of mandamus ordering a Circuit Court to exclude a statute empowering federal and state courts to set pensions for disabled Revolutionary War veterans. . . . [T]he New York Circuit, in 1791, with a bench consisting of Chief Justice Jay, Justice Cushing, and District Judge Duane, believed that individual judges acting not in their judicial capacities but as individual commissioners could exercise the duties conferred upon them by the statute. . . .

[*United States v. Ferreira,* 54 U.S. 40 (1852),] concerned a statute authorizing a Federal District Court in Florida to adjudicate claims for losses for which the United States was responsible under the 1819 treaty by which Spain ceded Florida to the United States. . . .

We did not conclude in *Ferreira* . . . that Congress could not confer on a federal judge the function of resolving administrative claims. On the contrary, we expressed general agreement with the view of some of the judges in *Hayburn's Case* that while such administrative duties could not be assigned to a court, or to judges acting as part of a court, such duties could be assigned to judges acting individually as commissioners. . . . *Ferreira,* like *Hayburn's Case,* suggests that Congress may authorize a federal judge, in an individual capacity, to perform an executive function without violating the separation of powers. *See United States v. Yale Todd* (1794) (unreported decision discussed in the margin of the opinion in *Ferreira,* 54 U.S. at 52–53).

. . . .

. . . Service on the Commission by any particular judge is voluntary. The Act does not conscript judges for the Commission. . . . [W]e simply do not face the question whether Congress may require a particular judge to undertake the extrajudicial duty of serving on the Commission. . . . [A]bsent a more specific threat to judicial independence, the fact that Congress has included federal judges on the Commission does not itself threaten the integrity of the Judicial Branch.

. . . While in the abstract a proliferation of commissions with congressionally mandated judiciary participation might threaten judicial independence by exhausting the resources of the Judicial Branch, that danger is far too remote for consideration here.

We are somewhat more troubled by petitioner's argument that the Judiciary's entanglement in the political work of the Commission undermines public confidence in the disinterestedness of the Judicial Branch. . . . The legitimacy of the Judicial Branch ultimately depends on its reputation for impartiality and nonpartisanship. That reputation may not be borrowed by the political Branches to cloak their work in the neutral colors of judicial action.

. . . Judicial contribution to the enterprise of creating rules to limit the discretion of sentencing judges does not enlist the resources or reputation of the Judicial Branch in either the legislative business of determining what conduct should be criminalized or the executive business of enforcing the law. . . .

C. *Presidential Control*

. . . .

. . . [T]he President's removal power under the Act is limited. In order to safeguard the independence of the Commission from executive control, Congress specified in the Act that the President may remove the Commission members only for good cause. Such congressional limitation on the President's removal power, like the removal provisions upheld in *Morrison v. Olson,* 487 U.S. 654 (1988), and *Humphrey's Executor v. United States,* 295 U.S. 602 (1935), is specifically crafted to prevent the President from exercising "coercive influence" over independent agencies. . . .

. . . .

V.

. . . .

The judgment of the U.S. District Court for the Western District of Missouri is affirmed.

JUSTICE SCALIA, dissenting.

. . . I dissent from today's decision because I can find no place within our constitutional system for an agency created by Congress to exercise no governmental power other than the making of laws.

I.

There is no doubt that the Sentencing Commission has established significant, legally binding prescriptions governing application of governmental power against private individuals . . . .

. . . Congress also gave the Commission discretion to determine whether 7 specified characteristics of offenses, and 11 specified characteristics of offenders, "have any relevance," and should be included among the factors varying the sentence. . . . Of the latter, it included only three among the factors required to be considered, and declared the remainder not ordinarily relevant. . . .

It should be apparent from the above that the decisions made by the Commission are far from technical, but are heavily laden (or ought to be) with value judgments and policy assessments. . . .

Petitioner's most fundamental and far-reaching challenge to the Commission is that Congress' commitment of such broad policy responsibility to any institution is an unconstitutional delegation of legislative power. . . . Our Members of Congress could not, even if they wished, vote all power to the President and adjourn *sine die.*

But while the doctrine of unconstitutional delegation is unquestionably a fundamental element of our constitutional system, it is not an element readily enforceable by the courts. Once it is conceded, as it must be, that no statute can be entirely precise, and that some judgments, even some judgments involving policy considerations, must be left to the officers executing the law and to the judges applying it, the debate over unconstitutional delegation becomes a debate not over a point of principle but over a question of degree. . . . [I]t is small wonder that we have almost never felt qualified to second-guess Congress regarding the permissible degree of policy judgment that can be left to those executing or applying the law. . . . What legislated standard, one must wonder, can possibly be too vague to survive judicial scrutiny, when we have repeatedly upheld, in various contexts, a "public interest" standard? . . .

In short, I fully agree with the Court's rejection of petitioner's contention that the doctrine of unconstitutional delegation of legislative authority has been violated because of the lack of intelligible, congressionally prescribed standards to guide the Commission.

II.

Precisely because the scope of delegation is largely uncontrollable by the courts, we must be particularly rigorous in preserving the Constitution's structural restrictions that deter excessive delegation. The major one, it seems to me, is that the power to make law cannot be exercised by anyone other than Congress, except in conjunction with the lawful exercise of executive or judicial power.

The whole theory of *lawful* congressional "delegation" is not that Congress is sometimes too busy or too divided and can therefore assign its responsibility of making law to someone else; but rather that a certain degree of discretion, and thus of lawmaking, *inheres* in most executive or judicial action, and it is up to Congress, by the relative specificity or generality of its statutory commands, to determine — up to a point — how small or how large that degree shall be. Thus, the courts could be given the power to say precisely what constitutes a "restraint of trade" . . . or to adopt rules of procedure . . . or to prescribe by rule the manner in which their officers shall execute their judgments . . . because that "lawmaking" was ancillary to their exercise of judicial powers. And the Executive could be given the power to adopt policies and rules specifying in detail what radio and television licenses will be in the "public interest, convenience or necessity," because that was ancillary to the exercise of its executive powers in granting and policing licenses and making a "fair and equitable allocation" of the electromagnetic spectrum. . . . Or to take examples closer to the case before us: Trial judges could be given the power to determine what factors justify a greater or lesser sentence within the statutorily prescribed limits because that was ancillary to their exercise of the judicial power of pronouncing sentence upon individual defendants. And the President, through the Parole Commission subject to his appointment and removal, could be given the power to issue Guidelines specifying when parole would be available, because that was ancillary to the President's exercise of the executive power to hold and release federal prisoners. . . .

As Justice Harlan wrote for the Court in *Field v. Clark*, 143 U.S. 649 (1892):

> The true distinction . . . is between the delegation of power to make the law, which necessarily involves a discretion as to what it shall be, and conferring authority or discretion *as to its execution*, to be exercised under and in pursuance of the law. The first cannot be done; to the latter no valid objection can be made.

Id. at 693–94 (emphasis added). . . .

. . . .

The focus of controversy, in the long line of our so-called excessive delegation cases, has been whether the *degree* of generality contained in the authorization for exercise of executive or judicial powers in a particular field is so unacceptably high as to *amount* to a delegation of legislative powers. I say "so-called excessive delegation" because although that convenient terminology is often used, what is really at issue is whether there has been *any* delegation of legislative power, which occurs (rarely) when Congress authorizes the exercise of executive or judicial power without adequate standards. Strictly speaking, there is *no* acceptable delegation of legislative power. As John Locke put it almost 300 years ago, "[t]he power of the *legislative* being derived from the people by a positive voluntary grant and institution, can be no other, than what the positive grant conveyed, which being only to make *laws*, and not to make *legislators*, the legislative can have no power to transfer their authority of making laws, and place it in other hands." JOHN LOCKE, SECOND TREATISE OF GOVERNMENT 87 (R. Cox. ed. 1982) (emphasis added). Or as we have less epigrammatically said: "That Congress cannot delegate legislative power to the President is a principle universally recognized as vital to the integrity and maintenance of the system of government ordained by the Constitution." *Field v. Clark,* 143 U.S. at 692. In the present case, however, a pure delegation of legislative power is precisely what we have before us. It is irrelevant whether the standards are adequate, because they are not standards related to the exercise of executive or judicial powers; they are, plainly and simply, standards for further legislation.

The lawmaking function of the Sentencing Commission is completely divorced from any responsibility for execution of the law or adjudication of private rights under the law. It is divorced from responsibility for execution of the law not only because the Commission is not said to be "located in the Executive Branch" . . . but, more importantly, because the Commission neither exercises any executive power on its own, nor is subject to the control of the President who does. The only functions it performs, apart from prescribing the law, . . . conducting the investigations useful and necessary for prescribing the law, . . . and clarifying the intended application of the law that it prescribes, . . . are data collection and intragovernmental advice giving and education . . . . These latter activities — similar to functions performed by congressional agencies and even congressional staff — neither determine nor affect private rights, and do not constitute an exercise of governmental power. *See Humphrey's Executor v. United States,* 295 U.S. 602 (1935). And the Commission's lawmaking is completely divorced from the exercise of judicial powers since, not being a court, it has no judicial powers itself, nor is it subject to the control of any other body with judicial powers. The power to make law at issue here, in other words, is not ancillary but quite naked. . . .

The delegation of lawmaking authority to the Commission is, in short, unsupported by any legitimating theory to explain why it is not a delegation of legislative power. To disregard structural legitimacy is wrong in itself — but since structure has purpose, the disregard also has adverse practical consequences. In this case, as suggested earlier, the consequence is to facilitate and encourage judicially uncontrollable delegation. . . .

By reason of today's decision, I anticipate that Congress will find delegation of its lawmaking powers much more attractive in the future. If rulemaking can be entirely unrelated to the exercise of judicial or executive powers, I foresee all manner of "expert" bodies, insulated from the political process, to which Congress will delegate various portions of its lawmaking responsibility. . . . This is an undemocratic precedent that we set — not because of the scope of the delegated power, but because its recipient is not one of the three Branches of Government. The only governmental power the Commission possesses is the power to make law; and it is not the Congress.

III.

The strange character of the body that the Court today approves, and its incompatibility with our constitutional institutions, is apparent from that portion of the Court's opinion entitled "Location of the Commission." This accepts at the outset that the Commission is a "body within the Judicial Branch" . . . . I am sure that Congress can divide up the Government any way it wishes, and employ whatever terminology it desires, for *non*constitutional purposes . . . . But since our subject here is the Constitution, to admit that that congressional designation "has [no] meaning for separation-of-powers analysis" is to admit that the Court must therefore decide for itself where the Commission *is* located for purposes of separation-of-powers analysis.

It would seem logical to decide the question of which Branch an agency belongs to on the basis of who controls its actions . . . . In *Humphrey's Executor v. United States,* we approved the concept of an agency that was controlled by (and thus within) none of the Branches. We seem to have assumed, however, that that agency (the old Federal Trade Commission, before it acquired many of its current functions) exercised no governmental power whatever, but merely assisted Congress and the courts in the performance of their functions. *See id.* at 628. Where no governmental power is at issue, there is no strict constitutional impediment to a "branchless" agency, since it is only "[a]ll legislative Powers," Art. I, § 1, "[t]he executive Power," Art. II, § 1, and "[t]he judicial Power," Art. III, § 1, which the Constitution divides into three departments. (As an example of a "branchless" agency exercising no governmental powers, one can conceive of an Advisory Commission charged with reporting to all three Branches, whose members are removable only for cause and are thus subject to the control of none of the Branches.) Over the years, however, *Humphrey's Executor* has come in general contemplation to stand for something quite different — not an "independent agency" in the sense of an agency independent of all three Branches, but an "independent agency" in the sense of an agency *within* the Executive Branch (and thus authorized to exercise executive powers) independent of the control of the President.

We approved that concept last Term in *Morrison. See* 487 U.S. at 688–91. I dissented in that case, essentially because I thought that concept illogical and destructive of the structure of the Constitution. I must admit, however, that today's next step — recognition of an independent agency in the *Judicial* Branch — makes *Morrison* seem, by comparison, rigorously logical. . . . [T]he concept of an "independent agency" simply does not translate into the legislative or judicial spheres. Although the Constitution says that "[t]he executive Power shall be vested in a President of the United States of America," Art. II, § 1, it was never thought that the President would have to exercise that power *personally*. He may generally authorize others to exercise executive powers, with full effect of law, in his place. . . . It is already a leap from the proposition that a person who is not the President may exercise executive powers to the proposition we accepted in *Morrison* that a person who is *neither* the President *nor* subject to the President's control may exercise executive powers. But with respect to the exercise of judicial powers . . . the platform for such a leap does not even exist. For unlike executive power, judicial and legislative powers have never been thought delegable. A judge may not leave the decision to his law clerk, or to a master. . . . Senators and Members of the House may not send delegates to consider and vote upon bills in their place. . . .[3]

Today's decision may aptly be described as the *Humphrey's Executor* of the Judicial Branch, and I think we will live to regret it. . . .

. . . .

Today's decision follows the regrettable tendency of our recent separation-of-powers jurisprudence, . . . to treat the Constitution as though it were no more than a generalized prescription that the functions of the Branches should not be

---

[3] There are of course agencies within the Judicial Branch (because they operate under the control of courts or judges) which are not themselves courts, *see, e.g.,* 28 U.S.C. § 601 *et seq.* (Administrative Office of the U.S. Courts), just as there are agencies within the Legislative Branch (because they operate under the control of Congress) which are not themselves Senators or Representatives, *see, e.g.,* 31 U.S.C. § 701 *et seq.* (General Accounting Office). But these agencies, unlike the Sentencing Commission, exercise no governmental powers, that is, they establish neither rights nor the prerogatives of the other Branches. They merely assist the courts and Congress in *their* exercise of judicial and legislative powers.

commingled too much — how much is too much to be determined, case-by-case, by this Court. The Constitution is not that. Rather, as its name suggests, it is a prescribed structure, a framework, for the conduct of government. In designing that structure, the Framers *themselves* considered how much commingling was, in the generality of things, acceptable, and set forth their conclusions in the document. . . .

I think the Court errs, in other words, not so much because it mistakes the degree of commingling, but because it fails to recognize that this case is not about commingling, but about the creation of a new Branch altogether, a sort of junior-varsity Congress. . . .

I respectfully dissent from the Court's decision . . . .

Exercise 8:

Consider the following matters in connection with *Mistretta v. United States*:

(1) What is the test that purports to determine whether federal legislation unconstitutionally confers too much discretion upon other branches of government?

(2) When did the Supreme Court last declare federal legislation was unconstitutional for violating the nondelegation doctrine? How, other than declaring legislation unconstitutional, has the Court effectuated the concerns underlying that doctrine?

(3) To the extent the Supreme Court has authorized broad delegation of discretion by Congress, how may exercises of that discretion be controlled? Who exercises that discretion? How is the person exercising that discretion accountable? Are officers like Commissioner Humphrey more or less accountable to Congress than the Secretary of State? Are officers like Commissioner Humphrey more or less accountable to the President than the Secretary of State?

(4) To the extent the Supreme Court has authorized broader delegations of discretion than in early congressional practice, should the Court permit Congress innovative means to hold officers accountable for the exercise of that discretion? To the extent those broader delegations are placed in the hands of "principal" officers who, like Commissioner Humphrey, are not subject to unlimited Presidential removal, is the problem of accountability greater or less than delegations to officers like the Secretary of State?

(5) The Sentencing Reform Act of 1984 (the "Act") created the U.S. Sentencing Commission and declared that it was "an independent commission in the judicial branch of the United States." May Congress simply declare that an agency is "independent" or that it is "in" a particular branch? Or, do the functions assigned to an agency dictate whether it is independent and in which branch it is placed?

(6) The process for appointing members of the Commission went beyond Presidential nomination and Senate approval. The Act required that the President nominate three of the seven voting members from the federal judiciary after considering a list of six judges recommended to the President by the judicial conference. Did the Act require that the President fill the three seats from judges on the list or did he remain free to nominate any federal judge after "considering" the list?

(a) Does Congress have the constitutional authority to limit the President's selection of appointees to a list of names provided to him?

(b) If so, could Congress require that the President fill vacancies on the U.S. Supreme Court by nominating an individual from a list of six names provided by the judicial conference?

(c) Does Congress have the constitutional authority to limit the President's selection of appointees, to positions in an agency that is not an Article III court, only to individuals who are federal judges? If so, could Congress further limit the President's field of choice by providing that nominees must be Justices serving on the U.S. Supreme Court?

(d) If Congress could limit the President to fill non-judicial offices only with federal judges, could Congress require that the President appoint only federal judges to the office of Attorney General?

(7) Congress sought to further limit the President's selection of nominees by providing that "[n]o more than four [of the seven] members of the Commission shall be members of the same political party." Is such a limitation consistent with the premise that federal judges act in a non-partisan manner? If the party affiliation of federal judges may properly be considered as a limit on the President's appointment power, could Congress require that no more than five (of the nine) members of the U.S. Supreme Court shall be members of the same political party?

(8) Congress sought to limit the President's selection of nominees in yet an additional manner. The Act provided that voting members of the Commission "may not serve more than two full terms." Could Congress require that the Secretary of State not serve in that capacity for more than four years?

(9) The Act provided that the "Attorney General, or his designee, is an ex officio non-voting member" of the Commission. Recall that the Act also asserted that the Commission is part of the judicial branch. Does the Constitution impose any limit on the power of Congress to place officers from one branch of government in non-voting positions in another branch of government?

(a) Could Congress provide that the Attorney General, or his designee, is a non-voting member of the U.S. Supreme Court, thereby permitting an executive officer to participate with the justices in conferences on the disposition of cases?

(b) Could Congress provide that the Speaker of the House, or his designee, is a non-voting member of the President's cabinet, thereby permitting a legislative officer to participate in discussions of executive policy?

(10) Do the responsibilities of the Commission satisfy the "test" of the non-delegation doctrine?

(11) In terms of the majority's separation of powers analysis, do you agree that the Act does not allow the judiciary to perform any tasks that are more properly accomplished by other branches of government?

(12) In terms of the majority's separation of powers analysis, do you agree that the Act does not impermissibly threaten the institutional integrity of the judicial branch?

(13) On what bases did the majority determine that there was no constitutional prohibition against federal judges serving simultaneously as members of the Commission? What types of arguments did the Court consider?

(14) If your instructor assigned Volume I, consider whether the majority fairly evaluated its precedents relating to Revolutionary War pensions.

(15) In dissent, Justice Scalia asserted that the Commission was unconstitutional. With what part of the majority's analysis did he disagree?

(16) In dissent, Justice Scalia asserted: "The whole theory of *lawful* congressional 'delegation' is not that Congress is sometimes too busy or too divided and can

therefore assign its responsibility of making law to someone else; but rather that a certain degree of discretion, and thus of lawmaking, *inheres* in most executive or judicial action . . . ." Assuming that Justice Scalia accurately described the rationale of the doctrine, which of the following matters, if any, violates the rationale of the nondelegation doctrine:

(a) the Gramm-Rudman-Hollings Act at issue in *Bowsher v. Synar*; or,

(B) the Federal Trade Act at issue in *Humphrey's Executor v. United States*.

(17) Do *Mistretta* and *Morrison v. Olson* authorize agencies that are "independent" in a sense different than *Humphrey's Executor v. United States*?

(18) Did Justice Scalia suggest a rationale for invalidating the Commission which would not have entailed invalidating agencies like the Federal Trade Commission or the Interstate Commerce Commission? How, if at all, does Justice Scalia's argument fit into the nondelegation doctrine?

(19) In dissent, Justice Scalia asserted that the Constitution specifies the permissible mixing of otherwise separated powers and that the Court, in several cases, inappropriately assumed the power to decide which additional measures were permissible. Do you agree with that description of recent cases? If so, is that a proper role for the judiciary?

INS v. CHADHA

462 U.S. 919 (1983)

CHIEF JUSTICE BURGER delivered the opinion of the Court.

. . . [These cases] present a challenge to the constitutionality of the provision in § 244(c)(2) of the Immigration and Nationality Act authorizing one House of Congress, by resolution, to invalidate the decision of the Executive Branch, pursuant to authority delegated by Congress to the Attorney General of the United States, to allow a particular deportable alien to remain in the United States.

I

Chadha is an East Indian who was born in Kenya and holds a British passport. He was lawfully admitted to the United States in 1966 on a nonimmigrant student visa. His visa expired on June 30, 1972. On October 11, 1973, the District Director of the Immigration and Naturalization Service ordered Chadha to show cause why he should not be deported for having "remained in the United States for a longer time than permitted." Pursuant to § 242(b) of the Immigration and Nationality Act (Act), 8 U.S.C. § 1252(b), a deportation hearing was held before an Immigration Judge on January 11, 1974. Chadha conceded that he was deportable for overstaying his visa and the hearing was adjourned to enable him to file an application for suspension of deportation under § 244(a)(1) of the Act. Section 244(a)(1), at the time in question, provided:

> As hereinafter prescribed in this section, the Attorney General may, in his discretion, suspend deportation and adjust the status to that of an alien lawfully admitted for permanent residence, in the case of an alien who applies to the Attorney General for suspension of deportation and —
>
> (1) is deportable under any law of the United States except the provisions specified in paragraph (2) of this subsection; has been physically present in the United States for a continuous period of not less than seven years immediately preceding the date of such application, and proves that

> during all of such period he was and is a person of good moral character; and is a person whose deportation would, in the opinion of the Attorney General, result in extreme hardship to the alien or to his spouse, parent, or child, who is a citizen of the United States or an alien lawfully admitted for permanent residence.[1]

After Chadha submitted his application for suspension of deportation, the deportation hearing was resumed . . . .

Pursuant to § 244(c)(1) of the Act, the Immigration Judge suspended Chadha's deportation and a report of the suspension was transmitted to Congress. Section 244(c)(1) provides:

> Upon application by any alien who is found by the Attorney General to meet the requirements of subsection (a) of this section the Attorney General may in his discretion suspend deportation of such alien. If the deportation of any alien is suspended under the provisions of this subsection, a complete and detailed statement of the facts and pertinent provisions of law in the case shall be reported to the Congress with the reasons for such suspension. . . .

Once the Attorney General's recommendation for suspension of Chadha's deportation was conveyed to Congress, Congress had the power under § 244(c)(2) of the Act to veto[2] the Attorney General's determination that Chadha should not be deported. Section 244(c)(2) provides:

> In the case of an alien specified in paragraph (1) of subsection (a) of this subsection —
>
> if . . . either the Senate or the House of Representatives passes a resolution stating in substance that it does not favor the suspension of such deportation, the Attorney General shall thereupon deport such alien . . . .

. . . For reasons not disclosed by the record, Congress did not exercise the veto authority reserved to it under § 244(c)(2) until the first session of the 94th Congress. This was the final session in which Congress, pursuant to § 244(c)(2), could act to veto the Attorney General's determination that Chadha should not be deported. . . .

On December 12, 1975, Representative Eilberg, Chairman of the Judiciary Subcommittee on Immigration, Citizenship, and International Law, introduced a resolution opposing "the granting of permanent residence in the United States to [six] aliens," including Chadha. . . . The resolution had not been printed and was not made available to other members of the House [other than the Committee on the Judiciary] prior to or at the time it was voted on. . . . The resolution was passed without debate or recorded vote. Since the House action was pursuant to § 244(c)(2), the resolution was not treated as an Art. I legislative act; it was not submitted to the Senate or presented to the President for his action.

[After the veto by the House, INS reopened Chadha's case and he was ordered

[1] Congress delegated the major responsibilities for enforcement of the Immigration and Nationality Act to the Attorney General. 8 U.S.C. § 1103(a). The Attorney General discharges his responsibilities through the Immigration and Naturalization Service (INS), a division of the Department of Justice. *Id.*

[2] In constitutional terms, "veto" is used to describe the President's power under Art. I, § 7, of the Constitution. It appears, however, that congressional devices of the type authorized by § 244(c)(2) have come to be commonly referred to as a "veto." We refer to the congressional "resolution" authorized by § 244(c)(2) as a "one-House veto" of the Attorney General's decision to allow a particular deportable alien to remain in the United States.

to be deported. Chadha argued to INS and on administrative appeal that § 244(c)(2) was unconstitutional. Chadha sought judicial review of that administrative action in the U.S. Court of Appeals for the Ninth Circuit. That court held the House action to be unconstitutional.]

II

[The Court determined that it had appellate jurisdiction, rejected the argument that § 244(c)(2) could not be severed from the remainder of that section, found that Chada had standing to challenge the constitutionality of the one-House veto provision of § 244(c)(2), concluded that any alternative form of relief available to Chadha was too speculative to permit the Court to avoid the constitutional issue, and held that the issue was presented by a final order within the jurisdiction of the Ninth Circuit. The Court also determined that the fact Chadha and the INS both took the same position on the constitutionality of the one-House veto did not deprive the Court of a case or controversy when both Houses of Congress intervened to defend the provision and when Chadha would be deported or not depending upon the ruling on the issue.

[The Court also considered the argument that the matter constituted a nonjusticiable political question. Relying upon the formulation in *Baker v. Carr*, 369 U.S. 186, 217 (1962), the Court explained that "Congress apparently directs its assertion of nonjusticiability to the first of the *Baker* factors by asserting that Chadha's claim is 'an assault on the legislative authority to enact Section 244(c)(2).'" The Court found that argument inadequate.]

. . . [I]f this turns the question into a political question virtually every challenge to the constitutionality of a statute would be a political question. Chadha indeed argues that one House of Congress cannot constitutionally veto the Attorney General's decision to allow him to remain in this country. No policy underlying the political question doctrine suggests that Congress or the Executive, or both acting in concert and in compliance with Art. I, can decide the constitutionality of a statute; that is a decision for the courts.[13]

Other *Baker* factors are likewise inapplicable to this case. As we discuss more fully below, Art. I provides the "judicially discoverable and manageable standards" of *Baker* for resolving the question presented by these cases. Those standards forestall reliance by this Court on nonjudicial "policy determinations" or any showing of disrespect for a coordinate branch. Similarly, if Chadha's arguments are accepted, § 244(c)(2) cannot stand, and, since the constitutionality of that statute is for this Court to resolve, there is no possibility of "multifarious pronouncements" on this question.

It is correct that this controversy may, in a sense, be termed "political." But the presence of constitutional issues with significant political overtones does not automatically invoke the political question doctrine. Resolution of litigation challenging the constitutional authority of one of the three branches cannot be evaded by courts because the issues have political implications in the sense urged by Congress. . . .

. . . .

[13] The suggestion is made that § 244(c)(2) is somehow immunized from constitutional scrutiny because the Act containing § 244(c)(2) was passed by Congress and approved by the President. *Marbury v. Madison*, 5 U.S. 137 (1803), resolved that question. . . . In any event, 11 Presidents, from Mr. Wilson through Mr. Reagan, who have been presented with this issue have gone on record at some point to challenge congressional vetoes as unconstitutional. . . .

III

A

We turn now to the question whether action of one House of Congress under § 244(c)(2) violates strictures of the Constitution. We begin, of course, with the presumption that the challenged statute is valid. Its wisdom is not the concern of the courts; if a challenged action does not violate the Constitution, it must be sustained: "Once the meaning of an enactment is discerned and its constitutionality determined, the judicial process comes to an end. We do not sit as a committee of review, nor are we vested with the power of veto." *TVA v. Hill*, 437 U.S. 153, 194–95 (1978).

By the same token, the fact that a given law or procedure is efficient, convenient, and useful in facilitating functions of government, standing alone, will not save it if it is contrary to the Constitution. Convenience and efficiency are not the primary objectives — or the hallmarks — of democratic government and our inquiry is sharpened rather than blunted by the fact that congressional veto provisions are appearing with increasing frequency in statutes which delegate authority to executive and independent agencies:

> Since 1932, when the first veto provision was enacted into law, 295 congressional veto-type procedures have been inserted in 196 different statutes as follows: from 1932 to 1939, five statutes were affected; from 1940–49, nineteen statutes; between 1950–59, thirty-four statutes; and from 1960–69, forty-nine. From the year 1970 through 1975, at least one hundred sixty-three such provisions were included in eighty-nine laws.

Abourezk, *The Congressional Veto: A Contemporary Response to Executive Encroachment on Legislative Prerogatives*, 52 Ind. L. Rev. 323, 324 (1977).

Justice White undertakes to make a case for the proposition that the one-House veto is a useful "political invention," and we need not challenge that assertion. We can even concede this utilitarian argument although the long-range political wisdom of this "invention" is arguable. . . . But policy arguments supporting even useful "political inventions" are subject to the demands of the Constitution which defines powers and, with respect to this subject, sets out just how those powers are to be exercised.

Explicit and unambiguous provisions of the Constitution prescribe and define the respective functions of the Congress and of the Executive in the legislative process. Since the precise terms of those familiar provisions are critical to the resolution of these cases, we set them out verbatim. Article I provides:

> "All legislative Powers herein granted shall be vested in a Congress of the United States, which shall consist of a Senate *and* House of Representatives." Art. I, § 1 (emphasis added).
>
> "Every Bill which shall have passed the House of Representatives *and* the Senate, *shall*, before it becomes a law, be presented to the President of the United States . . . ." Art. I, § 7, cl. 2 (emphasis added).
>
> "*Every* Order, Resolution, or Vote to which the Concurrence of the Senate and the House of Representatives may be necessary (except on a question of Adjournment) *shall be* presented to the President of the United States; and before the Same shall take Effect, *shall be* approved by him, or being disapproved by him, *shall be* repassed by two thirds of the Senate

> and House of Representatives, according to the Rules and Limitations prescribed in the Case of a Bill." Art. I, § 7, cl. 3 (emphasis added).

These provisions of Art. I are integral parts of the constitutional design for the separation of powers. We have recently noted that "[t]he principle of separation of powers was not simply an abstract generalization in the minds of the Framers: it was woven into the document that they drafted in Philadelphia in the summer of 1787." *Buckley v. Valeo,* 424 U.S. at 124. Just as we relied on the textual provision of Art. II, § 2, cl. 2, to vindicate the principle of separation of powers in *Buckley*, we see that the purposes underlying the Presentment Clauses, Art. I, § 7, cls. 2, 3, and the bicameral requirement of Art. I, § 1, and § 7, cl. 2, guide our resolution of the important question presented in these cases. The very structure of the Articles delegating and separating powers under Arts. I, II, and III exemplifies the concept of separation of powers, and we now turn to Art. I.

B. *The Presentment Clauses*

The records of the Constitutional Convention reveal that the requirement that all legislation be presented to the President before becoming law was uniformly accepted by the Framers. Presentment to the President and the Presidential veto were considered so imperative the draftsmen took special pains to assure that these requirements could not be circumvented. During the final debate on Art. I, § 7, cl. 2, James Madison expressed concern that it might easily be evaded by the simple expedient of calling a proposed law a "resolution" or "vote" rather than a "bill." 2 MAX FARRAND, THE RECORDS OF THE FEDERAL CONVENTION OF 1787, pp. 301–02 (1911). As a consequence, Art. I, § 7, cl. 3, was added. 2 MAX FARRAND, *supra,* at 304–05.

The decision to provide the President with a limited and qualified power to nullify proposed legislation by veto was based on the profound conviction of the Framers that the powers conferred on Congress were the powers to be most carefully circumscribed. . . .

The President's role in the lawmaking process also reflects the Framers' careful efforts to check whatever propensity a particular Congress might have to enact oppressive, improvident, or ill-considered measures.. . . The Court also has observed that the Presentment Clauses serve the important purpose of assuring that a "national" perspective is grafted on the legislative process . . . .

C. *Bicameralism*

The bicameral requirement of Art. I, §§ 1, 7, was of scarcely less concern to the Framers than was the Presidential veto . . . . By providing that no law could take effect without the concurrence of the prescribed majority of the Members of both Houses, the Framers reemphasized their belief, already remarked upon in connection with the Presentment Clauses, that legislation should not be enacted unless it has been carefully and fully considered by the Nation's elected officials. In the Constitutional Convention debates on the need for a bicameral legislature, James Wilson, later to become a Justice of this Court, commented:

> Despotism comes on mankind in different shapes, sometimes in an Executive, sometimes in a military, one. Is there danger of a Legislative despotism? Theory & practice both proclaim it. If the Legislative authority be not restrained, there can be neither liberty nor stability; and it can only be restrained by dividing it within itself, into distinct and independent branches. In a single house there is no check, but the inadequate one, of the virtue & good sense of those who compose it.

2 MAX FARRAND, *supra*, at 254.

Hamilton argued that a Congress comprised of a single House was antithetical to the very purposes of the Constitution. Were the Nation to adopt a Constitution providing for only one legislative organ, he warned:

> [W]e shall finally accumulate, in a single body, all the most important prerogatives of sovereignty, and thus entail upon our posterity one of the most execrable forms of government that human infatuation ever contrived. Thus we should create in reality that very tyranny which the adversaries of the new Constitution either are, or affect to be, solicitous to avert.

THE FEDERALIST NO. 82.

. . . These observations are consistent with what many of the Framers expressed, none more cogently than Madison in pointing up the need to divide and disperse power in order to protect liberty:

> In republican government, the legislative authority necessarily predominates. The remedy for this inconveniency is to divide the legislature into different branches; and to render them, by different modes of election and different principles of action, as little connected with each other as the nature of their common functions and their common dependence on the society will admit.

THE FEDERALIST NO. 51. . . .

However familiar, it is useful to recall that apart from their fear that special interests could be favored at the expense of public needs, the Framers were also concerned, although not of one mind, over the apprehensions of the smaller states. Those states feared a commonality of interest among the larger states would work to their disadvantage; representatives of the larger states, on the other hand, were skeptical of a legislature that could pass laws favoring a minority of the people. *See* 1 MAX FARRAND, *supra*, at 176–77, 484–91. It need hardly be repeated here that the Great Compromise, under which one House was viewed as representing the people and the other the states, allayed the fears of both the large and small states.

We see therefore that the Framers were actually conscious that the bicameral requirement and the Presentment Clauses would serve essential constitutional functions. The President's participation in the legislative process was to protect the Executive Branch from Congress and to protect the whole people from improvident laws. The division of the Congress into two distinctive bodies assures that the legislative power would be exercised only after opportunity for full study and debate in separate settings. The President's unilateral veto power, in turn, was limited by the power of two-thirds of both Houses of Congress to overrule a veto thereby precluding final arbitrary action of one person. *See id.* at 99–104. It emerges clearly that the prescription for legislative action in Art. I, §§ 1, 7, represents the Framers' decision that the legislative power of the Federal Government be exercised in accord with a single, finely wrought and exhaustively considered, procedure.

IV

The Constitution sought to divide the delegated powers of the new Federal Government into three defined categories, Legislative, Executive, and Judicial, to assure, as nearly as possible, that each branch of government would confine itself to its assigned responsibility. The hydraulic pressure inherent within each of the separate Branches to exceed the outer limits of its power, even to accomplish desirable objectives, must be resisted.

Although not "hermetically" sealed from one another, *Buckley* v. *Valeo*, 424 U.S. at 121, the powers delegated to the three Branches are functionally identifiable. When any Branch acts, it is presumptively exercising the power the Constitution has delegated to it. When the Executive acts, he presumptively acts in an executive or administrative capacity as defined in Art. II. And when, as here, one House of Congress purports to act, it is presumptively acting within its assigned sphere.

Beginning with this presumption, we must nevertheless establish that the challenged action under § 244(c)(2) is of the kind to which the procedural requirements of Art. I, § 7, apply. Not every action taken by either House is subject to the bicameralism and presentment requirements of Art. I. . . .

Examination of the action taken here by one House pursuant to § 244(c)(2) reveals that it was essentially legislative in purpose and effect. In purporting to exercise power defined in Art. I, § 8, cl. 4, to "establish an uniform Rule of Naturalization," the House took action that had the purpose and effect of altering the legal rights, duties, and relations of persons, including the Attorney General, Executive Branch officials and Chadha, all outside the Legislative Branch. Section 244(c)(2) purports to authorize one House of Congress to require the Attorney General to deport an individual alien whose deportation otherwise would be canceled under § 244. The one-House veto operated in these cases to overrule the Attorney General and mandate Chadha's deportation; absent the House action, Chadha would remain in the United States. Congress has *acted* and its action has altered Chadha's status.

The legislative character of the one-House veto in these cases is confirmed by the character of the congressional action it supplants. Neither the House of Representatives nor the Senate contends that, absent the veto provision in § 244(c)(2), either of them, or both of them acting together, could effectively require the Attorney General to deport an alien once the Attorney General, in the exercise of legislatively delegated authority,[16] had determined the alien should remain in the United States. Without the challenged provision in § 244(c)(2), this could have been achieved, if at all, only by legislation requiring deportation. Similarly, a veto by one House of Congress under § 244(c)(2) cannot be justified as an attempt at amending the standards set out in § 244(a)(1), or as a repeal of § 244 as applied to Chadha.

---

[16] Congress protests that affirming the Court of Appeals in these cases will sanction "lawmaking by the Attorney General. . . ." When the Attorney General performs his duties pursuant to § 244, he does not exercise "legislative" power. The bicameral process is not necessary as a check on the Executive's administration of the laws because his administrative activity cannot reach beyond the limits of the statute that created it — a statute duly enacted pursuant to Art. I, §§ 1, 7. The constitutionality of the Attorney General's execution of the authority delegated to him by § 244 involves only a question of delegation doctrine. . . . It is clear, therefore, that the Attorney General acts in his presumptively Art. II capacity when he administers the Immigration and Nationality Act. Executive action under legislatively delegated authority that might resemble "legislative" action in some respects is not subject to the approval of both Houses of Congress and the President for the reason that the Constitution does not so require. That kind of Executive action is always subject to check by the terms of the legislation that authorized it; and if that authority is exceeded it is open to judicial review as well as the power of Congress to modify or revoke the authority entirely. A one-House veto is clearly legislative in both character and effect and is not so checked; the need for the check provided by Art. I, §§ 1, 7, is therefore clear. Congress' authority to delegate portions of its power to administrative agencies provides no support for the argument that Congress can constitutionally control administration of the laws by way of a congressional veto.

Amendment and repeal of statutes, no less than enactment, must conform with Art. I.

The nature of the decision implemented by the one-House veto in these cases further manifests its legislative character. After long experience with the clumsy, time-consuming private bill procedure, Congress made a deliberate choice to delegate to the Executive Branch, and specifically to the Attorney General, the authority to allow deportable aliens to remain in this country in certain specified circumstances. It is not disputed that this choice to delegate authority is precisely the kind of decision that can be implemented only in accordance with the procedures set out in Art. I. Disagreement with the Attorney General's decision on Chadha's deportation — that is, Congress' decision to deport Chadha — no less than Congress' original choice to delegate to the Attorney General the authority to make that decision, involves determinations of policy that Congress can implement in only one way; bicameral passage followed by presentment to the President. Congress must abide by its delegation of authority until that delegation is legislatively altered or revoked.[19]

Finally, we see that when the Framers intended to authorize either House of Congress to act alone and outside of its prescribed bicameral legislative role, they narrowly and precisely defined the procedure for such action. There are four provisions in the Constitution,[20] explicit and unambiguous, by which one House may act alone with the unreviewable force of law, not subject to the President's veto:

(a) The House of Representatives alone was given the power to initiate impeachments. Art. I, § 2, cl. 5;

(b) The Senate alone was given the power to conduct trials following impeachment on charges initiated by the House and to convict following trial. Art. I, § 3, cl. 6;

(c) The Senate alone was given final unreviewable power to approve or to disapprove Presidential appointments. Art. II, § 2, cl. 2;

(d) The Senate alone was given unreviewable power to ratify treaties negotiated by the President. Art. II, § 2, cl. 2.

Clearly, when the Draftsmen sought to confer special powers on one House, independent of the other House, or of the President, they did so in explicit, unambiguous terms.[21] These carefully defined exceptions from presentment and bicameralism underscore the difference between legislative functions of Congress and other unilateral but important and binding one-House acts provided for in the Constitution. These exceptions are narrow, explicit, and separately justified; none of them authorize the action challenged here. On the contrary, they provide further support for the conclusion that congressional authority is not to be implied and for the conclusion that the veto provided for in § 244(c)(2) is not authorized by the

---

[19] . . . The Constitution provides Congress with abundant means to oversee and control its administrative creatures. Beyond the obvious fact that Congress ultimately controls administrative agencies in the legislation that creates them, other means of control, such as durational limits on authorizations and formal reporting requirements, lie well within Congress' constitutional power.

[20] *See also* U.S. Const., Art. II, § 1, & Amend. XII.

[21] An exception from the Presentment Clauses was ratified in *Hollingsworth v. Virginia*, 3 U.S. 378 (1798). There the Court held Presidential approval was unnecessary for a proposed constitutional amendment which had passed both Houses of Congress by the requisite two-thirds majority. *See* U.S. Const. Art. v.

. . . .

constitutional design of the powers of the Legislative Branch.

Since it is clear that the action by the House under § 244(c)(2) was not within any of the express constitutional exceptions authorizing one House to act alone, and equally clear that it was an exercise of legislative power, that action was subject to the standards prescribed in Art. I.[22] The bicameral requirement, the Presentment Clauses, the President's veto, and Congress' power to override a veto were intended to erect enduring checks on each Branch and to protect the people from the improvident exercise of power by mandating certain prescribed steps. To preserve those checks, and maintain the separation of powers, the carefully defined limits on the power of each Branch must not be eroded. To accomplish what has been attempted by one House of Congress in this case requires action in conformity with the express procedures of the Constitution's prescription for legislative action: passage by a majority of both Houses and presentment to the President.[23]

The veto authorized by § 244(c)(2) doubtless has been in many respects a convenient shortcut; the "sharing" with the Executive by Congress of its authority over aliens in this manner is, on its face, an appealing compromise. In purely practical terms, it is obviously easier for action to be taken by one House without submission to the President; but it is crystal clear from the records of the Convention, contemporaneous writings and debates, that the Framers ranked other values higher than efficiency. The records of the Convention and debates in the states preceding ratification underscore the common desire to define and limit the exercise of the newly created federal powers affecting the states and the people. There is unmistakable expression of a determination that legislation by the national Congress be a step-by-step, deliberate and deliberative process.

The choices we discern as having been made in the Constitutional Convention impose burdens on governmental processes that often seem clumsy, inefficient, even unworkable, but those hard choices were consciously made by men who had lived under a form of government that permitted arbitrary governmental acts to go unchecked. There is no support in the Constitution or decisions of this Court for the proposition that the cumbersomeness and delays often encountered in complying with explicit constitutional standards may be avoided, either by Congress or by the President. *See Youngstown Sheet & Tube Co. v. Sawyer*, 343 U.S. 579 (1952). With all the obvious flaws of delay, untidiness, and potential for abuse, we have not yet found a better way to preserve freedom than by making the exercise of power subject to the carefully crafted restraints spelled out in the Constitution.

---

[22] Justice Powell's position is that the one-House veto in this case is a *judicial* act and therefore unconstitutional as beyond the authority vested in Congress by the Constitution. . . . To be sure, it is normally up to the courts to decide whether an agency has complied with its statutory mandate. But the attempted analogy between judicial action and the one-House veto is less than perfect. Federal courts do not enjoy a roving mandate to correct alleged excesses of administrative agencies; we are limited by Art. III to hearing cases and controversies and no justiciable case or controversy was presented by the Attorney General's decision to allow Chadha to remain in this country. . . .

[23] Neither can we accept the suggestion that the one-House veto provision in § 244(c)(2) either removes or modifies the bicameralism and presentation requirements for the enactment of future legislation affecting aliens. The explicit prescription for legislative action contained in Art. I cannot be amended by legislation.

. . . .

V

We hold that the congressional veto provision in § 244(c)(2) is severable from the Act and that it is unconstitutional. Accordingly, the judgment of the Court of Appeals is affirmed.

JUSTICE POWELL, concurring in the judgment.

The Court's decision, based on the Presentment Clauses, Art. I, § 7, cls. 2 and 3, apparently will invalidate every use of the legislative veto. The breadth of this holding gives pause. Congress has included the veto in literally hundreds of statutes, dating back to the 1930's. Congress clearly views this procedure as essential to controlling the delegation of power to administrative agencies. One reasonably may disagree with Congress' assessment of the veto's utility, but the respect due its judgment as a coordinate branch of Government cautions that our holding should be no more extensive than necessary to deciding these cases. In my view, the cases may be decided on a narrower ground. When Congress finds that a particular person does not satisfy the statutory criteria for permanent residence in this country it has assumed a judicial function in violation of the principle of separation of powers. Accordingly, I concur only in the judgment.

. . . .

One abuse that was prevalent during the Confederation was the exercise of judicial power by the state legislatures. The Framers were well acquainted with the danger of subjecting the determination of the rights of one person to the "tyranny of shifting majorities." . . .

It was to prevent the recurrence of such abuses that the Framers vested the executive, legislative, and judicial powers in separate branches. Their concern that a legislature should not be able to unilaterally impose a substantial deprivation on one person was expressed not only in this general allocation of power, but also in more specific provisions, such as the Bill of Attainder Clause. Art. I, § 9, cl. 3. . . .

. . . .

On its face, the House's action appears clearly adjudicatory.[7] The House did not enact a general rule; rather it made its own determination that six specific persons did not comply with certain statutory criteria. It thus undertook the type of decision that traditionally has been left to other branches. Even if the House did not make a *de novo* determination, but simply reviewed the Immigration and Naturalization Service's findings, it still assumed a function ordinarily entrusted to the federal courts. Where, as here, Congress has exercised a power "that cannot possibly be regarded as merely in aid of the legislative function of Congress," *Buckley v. Valeo*, 424 U.S. at 138, the decisions of this Court have held that Congress impermissibly assumed a function that the Constitution entrusted to another branch. *See id.* at 138–41.

The impropriety of the House's assumption of this function is confirmed by the fact that its action raises the very danger the Framers sought to avoid — the exercise of unchecked power. In deciding whether Chadha deserves to be deported, Congress is not subject to any internal constraints that prevent it from arbitrarily depriving him of the right to remain in this country. Unlike the judiciary or an administrative agency, Congress is not bound by established substantive rules. Nor

[7] The Court concludes that Congress' action was legislative in character because each branch "presumptively act[s] within its assigned sphere." The Court's presumption provides a useful starting point, but does not conclude the inquiry. . . .

is it subject to the procedural safeguards, such as the right to counsel and a hearing before an impartial tribunal, that are present when a court or an agency adjudicates individual rights. The only effective constraint on Congress' power is political, but Congress is most accountable politically when it prescribes rules of general applicability. When it decides rights of specific persons, those rights are subject to "the tyranny of a shifting majority."

Chief Justice Marshall observed: "It is the peculiar province of the legislature to prescribe general rules for the government of society; the application of those rules to individuals in society would seem to be the duty of other departments." *Fletcher v. Peck*, 10 U.S. 87, 136 (1810). In my view, when Congress undertook to apply its rules to Chadha, it exceeded the scope of its constitutionally prescribed authority. I would not reach the broader question whether legislative vetoes are invalid under the Presentment Clauses.

JUSTICE WHITE, dissenting.

Today the Court not only invalidates § 244(c)(2) of the Immigration and Nationality Act, but also sounds the death knell for nearly 200 other statutory provisions in which Congress has reserved a "legislative veto." For this reason, the Court's decision is of surpassing importance. And it is for this reason that the Court would have been well advised to decide the cases, if possible, on the narrower grounds of separation of powers, leaving for full consideration the constitutionality of other congressional review statutes operating on such varied matters as war powers and agency rulemaking, some of which concern the independent regulatory agencies.

The prominence of the legislative veto mechanism in our contemporary political system and its importance to Congress can hardly be overstated. It has become a central means by which Congress secures accountability of executive and independent agencies. Without the legislative veto, Congress is faced with a Hobson's choice: either to refrain from delegating the necessary authority, leaving itself with a hopeless task of writing laws with the requisite specificity to cover endless special circumstances across the entire policy landscape, or in the alternative, to abdicate its lawmaking function to the Executive Branch and independent agencies. To choose the former leaves major national problems unresolved; to opt for the latter risks unaccountable policymaking by those not elected to fill that role. Accordingly, over the past five decades, the legislative veto has been placed in nearly 200 statutes. The device is known in every field of governmental concern: reorganization, budgets, foreign affairs, war powers, and regulation of trade, safety, energy, the environment, and the economy.

I

[Congress employed the first legislative veto in 1929, at the invitation of President Hoover, in the context of delegating authority to the Executive to reorganize the growing federal administrative state. In 1939 and thereafter, it was employed in various other contexts. The Roosevelt administration proposed legislation that included such provisions and argued that such provisions were constitutional. Later, Presidents Kennedy and Johnson proposed legislation that included legislative veto provisions and both took actions to defend its constitutionality. The record of the Nixon administration on the constitutionality of such procedures was mixed.]

Even this brief review suffices to demonstrate that the legislative veto is more than "efficient, convenient, and useful." It is an important if not indispensable political invention that allows the President and Congress to resolve major constitutional and policy differences, assures the accountability of independent regulatory agencies, and preserves Congress' control over lawmaking. Perhaps there are other means of accommodation and accountability, but the increasing reliance of Congress upon the legislative veto suggests that the alternatives to which Congress must now turn are not entirely satisfactory.[10]

The history of the legislative veto also makes clear that it has not been a sword with which Congress has struck out to aggrandize itself at the expense of the other branches — the concerns of Madison and Hamilton. Rather, the veto has been a means of defense, a reservation of the ultimate authority necessary if Congress is to fulfill its designated role under Art. I as the Nation's lawmaker. While the President has often objected to particular legislative vetoes, generally those left in the hands of congressional Committees, the Executive has more often agreed to legislative review as the price for a broad delegation of authority. To be sure, the President may have preferred unrestricted power, but that could be precisely why Congress thought it essential to retain a check on the exercise of delegated authority.

II

For all these reasons, the apparent sweep of the Court's decision today is regrettable. The Court's Art. I analysis appears to invalidate all legislative vetoes irrespective of form or subject. Because the legislative veto is commonly found as a check upon rulemaking by administrative agencies and upon broad-based policy decisions of the Executive Branch, it is particularly unfortunate that the Court reaches its decision in cases involving the exercise of a veto over deportation decisions regarding particular individuals. Courts should always be wary of striking statutes as unconstitutional; to strike an entire class of statutes based on consideration of a somewhat atypical and more readily indictable exemplar of the class is irresponsible. It was for cases such as these that Justice Brandeis wrote: "The Court will not 'formulate a rule of constitutional law broader than is required by the precise facts to which it is to be applied.' " *Ashwater v. TVA*, 297 U.S. 288, 347 (1936) (concurring opinion). Unfortunately, today's holding is not so limited.[11]

If the legislative veto were as plainly unconstitutional as the Court strives to suggest, its broad ruling today would be more comprehensible. But, the constitutionality of the legislative veto is anything but clear-cut. The issue divides scholars, courts, Attorneys General, and the two other branches of the National Government. If the veto devices so flagrantly disregard the requirements of Art. I as the Court today suggests, I find it incomprehensible that Congress, whose Members are bound by oath to uphold the Constitution, would have placed these mechanisms in nearly 200 separate laws over a period of 50 years.

The reality of the situation is that the constitutional question posed today is one

---

[10] While Congress could write certain statutes with greater specificity, it is unlikely that this is a realistic or even desirable substitute for the legislative veto. The controversial nature of many issues would prevent Congress from reaching agreement on many major problems if specificity were required in their enactments. . . .

Oversight hearings and congressional investigations have their purpose, but unless Congress is to be rendered a think tank or debating society, they are no substitute for the exercise of actual authority. . . .

Finally, the passage of corrective legislation after agency regulations take effect or Executive Branch officials have acted entails the drawbacks endemic to a retroactive response. . . .

[11] Perhaps I am wrong and the Court remains open to consider whether certain forms of the legislative veto are reconcilable with Art. I requirements. . . .

of immense difficulty over which the Executive and Legislative Branches — as well as scholars and judges — have understandably disagreed. That disagreement stems from the silence of the Constitution on the precise question: The Constitution does not directly authorize or prohibit the legislative veto. Thus, our task should be to determine whether the legislative veto is consistent with the purposes of Art. I and the principles of separation of powers which are reflected in that Article and throughout the Constitution.[15] We should not find the lack of a specific constitutional authorization for the legislative veto surprising, and I would not infer disapproval of the mechanism from its absence. From the summer of 1787 to the present the Government of the United States has become an endeavor far beyond the contemplation of the Framers. Only within the last half century has the complexity and size of the Federal Government's responsibilities grown so greatly that the Congress must rely on the legislative veto as the most effective if not the only means to insure its role as the Nation's lawmaker. But the wisdom of the Framers was to anticipate that the Nation would grow and new problems of governance would require different solutions. Accordingly, our Federal Government was intentionally chartered with the flexibility to respond to contemporary needs without losing sight of fundamental democratic principles. This was the spirit in which Justice Jackson penned his influential concurrence in the *Steel Seizure Case* . . . .

This is the perspective from which we should approach the novel constitutional questions presented by the legislative veto. In my view, neither Art. I of the Constitution nor the doctrine of separation of powers is violated by this mechanism by which our elected Representatives preserve their voice in the governance of the Nation.

III

. . . .

. . . The power to exercise a legislative veto is not the power to write new law without bicameral approval or Presidential consideration. The veto must be authorized by statute and may only negative what an Executive department or independent agency has proposed. On its face, the legislative veto no more allows one House of Congress to make law than does the Presidential veto confer such power upon the President. . . .

A

The terms of the Presentment Clauses suggest only that bills and their equivalent are subject to the requirements of bicameral passage and presentment to the President. . . .

Although [Art. 1, § 7, cl. 3] does not specify the actions for which the concurrences of both Houses is "necessary," the proceedings at the Philadelphia Convention suggest its purpose was to prevent Congress from circumventing the presentation requirement in the making of new legislation. James Madison observed that if the President's veto was confined to bills, it could be evaded by calling a proposed law a "resolution" or "vote" rather than a "bill." Accordingly, he proposed that "or resolve" should be added after "bill" in what is now Clause 2 of § 7. 2 MAX FARRAND,

---

[15] I limit my concern here to those legislative vetoes which require either one or both Houses of Congress to pass resolutions of approval or disapproval, and leave aside the questions arising from the exercise of such powers by Committees of Congress.

THE RECORDS OF THE FEDERAL CONVENTION OF 1787, pp. 301–02 (1911). After a short discussion on the subject, the amendment was rejected. On the following day, however, Randolph renewed the proposal in the substantial form as it now appears, and the motion passed. *Id.* at 304–05; 5 JONATHAN ELLIOT, DEBATES ON THE FEDERAL CONSTITUTION 431 (1845). The chosen language, Madison's comment, and the brevity of the Convention's consideration, all suggest a modest role was intended for the Clause and no broad restraint on congressional authority was contemplated. This reading is consistent with the historical background of the Presentment Clause itself which reveals only that the Framers were concerned with limiting the methods for enacting new legislation. The Framers were aware of the experience in Pennsylvania where the legislature had evaded the requirements attached to the passing of legislation by the use of "resolves," and the criticisms directed at this practice by the Council of Censors. There is no record that the Convention contemplated, let alone intended, that these Art. I requirements would someday be invoked to restrain the scope of congressional authority pursuant to duly enacted law.

When the Convention did turn its attention to the scope of Congress' lawmaking power, the Framers were expansive. The Necessary and Proper Clause, Art. I, § 8, cl. 18, vests Congress with the power "[t]o make all Laws which shall be necessary and proper for carrying into Execution the foregoing Powers [the enumerated powers of § 8] and all other Powers vested by this Constitution in the Government of the United States, or in any Department or Officer thereof." . . .

B

The Court heeded this counsel in approving the modern administrative state. The Court's holding today that all legislative-type action must be enacted through the lawmaking process ignores that legislative authority is routinely delegated to the Executive Branch, to the independent regulatory agencies, and to private individuals and groups. "The rise of administrative bodies probably has been the most significant legal trend of the last century. . . . They have become a veritable fourth branch of the Government, which has deranged our three-branch legal theories . . . ." *FTC v. Ruberoid Co.,* 343 U.S. 470, 487 (1952) (Jackson, J. dissenting).

This Court's decisions sanctioning such delegations make clear that Art. I does not require all action with the effect of legislation to be passed as a law.

Theoretically, agencies and officials were asked only to "fill up the details," and the rule was that "Congress cannot delegate any part of its legislative power except under the limitation of a prescribed standard." *United States v. Chicago, M., St. P. & P.R. Co.,* 282 U.S. 311, 324 (1931). Chief Justice Taft elaborated the standard in *J.W. Hampton & Co. v. United States,* 276 U.S. 394, 409, Treas. Dec. 42706 (1928): "If Congress shall lay down by legislative act an intelligible principle to which the person or body authorized to fix such rates is directed to conform, such legislative action is not a forbidden delegation of legislative power." In practice, however, restrictions on the scope of the power that could be delegated diminished and all but disappeared. In only two instances did the Court find an unconstitutional delegation. *Panama Refining Co. v. Ryan,* 293 U.S. 388 (1935); *A.L.A. Schechter Poultry Corp. v. United States,* 295 U.S. 495 (1935). . . .

The wisdom and the constitutionality of these broad delegations are matters that still have not been put to rest. But for present purposes, these cases establish by virtue of congressional delegation, legislative power can be exercised by independent agencies and Executive departments without the passage of new legislation.

For some time, the sheer amount of law — the substantive rules that regulate private conduct and direct the operation of government — made by the agencies has far outnumbered the lawmaking engaged in by Congress through the traditional process. There is no question but that agency rulemaking is lawmaking in any functional or realistic sense of the term. . . . In sum, they have the force of law.

If Congress may delegate lawmaking power to independent and Executive agencies, it is most difficult to understand Art. I as prohibiting Congress from also reserving a check on legislative power for itself. Absent the veto, the agencies receiving delegations of legislative or quasi-legislative power may issue regulations having the force of law without bicameral approval and without the President's signature. It is thus not apparent why reservation of a veto over the exercise of that legislative power must be subject to a more exacting test. In both cases, it is enough that the initial statutory authorization comply with the Art. I requirements.

. . . .

. . . If the effective functioning of a complex modern government requires the delegation of vast authority which, by virtue of its breadth, is legislative or "quasi-legislative" in character, I cannot accept that Art. I — which is, after all, the source of the nondelegation doctrine — should forbid Congress to qualify that grant with a legislative veto.[21]

C

The Court also takes no account of perhaps the most relevant consideration: However resolutions of disapproval under § 244(c)(2) are formally characterized, in reality, a departure from the status quo occurs only upon the concurrence of opinion among the House, Senate, and President. Reservations of legislative authority to be exercised by Congress should be upheld if the exercise of such reserved authority is consistent with the distribution of and limits upon legislative power that Art. I provides.

1

. . . .

The history of the Immigration and Nationality Act makes clear that § 244(c)(2) did not alter the division of the actual authority between Congress and the Executive. At all times, whether through private bills, or through affirmative concurrent resolutions, or through the present one-House veto, a permanent change in a deportable alien's status could be accomplished only with the agreement of the Attorney General, the House, and the Senate.

---

21 . . . .

The Court also argues that the legislative character of the challenged action of one House is confirmed by the fact that "when the Framers intended to authorize either House of Congress to act alone and outside of its prescribed bicameral legislative role, they narrowly and precisely defined the procedure for such action." Leaving aside again the above-refuted premise that all action with a legislative character requires passage in a law, the short answer is that all of these carefully defined exceptions to the presentment and bicameralism strictures do not involve action of the Congress pursuant to a duly enacted statute. Indeed, for the most part these powers — those of impeachment, review of appointments, and treaty ratification — are not legislative powers at all. . . .

2

The central concern of the presentment and bicameralism requirements of Art. I is that when a departure from the legal status quo is undertaken, it is done with the approval of the President and both Houses of Congress. . . . This interest is fully satisfied by the operation of § 244(c)(2). The President's approval is found in the Attorney General's action in recommending to Congress that the deportation order for a given alien be suspended. The House and the Senate indicate their approval of the Executive's action by not passing a resolution of disapproval within the statutory period. Thus, a change in the legal status quo — the deportability of the alien — is consummated only with the approval of each of the three relevant actors. The disagreement of any one of the three maintains the alien's pre-existing status. . . .

The very construction of the Presentment Clauses which the Executive Branch now rejects was the basis upon which the Executive branch defended the constitutionality of the Reorganization Act . . . . When the Department of Justice advised the Senate on the constitutionality of congressional review in reorganization legislation in 1949, it stated: "In this procedure there is no question involved of the Congress taking legislative action beyond its initial passage of the Reorganization Act." This also represents the position of the Attorney General more recently.[22]

. . . .

IV

. . . It is true that the purpose of separating the authority of the Government is to prevent unnecessary and dangerous concentration of power in one branch. For that reason, the Framers saw fit to divide and balance the powers of Government so that each branch would be checked by the others. Virtually every part of our constitutional system bears the mark of this judgment.

But the history of the separation-of-powers doctrine is also a history of accommodation and practicality. Apprehensions of an overly powerful branch have not led to undue prophylactic measures that handicap the effective working of the National Government as a whole. The Constitution does not contemplate total separation of the three branches of Government. *Buckley v. Valeo,* 424 U.S. 1, 121 (1976). "[A] hermetic sealing off of the three branches of Government from one another would preclude the establishment of a Nation capable of governing itself effectively." *Id.*

Our decisions reflect this judgment. . . . The separation-of-powers doctrine has therefore led to the invalidation of Government action only when the challenged

---

[22] In his opinion on the constitutionality of the legislative review provisions of the most recent reorganization statute Attorney General Bell stated that "the statements in Article I, § 7, of the procedural steps to be followed in the enactment of legislation does not exclude other forms of action by Congress. . . . The procedures prescribed in Article I § 7, for congressional action are not exclusive." 43 Op. Atty. Gen. No. 10, pp. 2–3 (1977). "[I]f the procedures provided in a given statute have no effect on the constitutional distribution of power between the legislature and the executive," then the statute is constitutional. *Id.* at 3. In the case of the reorganization statute, the power of the President to refuse to submit a plan, combined with the power of either House of Congress to reject a submitted plan, suffices under the standard to make the statute constitutional. Although the Attorney General sought to limit his opinion to the reorganization statute, and the Executive opposes the instant statute, I see no Art. I basis to distinguish between the two.

action violated some express provision in the Constitution.

This is the teaching of *Nixon v. Administrator of General Services*, 433 U.S. 425 (1977), which, in rejecting a separation-of-powers objection to a law requiring that the Administrator take custody of certain Presidential papers, set forth a framework for evaluating such claims:

> [I]n determining whether the Act disrupts the proper balance between coordinate branches, the proper inquiry focuses on the extent to which it prevents the Executive Branch from accomplishing its constitutionally assigned functions. *United States v. Nixon*, 418 U.S. at 711–12. Only where the potential for disruption is present must we then determine whether that impact is justified by an overriding need to promote objectives within the constitutional authority of Congress.

Id. at 443.

Section 244(c)(2) survives this test. The legislative veto provision does not "preven[t] the Executive Branch from accomplishing its constitutionally assigned functions." . . .

. . . In comparison to private bills, which must be initiated in the Congress and which allow a Presidential veto to be overridden by a two-thirds majority in both Houses of Congress, § 244 augments rather than reduces the Executive Branch's authority. So understood, congressional review does not undermine, as the Court of Appeals thought, the "weight and dignity" that attends the decisions of the Executive Branch.

Nor does § 244 infringe on the judicial power, as Justice Powell would hold. Section 244 makes clear that Congress has reserved its own judgment as part of the statutory process. Congressional action does not substitute for judicial review of the Attorney General's decisions. The Act provides for judicial review of the refusal of the Attorney General to suspend a deportation and to transmit a recommendation to Congress. . . .

I do not suggest that all legislative vetoes are necessarily consistent with separation-of-powers principles. A legislative check on an inherently executive function, for example, that of initiating prosecutions, poses an entirely different question. But the legislative veto device here — and in many other settings — is far from an instance of legislative tyranny over the Executive. It is a necessary check on the unavoidably expanding power of the agencies, both Executive and independent, as they engage in exercising authority delegated by Congress.

V

. . . Today's decision strikes down in one fell swoop provisions in more laws enacted by Congress than the Court has cumulatively invalidated in its history. I fear it will now be more difficult to "insur[e] that the fundamental policy decisions in our society will be made not by an appointed official but by the body immediately responsible to the people," *Arizona v. California*, 373 U.S. 546, 626 (1963) (Harlan, J., dissenting in part). I must dissent.

JUSTICE REHNQUIST, with whom JUSTICE WHITE joins, dissenting.

. . . Because I believe that Congress did not intend the one-House veto provision of § 244(c)(2) to be severable, I dissent.

Exercise 9:

Consider the following questions in connection with *INS v. Chadha*:

(1) The Court asserted that "[c]onvenience and efficiency are not the primary objectives . . . of democratic government." Is that true? If so, should innovation be available so as to minimize the inconvenience and inefficiency inherent in the system?

(2) The Court asserted that the fact a law "is efficient, convenient, and useful" is not sufficient to justify a departure from the constitutional design. Throughout the remainder of the course, ascertain whether the Court (or another coordinate branch of government) seeks to justify a departure from the Constitution on such a basis.

(3) The Court asserted that the first legislative veto provision was enacted in 1932. From 1789 until 1932 — a period of 143 years — Congress did not employ the device. (Justice White, in dissent, asserts the legislative veto was first used in 1929.) What structural changes, if any, prompted the introduction and rapid expansion of the device?

(4) The Court interpreted the procedure described in Article I, Section 7 of the Constitution as the exclusive method — rather than merely one (and, perhaps, the preferred) manner — for enactment of legislation. Does the text of the Constitution support that conclusion? Have we examined other examples of procedures explicit in the Constitution that the Court has held did not imply an absence of alternative procedures? Or, has the Court consistently viewed one express procedure to constitute the exclusive permissible means?

(5) The Court asserted that each house of Congress may take some actions that are not "subject to the bicameralism and presentment requirements." What are examples of such actions? What is the test formulated by the Court to ascertain which actions are subject to the bicameralism and presentment requirements?

(6) The Court explained that before Congress sought to address decisions of the Attorney General regarding deportation of specific aliens, Congress relied upon a "private bill procedure." What are so-called private bills? Once Congress authorized the Attorney General to consider the requests of deportable aliens to remain in this country, did Congress retain the power to employ the prior private bill procedure? If so, how would that procedure differ from the procedure actually employed in Chadha's case?

(7) To the extent that the Attorney General's decision with respect to a specific individual is subject to judicial review, how, if at all, is use of the private bill procedure after such review consistent with the precedents relating to Revolutionary War pensions discussed in Volume 1?

(8) The Court identified four examples where the Constitution expressly permits one house of Congress to act alone. Are those the only such examples?

(9) Justice Powell reached the same result as the Court but on a different line of reasoning. He was concerned that Congress was engaged in adjudication rather than formulation of a rule of general applicability. When Congress enacts a private bill — employing bicameralism and presentment — is the same concern present as when it employs the procedure actually at issue in the case?

(10) In dissent, Justice White asserted that the Court's decision "sound[ed] the death knell for nearly 200 other statutory provisions." Is that true or does the Court's reasoning provide potential grounds to distinguish among various forms of

legislative vetoes? Justice White asserted that, in view of that impact, "the Court would have been well-advised to decide the case, if possible, on the narrower grounds of separation of powers." Was a narrower rationale available to the Court?

(11) In dissent, Justice White asserted that, without a legislative veto, Congress confronts the dilemma of selecting between (a) "writing laws with the requisite specificity to cover endless special circumstances across the entire policy landscape" which would leave "major national problems unresolved" or (b) "abdicat[ing] its law-making function to the executive branch and independent agencies" which would "risk[] unaccountable policymaking by those not elected to fill that role." Does Congress really face such a dilemma or are there other alternatives aside from a legislative veto?

(12) In dissent, Justice White asserted that the legislative veto was "important if not indispensable" to "assure[] the accountability of independent regulatory agencies" and ensure that such agencies did not escape "Congress' control over lawmaking." If the constitutional text and views of the Framers do not permit a legislative veto, how did the Framers anticipate that Congress would retain control over policymaking and that those entrusted by Congress would remain accountable?

(13) In dissent, Justice White asserted that the legislative veto "has not been a sword with which Congress has struck out to aggrandize itself at the expense of the other branches." Can the same be said about the creation of "independent regulatory agencies" in lieu of Executive Departments and/or Article III courts? Stated otherwise, does Congress gain additional power beyond that in the structure established by the Framers when it establishes independent agencies? Why or why not?

(14) In dissent, Justice White asserted that Presidents often signed legislation which contained legislative veto provisions. Should that make a difference in evaluating whether the practice is constitutional? Why or why not? Justice White further asserted that Presidents often signed legislation containing such provisions "as the price for a broad delegation of authority." To the extent the Executive thus obtained some authority in exchange for agreeing to limitation of that authority through the legislative veto, should such an exchange make a difference in evaluating whether the legislative vetoes are constitutional? (If, in fact, the "broad delegation of authority" was to an "independent regulatory agency," did the Executive gain anything in exchange for agreeing to the legislative veto?)

(15) In dissent, Justice White asserted: "Only within the last half century has the complexity and size of the Federal Government's responsibilities grown so greatly that the Congress must rely on the legislative veto as the most effective if not the only means to insure their role as the nation's lawmakers." Which constitutional amendments in the fifty or so years prior to 1983 accounted for the growth in the "complexity and size of the Federal Government's responsibilities"? To the extent that constitutional amendments alone do not fully explain the growth in responsibilities, what does?

(16) In dissent, Justice White asserted that the Framers provided "expansive" lawmaking powers to Congress. Do you agree?

(17) In dissent, Justice White asserted that the Court "approv[ed] the modern administrative state." Did it do so? If so, when? Justice White identified "routine[] delegat[ion] to the Executive branch, to the independent regulatory agencies" and others of "legislative authority" as the key to the "rise of administrative bodies."

What developments of constitutional law — apart from the Court's nondelegation doctrine jurisprudence — were essential to the development of the modern administrative state?

(18) In dissent, Justice White quoted Justice Jackson, from 1952, for the proposition that the rise of the modern administrative state introduced "a veritable fourth branch of the Government, which has deranged our three-branch legal theories." To the extent the constitutional text, its structure, the drafting and ratification history, and early precedents were all premised upon "three-branch legal theories," upon what basis can the judiciary determine whether actions of Congress and/or the Executive comply with the Constitution? What are the constraints, if any, on the judiciary in declaring the appropriate separation of powers once "three-branch legal theories" are discarded as obsolete?

(19) In dissent, Justice White asserted that "restrictions on the scope of the [legislative] power that could be delegated [by Congress] diminished and all but disappeared." Is that your understanding of the nondelegation doctrine? If so, how did that happen?

(20) In dissent, Justice White asserted "that agency rulemaking is lawmaking in any functional or realistic sense of the term." Is that statement consistent with your understanding of the nondelegation doctrine? If so, is there any reason to prohibit Congress, in legislation complying with bicameralism and presentment requirements, from delegating legislative power to a single house of Congress acting alone? If that would be permissible, could Congress so delegate legislative power to the appropriate committee of a single house of Congress? If that would be permissible, could Congress so delegate legislative power to the chair of the appropriate committee of a single house of Congress? If Congress could so delegate legislative power to one house alone, could it so authorize not only a "legislative veto" reacting to executive activity (or the activity of an independent agency) but affirmative legislation without any trigger from executive activity?

(21) In dissent, Justice White asserted that "in reality, a departure from the status quo occurs only upon the concurrence of opinion among the House, Senate, and President." Is that true? If so, what is the status quo to which it refers: Chadha's presence in the United States, Chadha's deportability for remaining in the United States after the expiration of his visa, the determination of the immigration judge that Chadha qualified for an exception to deportation, the determination of the Attorney General that Chadha qualified for an exception to deportation, or the determination of the House of Representatives that Chadha should be deported?

(22) In dissent, Justice White asserted that upholding the legislative veto before the Court would not necessarily justify legislative vetoes over other forms of executive action. Do you agree? Justice White identified, for example, the "inherently executive function" of "initiating prosecutions." Do you agree that the example constitutes an "inherently executive function"? If so, do you agree that separation of powers principles would prohibit Congress from intruding (or authorizing anyone else to intrude) on the executive's decision whether to initiate prosecutions?

(23) In dissent, Justice White asserted that the legislative veto was a "necessary check on the unavoidably expanding power of the agencies." Do you agree that the expanding power of federal agencies is "unavoidabl[e]"? If so, why? If not, who is capable of avoiding such expansions of power?

(24) Without a legislative veto, how could Congressman Eilberg (or his Committee or the House of Representatives) have obtained (or encouraged) the

deportation of Chadha? How could he (or they) more broadly supervise the Attorney General's exercise of discretionary authority?

The Legislative Veto After *Chadha*

In light of the rationale of the majority in *Chadha*, one might think that a different result would follow if both Houses of Congress together exercised a "legislative veto," as that would satisfy the bicameralism requirement of the Constitution. Two weeks after the *Chadha* decision was announced, however, the Court summarily affirmed other cases[1] including one which invalidated a two-House legislative veto provision[2] and two of which invalidated legislative vetoes of agency rulemaking (that is, *quasi*-legislative action) rather than adjudication (that is, *quasi*-judicial action).[3] To the extent Justice Powell's concurring opinion in *Chadha* sought to rely on the "narrower ground" that the exercise of the legislative veto there at issue infringed on judicial power, the summary application of *Chadha* to agency rulemaking limited the Court's ability to later recharacterize the Court's holding.

Reading *Chadha* through the lens of those summary affirmances, one might conclude that legislative veto provisions are relics of an earlier age, now condemned. In fact, it has been asserted that Congress included 500 legislative veto provisions in statutes codified between 1983 and 2005,[4] or more than twice the number of such provisions cumulatively enacted in the decades prior to *Chadha*.

After *Chadha*, how should the President react when presented with a bill that includes a legislative veto provision? If the President favors the substance of the bill, is there any method for him to disapprove the legislative veto provision while signing the bill into law?

For a recent examination of these matters, see Anthony M. Bottenfield, *Congressional Creativity: The Post-*Chadha *Struggle for Agency Control in the Era of Presidential Signing Statements*, 112 PENN. ST. L. REV. 1125 (2008).

To the extent the *Chadha* Court relied on an *expresio unius* argument based on explicit textual provisions permitting Congress (or one House thereof) to act outside of the framework of bicameralism and presentment, to what extent is that line of reasoning undermined by judicial precedent recognizing that (1) presentment was not required for a proposed constitutional amendment[5] and (2) that neither bicameralism nor presentment were required for legislative investigations

---

[1] *Chadha* was decided June 23, 1983. *See* 462 U.S. 919 (1983). On July 6, 1983, the Court issued summary orders affirming eight cases including *Process Gas Consumers Group v. Consumer Energy Council*, 463 U.S. 1216 (1983) (No. 81-2008), and *United States Senate v. Federal Trade Commission*, 463 U.S. 1216 (1983) (No. 82-935). Justice White published a dissent from those summary dispositions. *Id.* at 1217–19.

[2] Justice White explained in his dissent that *United States Senate v. Federal Trade Commission* involved a statute with a joint, two-House legislative veto provision. 463 U.S. at 1218.

[3] Justice White explained in his dissent that *Process Gas Consumers Group* arose in the context of rulemaking (specifically, ratemaking) by the Federal Energy Regulatory Commission. 463 U.S. at 1217–18. His description of *United States Senate v. Federal Trade Commission* also indicated that rulemaking was involved in that case as well.

[4] *See* LOUIS FISHER & NEAL DEVINS, POLITICAL DYNAMICS OF CONSTITUTIONAL LAW 121 (4th Ed. 2006).

[5] *See Hollingsworth v. Virginia*, 3 U.S. 378 (1798) (holding that the Eleventh Amendment was adopted in accordance with the Constitution despite the objection that Congress did not submit the proposal to the President prior to sending it to States for ratification), discussed in *Chadha*, 462 U.S. at 955 n.21.

and oversight[6] of the Executive? For an argument that these exceptions "illustrate that there is a category of congressional powers not mentioned in the text in addition to the power to pass statutes" that invalidates reliance on the *expresio unius* rationale, see E. Donald Elliott, *INS v. Chadha: The Administrative Constitution, The Constitution, and the Legislative Veto,* 1983 SUP. CT. REV. 125, 139–44 (1983).

For a recent defense of the holding in *Chadha* based on "a more complete rationale" connected "to the purposes of bicameralism and presentment," see Harold H. Bruff, *The Incompatibility Principle,* 59 ADMIN. L. REV. 225, 246–48 (2007).

CLINTON v. CITY OF NEW YORK

524 U.S. 417 (1998)

[This case involves the challenge to the Line Item Veto Act. An earlier challenge to the Act was dismissed because it was brought by Senators who opposed the Act who lacked the necessary standing. *See Raines v. Byrd,* 521 U.S. 811 (1997). Two months later, President Clinton "cancelled" provisions in two statutes by following the procedures of the Act. The City of New York and Snake River Potato Growers claimed they were injured by the cancellations.]

JUSTICE STEVENS delivered the opinion of the Court.

. . . .

On the merits, the District Court held that the cancellations did not conform to the constitutionally mandated procedures for the enactment or repeal of laws in two respects. First, the laws that resulted after the cancellations "were different from those consented to by both Houses of Congress." Moreover, the President violated Article I "when he unilaterally canceled provisions of duly enacted statutes." As a separate basis for its decision, the District Court also held that the Act "impermissibly disrupts the balance of powers among the three branches of government."

. . . .

[The Court first concluded that the appellees had standing and that expedited review was proper in this case. The Court also held that the appellees' injuries were not too speculative to permit them to raise issues that more directly concerned non-parties.]

. . . Once it is determined that a particular plaintiff is harmed by the defendant, and that the harm will likely be redressed by a favorable decision, that plaintiff has standing — regardless of whether there are others who would also have standing

---

[6] *See McGrain v. Daugherty,* 273 U.S. 135, 173 (1927) (stating "that the two houses of Congress, in their separate relations, possess not only such powers as are expressly granted to them by the Constitution, but such auxiliary powers as are necessary and appropriate to make the express powers effective" and concluding that the Senate may authorize a committee to subpoena the appearance of a private citizen to testify in an investigation into "various charges of misfeasance and nonfeasance in the Department of Justice" and, upon failure to appear, find the individual in contempt, and issue a warrant for the Sergeant at Arms to seize the individual and bring him before the Senate and hold him in jail until the individual testified); *Barenblatt v. United States,* 360 U.S. 109, 111 (1959) (sustaining misdemeanor judicial conviction for contempt of Congress resulting in a $250 fine and six-month prison sentence to a private individual who, on bases addressing the Committee's jurisdiction including separation of powers violations, refused to answer questions before a subcommittee of the House Un-American Activities Committee relating to his past or then-present membership in the Communist Party).

to sue. Thus, we are satisfied that both of these actions are Article III "Cases" that we have a duty to decide.

IV

The Line Item Veto Act gives the President the power to "cancel in whole" three types of provisions that have been signed into law: "(1) any dollar amount of discretionary budget authority; (2) any item of new direct spending; or (3) any limited tax benefit." 2 U.S.C. § 691(a). It is undisputed that the New York case involves an "item of new direct spending" and that the Snake River case involves a "limited tax benefit" as those terms are defined in the Act. It is also undisputed that each of those provisions had been signed into law pursuant to Article I, § 7, of the Constitution before it was canceled.

The Act requires the President to adhere to precise procedures whenever he exercises his cancellation authority. In identifying items for cancellation he must consider the legislative history, the purposes, and other relevant information about the items. *See* 2 U.S.C. § 691(b). He must determine, with respect to each cancellation, that it will "(i) reduce the Federal budget deficit; (ii) not impair any essential Government functions; and (iii) not harm the national interest." § 691(a)(3)(A). Moreover, he must transmit a special message to Congress notifying it of each cancellation within five calendar days (excluding Sundays) after the enactment of the canceled provision. *See* § 691(a)(3)(B). It is undisputed that the President meticulously followed these procedures in these cases.

A cancellation takes effect upon receipt by Congress of the special message from the President. *See* § 691b(a). If, however, a "disapproval bill" pertaining to a special message is enacted into law, the cancellations set forth in that message become "null and void." *Id.* The Act sets forth a detailed expedited procedure for the consideration of a "disapproval bill," *see* § 691d, but no such bill was passed for either of the cancellations involved in these cases. A majority vote of both Houses is sufficient to enact a disapproval bill. The Act does not grant the President the authority to cancel a disapproval bill, *see* § 691(c), but he does, of course, retain his constitutional authority to veto such a bill.

The effect of a cancellation is plainly stated in § 691e, which defines the principal terms used in the Act. With respect to both an item of new direct spending and a limited tax benefit, the cancellation prevents the item "from having legal force or effect." §§ 691e(4)(B)-(C). Thus, under the plain text of the statute, the two actions of the President that are challenged in these cases prevented one section of the Balanced Budget Act of 1997 and one section of the Taxpayer Relief Act of 1997 "from having legal force or effect." The remaining provisions of those statutes . . . continue to have the same force and effect as they had when signed into law.

In both legal and practical effect, the President has amended two Acts of Congress by repealing a portion of each. "[R]epeal of statutes, no less than enactment, must conform with Art. I." *INS v. Chadha,* 462 U.S. 919, 954 (1983). There is no provision in the Constitution that authorizes the President to enact, to amend, or to repeal statutes. Both Article I and Article II assign responsibilities to the President that directly relate to the lawmaking process, but neither addresses the issue presented by these cases. The President "shall from time to time give to the Congress Information on the State of the Union, and recommend to their Consideration such Measures as he shall judge necessary and expedient . . . ." Art. II, § 3. Thus, he may initiate and influence legislative proposals. Moreover, after a bill has passed both Houses of Congress, but "before it become[s] a Law," it must be presented to the President. If he approves it, "he shall sign it, but if not he shall return it, with his Objections to that House in which it shall have originated, who shall enter the Objections at large on their Journal, and proceed to reconsider it." Art. I, § 7, cl. 2. His "return" of a bill, which is usually described as a "veto," is subject to being overridden by a two-thirds vote in each House.

There are important differences between the President's "return" of a bill pursuant to Article I, § 7, and the exercise of the President's cancellation authority pursuant to the Line Item Veto Act. The constitutional return takes place *before* the bill becomes law; the statutory cancellation occurs *after* the bill becomes law. The constitutional return is of the entire bill; the statutory cancellation is of only a part. Although the Constitution expressly authorizes the President to play a role in the process of enacting statutes, it is silent on the subject of unilateral Presidential action that either repeals or amends parts of duly enacted statutes.

There are powerful reasons for construing constitutional silence on this profoundly important issue as equivalent to an express prohibition. The procedures governing the enactment of statutes set forth in the text of Article I were the product of the great debates and compromises that produced the Constitution itself. Familiar historical materials provide abundant support for the conclusion that the power to enact statutes may only "be exercised in accord with a single, finely wrought and exhaustively considered, procedure." *Chadha,* 462 U.S. at 951. Our first President understood the text of the Presentment Clause as requiring that he either "approve all the parts of a Bill, or reject it in toto."[30] What has emerged in these cases from the President's exercise of his statutory cancellation powers, however, are truncated versions of two bills that passed both Houses of Congress. They are not the product of the "finely wrought" procedure that the Framers designed.

. . . .

V

The Government advances two related arguments to support its position that despite the unambiguous provisions of the Act, cancellations do not amend or repeal properly enacted statutes in violation of the Presentment Clause. First, relying primarily on *Field v. Clark,* 143 U.S. 649 (1892), the Government contends that the cancellations were merely exercises of discretionary authority granted to the President by the Balanced Budget Act and the Taxpayer Relief Act read in light of the previously enacted Line Item Veto Act. Second, the Government submits that the substance of the authority to cancel tax and spending items "is, in practical effect, no more and no less than the power to 'decline to spend' specified sums of money, or to 'decline to implement' specified tax measures." Neither argument is persuasive.

In *Field v. Clark,* the Court upheld the constitutionality of the Tariff Act of 1890. That statute contained a "free list" of almost 300 specific articles that were exempted from import duties "unless otherwise specially provided for in this act." 143 U.S. at 602. Section 3 was a special provision that directed the President to suspend that exemption for sugar, molasses, coffee, tea, and hides "whenever, and so often" as he should be satisfied that any country producing and exporting those

---

[30] 33 WRITINGS OF GEORGE WASHINGTON 96 (J. Fitzpatrick ed. 1940); *see also* W. TAFT, THE PRESIDENCY: ITS DUTIES, ITS POWERS, ITS OPPORTUNITIES AND ITS LIMITATIONS 11 (1916) (stating that the President "has no power to veto part of a bill and let the rest become a law"); *cf.* 1 W. BLACKSTONE, COMMENTARIES *154 ("The crown cannot begin of itself any alterations in the present established law; but it may approve or disapprove of the alterations suggested and consented to by the two houses").

products imposed duties on the agricultural products of the United States that he deemed to be "reciprocally unequal and unreasonable . . . ." The section then specified the duties to be imposed on those products during any such suspension. The Court provided this explanation for its conclusion that § 3 had not delegated legislative power to the President:

> Nothing involving the expediency or the just operation of such legislation was left to the determination of the President. . . . [W]hen he ascertained the fact that duties and exactions, reciprocally unequal and unreasonable, were imposed upon the agricultural or other products of the United States by a country producing and exporting sugar, molasses, coffee, tea or hides, it became his duty to issue a proclamation declaring the suspension, as to that country, which Congress had determined should occur. He had no discretion in the premises except in respect to the duration of the suspension so ordered. But that related only to the enforcement of the policy established by Congress. As the suspension was absolutely required when the President ascertained the existence of a particular fact, it cannot be said that in ascertaining that fact and in issuing his proclamation, in obedience to the legislative will, he exercised the function of making laws. . . . It was a part of the law itself as it left the hands of Congress that the provisions, full and complete in themselves, permitting the free introduction of sugars, molasses, coffee, tea and hides, from particular countries, should be suspended, in a given contingency, and that in case of such suspensions certain duties should be imposed.

Id. at 693.

This passage identifies three critical differences between the power to suspend the exemption from import duties and the power to cancel portions of a duly enacted statute. First, the exercise of the suspension power was contingent upon a condition that did not exist when the Tariff Act was passed: the imposition of "reciprocally unequal and unreasonable" import duties by other countries. In contrast, the exercise of the cancellation power within five days after the enactment of the Balanced Budget and Tax Reform Acts necessarily was based on the same conditions that Congress evaluated when it passed those statutes. Second, under the Tariff Act, when the President determined that the contingency had arisen, he had a duty to suspend; in contrast, while it is true that the President was required by the Act to make three determinations before he canceled a provision, *see* 2 U.S.C. § 691(a)(A), those determinations did not qualify his discretion to cancel or not to cancel. Finally, whenever the President suspended an exemption under the Tariff Act, he was executing the policy that Congress had embodied in the statute. In contrast, whenever the President cancels an item of new direct spending or a limited tax benefit he is rejecting the policy judgment made by Congress and relying on his own policy judgment. Thus, the conclusion in *Field v. Clark* that the suspensions mandated by the Tariff Act were not exercises of legislative power does not undermine our opinion that cancellations pursuant to the Line Item Veto Act are the functional equivalent of partial repeals of Acts of Congress that fail to satisfy Article I, § 7.

. . . .

The cited statutes all relate to foreign trade, and this Court has recognized that in the foreign affairs arena, the President has "a degree of discretion and freedom from statutory restriction which would not be admissible were domestic affairs alone involved." *United States v. Curtiss-Wright Export Corp.*, 299 U.S. 304, 320 (1936). "Moreover, he, not Congress, has the better opportunity of knowing the conditions which prevail in foreign countries." *Id.* . . . The Line Item Veto Act authorizes the President himself to effect the repeal of laws, for his own policy reasons, without observing the procedures set out in Article I, § 7. The fact that Congress intended such a result is of no moment. Although Congress presumably anticipated that the President might cancel some of the items in the Balanced Budget Act and in the Taxpayer Relief Act, Congress cannot alter the procedures set out in Article I, § 7, without amending the Constitution.

Neither are we persuaded by the Government's contention that the President's authority to cancel new direct spending and tax benefit items is no greater than his traditional authority to decline to spend appropriated funds. The Government has reviewed in some detail the series of statutes in which Congress has given the Executive broad discretion over the expenditure of appropriated funds. For example, the First Congress appropriated "sum[s] not exceeding" specified amounts to be spent on various Government operations. *See, e.g.,* Act of Sept. 29, 1789, ch. 23, § 1, 1 Stat. 95; Act of Mar. 26, 1790, ch. 4, § 1, 1 Stat. 104; Act of Feb. 11, 1791, ch. 6, 1 Stat. 190. In those statutes, as in later years, the President was given wide discretion with respect to both the amounts to be spent and how the money would be allocated among different functions. It is argued that the Line Item Veto Act merely confers comparable discretionary authority over the expenditure of appropriated funds. The critical difference between this statute and all of its predecessors, however, is that unlike any of them, this Act gives the President the unilateral power to change the text of duly enacted statutes. None of the Act's predecessors could even arguably have been construed to authorize such a change.

VI

. . . .

. . . [O]ur decision rests on the narrow ground that the procedures authorized by the Line Item Veto Act are not authorized by the Constitution. The Balanced Budget Act of 1997 is a 500-page document that became "Public Law 105-33" after three procedural steps were taken: (1) a bill containing its exact text was approved by a majority of the Members of the House of Representatives; (2) the Senate approved precisely the same text; and (3) that text was signed into law by the President. The Constitution explicitly requires that each of those three steps be taken before a bill may "become a law." Art. I, § 7. If one paragraph of that text had been omitted at any one of those three stages, Public Law 105-33 would not have been validly enacted. If the Line Item Veto Act were valid, it would authorize the President to create a different law — one whose text was not voted on by either House of Congress or presented to the President for signature. Something that might be known as "Public Law 105-33 as modified by the President" may or may not be desirable, but it is surely not a document that may "become a law" pursuant to the procedures designed by the Framers of Article I, § 7, of the Constitution.

If there is to be a new procedure in which the President will play a different role in determining the final text of what may "become a law," such change must come not by legislation but through the amendment procedures set forth in Article V of the Constitution.

The judgment of the District Court is affirmed.

JUSTICE KENNEDY, concurring.

A Nation cannot plunder its own treasury without putting its Constitution and its survival in peril. The statute before us, then, is of first importance, for it seems undeniable the Act will tend to restrain persistent excessive spending. Nevertheless, for the reasons given by Justice Stevens in the opinion for the Court, the statute must be found invalid. Failure of political will does not justify unconstitutional remedies.

I write to respond to my colleague Justice Breyer, who observes that the statute does not threaten the liberties of individual citizens, a point on which I disagree. The argument is related to his earlier suggestion that our role is lessened here because the two political branches are adjusting their own powers between themselves. To say the political branches have a somewhat free hand to reallocate their own authority would seem to require acceptance of two premises: first, that the public good demands it, and second, that liberty is not at risk. The former premise is inadmissible. The Constitution's structure requires a stability which transcends the convenience of the moment. *See Bowsher v. Synar,* 478 U.S. 714, 736 (1986); *INS v. Chadha,* 462 U.S. 919, 944–45 (1983). The latter premise, too, is flawed. Liberty is always at stake when one or more of the branches seek to transgress the separation of powers.

Separation of powers was designed to implement a fundamental insight: Concentration of power in the hands of a single branch is a threat to liberty. The Federalist states the axiom in these explicit terms: "The accumulation of all powers, legislative, executive, and judiciary, in the same hands . . . may justly be pronounced the very definition of tyranny." THE FEDERALIST NO. 47 . . . .

. . . [The Founders] used the principles of separation of powers and federalism to secure liberty in the fundamental political sense of the term, quite in addition to the idea of freedom from intrusive governmental acts. The idea and the promise were that when the people delegate some degree of control to a remote central authority, one branch of government ought not possess the power to shape their destiny without a sufficient check from the other two. In this vision, liberty demands limits on the ability of any one branch to influence basic political decisions. . . .

. . . .

The principal object of the statute, it is true, was not to enhance the President's power to reward one group and punish another, to help one set of taxpayers and hurt another, to favor one State and ignore another. Yet these are its undeniable effects. The law establishes a new mechanism which gives the President the sole ability to hurt a group that is a visible target, in order to disfavor the group or to extract further concessions from Congress. The law is the functional equivalent of a line item veto and enhances the President's powers beyond what the Framers would have endorsed.

It is no answer, of course, to say that Congress surrendered its authority by its own hand; nor does it suffice to point out that a new statute, signed by the President or enacted over his veto, could restore to Congress the power it now seeks to relinquish. That a congressional cession of power is voluntary does not make it innocuous. The Constitution is a compact enduring for more than our time, and one Congress cannot yield up its own powers, much less those of other Congresses to follow. *See Freytag v. Commissioner,* 501 U.S. 868, 880 (1991); *cf. Chadha,* 462 U.S. at 942 n.13. Abdication of responsibility is not part of the constitutional design.

Separation of powers helps to ensure the ability of each branch to be vigorous in asserting its proper authority. In this respect the device operates on a horizontal axis to secure a proper balance of legislative, executive, and judicial authority. Separation of powers operates on a vertical axis as well, between each branch and the citizens in whose interest powers must be exercised. The citizen has a vital interest in the regularity of the exercise of governmental power. If this point was not clear before *Chadha,* it should have been so afterwards. Though *Chadha* involved the deportation of a person, while the case before us involves the expenditure of money or the grant of a tax exemption, this circumstance does not mean that the vertical operation of the separation of powers is irrelevant here. By increasing the power of the President beyond what the Framers envisioned, the statute compromises the political liberty of our citizens, liberty which the separation of powers seeks to secure.

The Constitution is not bereft of controls over improvident spending. Federalism is one safeguard, for political accountability is easier to enforce within the States than nationwide. The other principal mechanism, of course, is control of the political branches by an informed and responsible electorate. Whether or not federalism and control by the electorate are adequate for the problem at hand, they are two of the structures the Framers designed for the problem the statute strives to confront. . . . The fact that these mechanisms, plus the proper functioning of the separation of powers itself, are not employed, or that they prove insufficient, cannot validate an otherwise unconstitutional device. With these observations, I join the opinion of the Court.

JUSTICE SCALIA, with whom JUSTICE O'CONNOR joins, and with whom JUSTICE BREYER joins as to Part III, concurring in part and dissenting in part.

[Justice Scalia disagreed both that some of the appellees had standing and that the statute granted some of the appellees expedited review.]

. . . .

III

. . . .

The Presentment Clause requires, in relevant part, that "[e]very Bill which shall have passed the House of Representatives and the Senate, shall, before it become a Law, be presented to the President of the United States; If he approve he shall sign it, but if not he shall return it." U.S. Const., Art. I, § 7, cl. 2. There is no question that enactment of the Balanced Budget Act complied with these requirements: the House and Senate passed the bill, and the President signed it into law. It was only *after* the requirements of the Presentment Clause had been satisfied that the President exercised his authority under the Line Item Veto Act to cancel the spending item. Thus, the Court's problem with the Act is not that it authorizes the President to veto parts of a bill and sign others into law, but rather that it authorizes him to "cancel" — prevent from "having legal force or effect" — certain parts of duly enacted statutes.

Article I, § 7, of the Constitution obviously prevents the President from canceling a law that Congress has not authorized him to cancel. Such action cannot possibly be considered part of his execution of the law, and if it is legislative action, as the Court observes, "repeal of statutes, no less than enactment, must conform with Art. I." But that is not this case. It was certainly arguable, as an original matter, that Art. I, § 7, also prevents the President from canceling a law which itself *authorizes* the President to cancel it. But as the Court acknowledges, that argument has long since been made and rejected. In 1809, Congress passed a law authorizing the President to cancel trade restrictions against Great Britain and France if either revoked edicts directed at the United States. Joseph Story regarded the conferral of that authority as entirely unremarkable in *The Orono*, 18 F. Cas. 830 (No. 10,585) (C.C.D. Mass. 1812). The Tariff Act of 1890 authorized the President to "suspend, by proclamation to that effect" certain of its provisions if he determined that other countries were imposing "reciprocally unequal and unreasonable" duties. This

Court upheld the constitutionality of that Act in *Field v. Clark*, 143 U.S. 649 (1892), reciting the history since 1798 of statutes conferring upon the President the power to, *inter alia*, "discontinue the prohibitions and restraints hereby enacted and declared," *id.* at 684, "suspend the operation of the aforesaid act," *id.* at 685, and "declare the provisions of this act to be inoperative," *id.* at 688.

As much as the Court goes on about Art. I, § 7, therefore, that provision does not demand the result the Court reaches. It no more categorically prohibits the Executive *reduction* of congressional dispositions in the course of implementing statutes that authorize such reduction, than it categorically prohibits the Executive *augmentation* of congressional dispositions in the course of implementing statutes that authorize such augmentation — generally known as substantive rulemaking. There are, to be sure, limits upon the former just as there are limits upon the latter — and I am prepared to acknowledge that the limits upon the former may be much more severe. Those limits are established, however, not by some categorical prohibition of Art. I, § 7, which our cases conclusively disprove, but by what has come to be known as the doctrine of unconstitutional delegation of legislative authority: When authorized Executive reduction or augmentation is allowed to go too far, it usurps the nondelegable function of Congress and violates the separation of powers.

It is this doctrine, and not the Presentment Clause, that was discussed in the *Field* opinion, and it is this doctrine, and not the Presentment Clause, that is the issue presented by the statute before us here. That is why the Court is correct to distinguish prior authorizations of Executive cancellation, such as the one involved in *Field*, on the ground that they were contingent upon an Executive finding of fact, and on the ground that they related to the field of foreign affairs, an area where the President has a special "degree of discretion and freedom." These distinctions have nothing to do with whether the details of Art. I, § 7, have been complied with, but everything to do with whether the authorizations went too far by transferring to the Executive a degree of political, lawmaking power that our traditions demand be retained by the Legislative Branch.

I turn, then, to the crux of the matter: whether Congress's authorizing the President to cancel an item of spending gives him a power that our history and traditions show must reside exclusively in the Legislative Branch. . . .

Insofar as the degree of political, "lawmaking" power conferred upon the Executive is concerned, there is not a dime's worth of difference between Congress's authorizing the President to *cancel* a spending item, and Congress's authorizing money to be spent on a particular item at the President's discretion. And the latter has been done since the founding of the Nation. From 1789–1791, the First Congress made lump-sum appropriations for the entire Government — "sum[s] not exceeding" specified amounts for broad purposes. Act of Sept. 29, 1789, ch. 23, 1 Stat. 95; Act of Mar. 26, 1790, ch. 4, § 1, 1 Stat. 104; Act of Feb. 11, 1791, ch. 6, 1 Stat. 190. From a very early date Congress also made permissive individual appropriations, leaving the decision whether to spend the money to the President's unfettered discretion. . . .

Certain Presidents have claimed Executive authority to withhold appropriated funds even *absent* an express conferral of discretion to do so. In 1876, for example, President Grant reported to Congress that he would not spend money appropriated for certain harbor and river improvements because "[u]nder no circumstances [would he] allow expenditures upon works not clearly national," and in his view, the appropriations were for "works of purely private or local interest, in no sense national," 4 Cong. Rec. 5628. President Franklin D. Roosevelt impounded funds appropriated for a flood control reservoir . . . . President Truman ordered the impoundment of hundreds of millions of dollars that had been appropriated for military aircraft. President Nixon . . . asserted at a press conference in 1973 that his "constitutional right" to impound appropriated funds was "absolutely clear." Our decision two years later in *Train v. City of New York,* 420 U.S. 35 (1975), proved him wrong, but it implicitly confirmed that Congress may confer discretion upon the Executive to withhold appropriated funds, even funds appropriated for a specific purpose. The statute at issue in *Train* authorized spending "not to exceed" specified sums for certain projects, and directed that such "[s]ums authorized to be appropriated . . . shall be allotted" by the Administrator of the Environmental Protection Agency. Upon enactment of this statute, the President directed the Administrator to allot no more than a certain part of the amount authorized. This Court held, as a matter of statutory interpretation, that the statute *did not grant* the Executive discretion to withhold the funds, but required allotment of the full amount authorized. *Id.* at 44–47.

The short of the matter is this: Had the Line Item Veto Act authorized the President to "decline to spend" any item of spending contained in the Balanced Budget Act of 1997, there is not the slightest doubt that authorization would have been constitutional. What the Line Item Veto Act does instead — authorizing the President to "cancel" an item of spending — is technically different. But the technical difference does *not* relate to the technicalities of the Presentment Clause, which have been fully complied with; and the doctrine of unconstitutional delegation, which *is* at issue here, is preeminently *not* a doctrine of technicalities. The title of the Line Item Veto Act, which was perhaps designed to simplify for public comprehension, or perhaps merely to comply with the terms of a campaign pledge, has succeeded in faking out the Supreme Court. The President's action it authorizes in fact is not a line-item veto and thus does not offend Art. I, § 7; and insofar as the substance of that action is concerned, it is no different from what Congress has permitted the President to do since the formation of the Union.

. . . .

For the foregoing reasons, I respectfully dissent.

JUSTICE BREYER, with whom JUSTICE O'CONNOR and JUSTICE SCALIA join as to Part III, dissenting.

I

. . . In my view the Line Item Veto Act (Act) does not violate any specific textual constitutional command, nor does it violate any implicit separation-of-powers principle. Consequently, I believe that the Act is constitutional.

II

. . . *First,* the Act represents a legislative effort to provide the President with the power to give effect to some, but not to all, of the expenditure and revenue-diminishing provisions contained in a single massive appropriations bill. And this objective is constitutionally proper.

. . . .

. . . [Today,] a typical budget appropriations bill may have a dozen titles, hundreds of sections, and spread across more than 500 pages of the Statutes at Large. Congress cannot divide such a bill into thousands, or tens of thousands, of separate appropriations bills, each one of which the President would have to sign, or to veto, separately. Thus, the question is whether the Constitution permits

Congress to choose a particular novel *means* to achieve this same, constitutionally legitimate, *end*.

Second, the case in part requires us to focus upon the Constitution's generally phrased structural provisions, provisions that delegate all "legislative" power to Congress and vest all "executive" power in the President. The Court, when applying these provisions, has interpreted them generously in terms of the institutional arrangements that they permit. *See, e.g., Mistretta v. United States*, 488 U.S. 361, 412 (1989) (upholding delegation of authority to Sentencing Commission to promulgate Sentencing Guidelines); *Crowell v. Benson*, 285 U.S. 22, 53-54 (1932) (permitting non-Article III commission to adjudicate factual disputes arising under federal dock workers' compensation statute).

Indeed, Chief Justice Marshall, in a well-known passage, explained,

> To have prescribed the means by which government should, in all future time, execute its powers, would have been to change, entirely, the character of the instrument, and give it the properties of a legal code. It would have been an unwise attempt to provide, by immutable rules, for exigencies which, if foreseen at all, must have been seen dimly, and which can be best provided for as they occur.

McCulloch v. Maryland, 17 U.S. 316, 415 (1819). This passage, like the cases I have just mentioned, calls attention to the genius of the Framers' pragmatic vision, which this Court has long recognized in cases that find constitutional room for necessary institutional innovation.

Third, we need not here referee a dispute among the other two branches. . . . *Cf. Youngstown Sheet and Tube Co. v. Sawyer*, 343 U.S. 579, 635 (1952) (Jackson, J., concurring) ("Presidential powers are not fixed but fluctuate, depending on their disjunction or conjunction with those of Congress . . . [and when] the President acts pursuant to an express or implied authorization of Congress, his authority is at its maximum").

These three background circumstances mean that, when one measures the *literal* words of the Act against the Constitution's *literal* commands, the fact that the Act may closely resemble a different, literally unconstitutional, arrangement is beside the point. To drive exactly 65 miles per hour on an interstate highway closely resembles an act that violates the speed limit. But it does not violate that limit, for small differences matter when the question is one of literal violation of law. No more does this Act literally violate the Constitution's words.

The background circumstances also mean that we are to interpret nonliteral separation-of-powers principles in light of the need for "workable government." *Youngstown Sheet and Tube Co.*, 343 U.S. at 635 (Jackson, J., concurring). If we apply those principles in light of that objective, as this Court has applied them in the past, the Act is constitutional.

III

The Court believes that the Act violates the literal text of the Constitution. A simple syllogism captures its basic reasoning:

> Major Premise: The Constitution sets forth an exclusive method for enacting, repealing, or amending laws.
>
> Minor Premise: The Act authorizes the President to "repea[l] or amen[d]" laws in a different way, namely by announcing a cancellation of a portion of a previously enacted law.

Conclusion: The Act is inconsistent with the Constitution.

I find this syllogism unconvincing, however, because its Minor Premise is faulty. When the President "canceled" the two appropriation measures now before us, he did not *repeal* any law nor did he *amend* any law. He simply *followed* the law, leaving the statutes, as they are literally written, intact.

To understand why one cannot say, *literally speaking,* that the President has repealed or amended any law, imagine how the provisions of law before us might have been, but were not, written. Imagine that the canceled New York health care tax provision at issue here had instead said the following:

> Section One. Taxes . . . that were collected by the State of New York from a health care provider before June 1, 1997, and for which a waiver of the provisions [requiring payment] have been sought . . . are deemed to be permissible health care related taxes . . . *provided however that the President may prevent the just-mentioned provision from having legal force or effect if he determines x, y, and z.* (Assume x, y and z to be the same determinations required by the Line Item Veto Act).

Whatever a person might say, or think, about the constitutionality of this imaginary law, there is one thing the English language would prevent one from saying. One could not say that a President who "prevent[s]" the deeming language from "having legal force or effect," *see* 2 U.S.C. § 691e(4)(B), has either *repealed* or *amended* this particular hypothetical statute. Rather, the President has *followed* that law to the letter. He has exercised the power it explicitly delegates to him. He has executed the law, not repealed it.

It could make no significant difference to this linguistic point were the italicized proviso to appear, not as part of what I have called Section One, but, instead, at the bottom of the statute page, say, referenced by an asterisk, with a statement that it applies to every spending provision in the Act next to which a similar asterisk appears. And that being so, it could make no difference if that proviso appeared, instead, in a different, earlier enacted law, along with legal language that makes it applicable to every future spending provision picked out according to a specified formula.

But, of course, this last mentioned possibility is this very case. The earlier law, namely, the Line Item Veto Act, says that "the President may . . . prevent such [future] budget authority from having legal force or effect." 2 U.S.C. §§ 691(a), 691e(4)(B). Its definitional sections make clear that it applies to the 1997 New York health care provision, *see* § 691e(8), just as they give a special legal meaning to the word "cancel," § 691e(4). For that reason, one cannot dispose of this case through a purely literal analysis as the majority does. Literally speaking, the President has not "repealed" or "amended" anything. He has simply *executed* a power conferred upon him by Congress, which power is contained in laws that were enacted in compliance with the exclusive method set forth in the Constitution. *See Field v. Clark,* 143 U.S. 649, 693 (1892) (President's power to raise tariff rates "*was a part of the law itself, as it left the hands of Congress*" (emphasis added)).

Nor can one dismiss this literal compliance as some kind of formal quibble, as if it were somehow "obvious" that what the President has done "amounts to," "comes close to," or is "analogous to" the repeal or amendment of a previously enacted law. That is because the power the Act grants the President (to render designated appropriations items without "legal force or effect") also "amounts to," "comes close to," or is "analogous to" a different legal animal, the delegation of a power to choose one legal path as opposed to another, such as a power to appoint.

. . . .

IV

Because I disagree with the Court's holding of literal violation, I must consider whether the Act nonetheless violates separation-of-powers principles — principles that arise out of the Constitution's vesting of the "executive Power" in "a President," U.S. Const., Art. II, § 1, and "[a]ll legislative Powers" in "a Congress," Art. I, § 1. There are three relevant separation-of-powers questions here: (1) Has Congress given the President the wrong kind of power, *i.e.*, "non-Executive" power? (2) Has Congress given the President the power to "encroach" upon Congress' own constitutionally reserved territory? (3) Has Congress given the President too much power, violating the doctrine of "nondelegation?" . . .

A

Viewed conceptually, the power the Act conveys is the right kind of power. It is "executive." As explained above, an exercise of that power "executes" the Act. Conceptually speaking, it closely resembles the kind of delegated authority — to spend or not to spend appropriations, to change or not to change tariff rates — that Congress has frequently granted the President, any differences being differences in degree, not kind.

The fact that one could also characterize this kind of power as "legislative," say, if Congress itself (by amending the appropriations bill) prevented a provision from taking effect, is beside the point. This Court has frequently found that the exercise of a particular power, such as the power to make rules of broad applicability or to adjudicate claims, can fall within the constitutional purview of more than one branch of Government. *See Wayman v. Southard*, 23 U.S. 1, 43 (1825) (Marshall, C.J.) ("Congress may certainly delegate to others, powers which the legislature may rightfully exercise itself"). The Court does not "carry out the distinction between legislative and executive action with mathematical precision" or "divide the branches into watertight compartments," for, as others have said, the Constitution "blend[s]" as well as "separat[es]" powers in order to create a workable government.

The Court has upheld congressional delegation of rulemaking power and adjudicatory power to federal agencies, guideline-writing power to a Sentencing Commission, *Mistretta v. United States*, 488 U.S. at 412, and prosecutor-appointment power to judges, *Morrison v. Olson*, 487 U.S. 654, 696–97 (1988). It is far easier *conceptually* to reconcile the power at issue here with the relevant constitutional description ("executive") than in many of these cases. And cases in which the Court may have found a delegated power and the basic constitutional function of another branch conceptually irreconcilable are yet more distant. *See, e.g., Federal Radio Comm'n v. General Elec. Co.*, 281 U.S. 464 (1930) (power to award radio licenses not a "judicial" power).

If there is a separation-of-powers violation, then, it must rest, not upon purely conceptual grounds, but upon some important conflict between the Act and a significant separation-of-powers objective.

B

The Act does not undermine what this Court has often described as the principal function of the separation of powers, which is to maintain the tripartite structure of the Federal Government — and thereby protect individual liberty — by providing a "safeguard against the encroachment or aggrandizement of one branch at the expense of the other." *Buckley v. Valeo,* 424 U.S. 1, 122 (1976) (per curiam); *Mistretta v. United States,* 488 U.S. at 380–382.

In contrast to these cases, one cannot say that the Act "encroaches" upon Congress' power, when Congress retained the power to insert, by simple majority, into any future appropriations bill, into any section of any such bill, or into any phrase of any section, a provision that says the Act will not apply. *See* 2 U.S.C. § 691f(c)(1); *Raines v. Byrd,* 521 U.S. 811, 824 (1997) (Congress can "exempt a given appropriations bill (or a given provision in an appropriations bill) from the Act"). Congress also retained the power to "disapprov[e]," and thereby reinstate, any of the President's cancellations. *See* 2 U.S.C. § 691b(a). And it is Congress that drafts and enacts the appropriations statutes that are subject to the Act in the first place — and thereby defines the outer limits of the President's cancellation authority. Thus *this* Act is not the sort of delegation "without . . . sufficient check" that concerns Justice Kennedy. Indeed, the President acts only in response to, and on the terms set by, the Congress.

Nor can one say that the Act's basic substantive objective is constitutionally improper, for the earliest Congresses could and often did, confer on the President this sort of discretionary authority over spending. . . .

Nor can one say the Act's grant of power "aggrandizes" the Presidential office. The grant is limited to the context of the budget. It is limited to the power to spend, or not to spend, particular appropriated items, and the power to permit, or not to permit, specific limited exemptions from generally applicable tax law from taking effect. . . .

C

The "nondelegation" doctrine represents an added constitutional check upon Congress' authority to delegate power to the Executive Branch. And it raises a more serious constitutional obstacle here. The Constitution permits Congress to "see[k] assistance from another branch" of Government, the "extent and character" of that assistance to be fixed "according to common sense and the inherent necessities of the governmental co-ordination." *J.W. Hampton & Co. v. United States,* 276 U.S. 394, 406, Treas. Dec. 42706 (Taft, C.J.). But there are limits on the way in which Congress can obtain such assistance; it "cannot delegate any part of its legislative power except under the limitation of a prescribed standard." *United States v. Chicago, M., St. P. & P.R. Co.,* 282 U.S. 311, 324 (1931). Or, in Chief Justice Taft's more familiar words, the Constitution permits only those delegations where Congress "shall lay down by legislative act an *intelligible principle* to which the person or body authorized to [act] is directed to conform." *J.W. Hampton,* 276 U.S. at 409 (emphasis added).

The Act before us seeks to create such a principle in three ways. The first is procedural. The Act tells the President that, in "identifying dollar amounts [or] . . . items . . . for cancellation" (which I take to refer to his selection of the amounts or items he will "prevent from having legal force or effect"), he is to "consider" [certain specified things] . . . .

The second is purposive. The clear purpose behind the Act, confirmed by its legislative history, is to promote "greater fiscal accountability" and to "eliminate wasteful federal spending and . . . special tax breaks."

The third is substantive. The President must determine that, to "prevent" the item or amount "from having legal force or effect" will "reduce the Federal budget deficit; . . . not impair any essential Government functions; and . . . not harm the national interest." 2 U.S.C. § 691(a)(A).

The resulting standards are broad. But this Court has upheld standards that are equally broad, or broader. *See, e.g., National Broadcasting Co. v. United States,* 319 U.S. 190, 225–26 (1943) (upholding delegation to Federal Communications Commission to regulate broadcast licensing as "public interest, convenience, or necessity" require); *FPC v. Hope Natural Gas Co.,* 320 U.S. 591, 600-03 (1944) (upholding delegation to Federal Power Commission to determine "just and reasonable" rates). . . .

Indeed, the Court has only twice in its history found that a congressional delegation of power violated the "nondelegation" doctrine. One such case, *Panama Refining Co. v. Ryan,* 293 U.S. 388 (1935), was in a sense a special case, for it was discovered in the midst of the case that the particular exercise of the power at issue, the promulgation of a Petroleum Code under the National Industrial Recovery Act, did not contain any legally operative sentence. *Id.* at 412–413. The other case, *A.L.A. Schechter Poultry Corp. v. United States,* 295 U.S. 495 (1935), involved a delegation through the National Industrial Recovery Act that contained not simply a broad standard ("fair competition"), but also the conferral of power on private parties to promulgate rules applying that standard to virtually all of American industry, *id.* at 521–525. . . .

The case before us does not involve any such "roving commission," nor does it involve delegation to private parties, nor does it bring all of American industry within its scope. . . .

1

. . . [T]he Act is aimed at a discrete problem: namely, a particular set of expenditures within the federal budget. The Act concerns, not the entire economy, *cf. Schechter Poultry Corp.,* but the annual federal budget. Within the budget it applies only to *discretionary* budget authority and *new* direct spending items, that together amount to approximately a third of the current annual budget outlays and to "limited tax benefits" that . . . amount to a tiny fraction of federal revenues and appropriations. . . .

. . . .

[I]nsofar as monetary expenditure (but not "tax expenditure") is at issue, the President acts in an area where history helps to justify the discretionary power that Congress has delegated, and where history may inform his exercise of the Act's delegated authority. Congress has frequently delegated the President the authority to spend, or not to spend, particular sums of money. . . .

[T]he Constitution permits Congress to rely upon context and history as providing the necessary standard for the exercise of the delegated power. *See e.g., Federal Radio Comm'n v. Nelson Brothers Bond & Mortgage Co. (Station WIBO),* 289 U.S. 266, 285 (1933) ("public interest, convenience, or necessity [standard] . . . is to be interpreted by its context"); *Fahey v. Mallonee,* 332 U.S. 245, 253 (1947) (otherwise vague delegation to regulate banks was "sufficiently explicit, against the background of custom, to be adequate"). Relying upon context, Congress has sometimes granted the President broad discretionary authority over spending in laws that mention no standard at all. *See e.g.,* Act of Mar. 3, 1809, ch. 28, § 1, 2 Stat. 535–36 (granting the President recess authority to transfer money "appropriated for a particular branch of expenditure in [a] department" to be "applied [instead] to another branch of expenditure in the same department"). . . .

On the other hand, I must recognize that there are important differences between the delegation before us and other broad, constitutionally acceptable delegations to Executive Branch agencies — differences that argue against my conclusion. In particular, a broad delegation of authority to an administrative agency differs from the delegation at issue here in that agencies often develop subsidiary rules under the statute, rules that explain the general "public interest" language. . . .

While I believe that these last mentioned considerations are important, they are not determinative. The President, unlike most agency decisionmakers, is an elected official. He is responsible to the voters, who, in principle, will judge the manner in which he exercises his delegated authority. Whether the President's expenditure decisions, for example, are arbitrary is a matter that in the past has been left primarily to those voters to consider. And this Court has made clear that judicial review is less appropriate when the President's own discretion, rather than that of an agency, is at stake. *See Dalton v. Specter*, 511 U.S. 462, 476 (1994) (Presidential decision on military base closure recommendations not reviewable; President could "approv[e] or disapprov[e] the recommendations for whatever reason he sees fit") . . . .

. . . .

V

In sum, I recognize that the Act before us is novel. In a sense, it skirts a constitutional edge. But that edge has to do with means, not ends. The means chosen do not amount literally to the enactment, repeal, or amendment of a law. Nor, for that matter, do they amount literally to the "line item veto" that the Act's title announces. Those means do not violate any basic separation-of-powers principle. They do not improperly shift the constitutionally foreseen balance of power from Congress to the President. Nor, since they comply with separation-of-powers principles, do they threaten the liberties of individual citizens. They represent an experiment that may, or may not, help representative government work better. The Constitution, in my view, authorizes Congress and the President to try novel methods in this way. Consequently, with respect, I dissent.

Exercise 10:

In light of *Clinton v. City of New York*, consider the following questions:

(1) Why was the first judicial challenge to the Line Item Veto Act unsuccessful?

(2) The majority of the Court asserted that President Clinton's actions had the "legal and practical effect" of "repealing a portion" of the statutes at issue. Is that true?

(3) How, if at all, did the procedure followed by President Clinton differ from the procedure specified by Congress? How, if at all, did the procedure followed by President Clinton differ from the procedure historically employed to "veto" legislation?

(4) The majority of the Court asserted that "constitutional silence" should be construed "as equivalent to an express prohibition" of enactment of legislation in any manner other than the one specified by the Constitution. Is that a fair inference? If so, should constitutional silence regarding removal of a non-judicial officer from office by means other than impeachment be construed to prohibit alternative means of removal? Why or why not?

(5) The majority of the Court based its conclusion, in part, on the fact that President Washington "understood the text of the Presentment Clause as requiring that he either 'approve all the parts of a Bill, or reject it in toto.' " Could the text of the Presentment Clause support any alternative construction? Why or why not? How much weight, if any, should be given in 1998 to President Washington's views and historical practice? Why?

(6) The majority of the Court distinguished on three bases numerous precedents authorizing limited "delegation" to the Executive. One basis of distinction suggested by the Court was that "the suspension power [at issue in *Field v. Clark*] was contingent upon a condition that did not exist" when the statute was enacted. A second basis of distinction suggested by the Court was that "when the President determined that the contingency had arisen, he had a duty to suspend" under the statute at issue in *Field v. Clark*, rather than retaining "discretion" whether to act. Assume that on April 5, 1952, Congress enacted a statute providing that "the President may seize control of the means of production of any commodities for up to one year upon certifying that (a) a nation-wide disruption of production was imminent and (b) each such commodity was essential to national defense." Could President Truman have relied upon that statute to seize the steel mills on April 9, or would the statute be unconstitutional because the crisis existed at the time Congress legislated? Would the statute have been unconstitutional because it did not mandate seizure whenever the President certified the two conditions were satisfied?

(7) The third basis for distinguishing precedent identified by the majority of the Court was that "whenever the President suspended an exemption [under the statute at issue in *Field v. Clark*], he was executing the policy that Congress had embodied in the statute." Is it not equally true that President Clinton was executing the policy that Congress embodied in the Line Item Veto Act? Is there some reason for distinguishing between the policy of Congress in the Line Item Veto Act and the policy of Congress in the statutes as to which President Clinton asserted "cancellation" authority? If so, would a different result follow if, instead of enacting the Line Item Veto Act, Congress had written its provisions directly into the Balanced Budget Act of 1997 and the Taxpayer Relief Act of 1997? Why or why not?

(8) A possible fourth basis for distinguishing precedent identified by the majority of the Court is that the statutes cited by the government "all relate to foreign trade" as distinguished from "domestic affairs alone." Is that distinction pertinent to analysis under the Presentment Clause? Why or why not?

(9) The majority of the Court asserted that it was irrelevant "that Congress intended" to convey discretion upon the President absent its "amending the Constitution." Why is the view of Congress in 1996 that such a procedure was constitutionally permissible "of no moment" but the views of President Washington were persuasive in eliminating a constitutional power in the executive to make partial vetoes?

(10) The majority of the Court identified "three procedural steps" which are "explicitly require[d]" by the Constitution so that "[i]f one paragraph of [the text of the bill] had been omitted at any one of those three stages, Public Law 105-33 would not have been validly enacted" and was "surely not a document that may 'become a law' " under the Constitution. How are those statements consistent with the scope of judicial review expressed in *Field v. Clark*? In light of the extensive discussion of that precedent in the majority's opinion, albeit on a different issue, is it reasonable to believe the Court overlooked the matter? Did Congress and the

President make a mistake in enacting and operating under the Line Item Veto Act instead of simply conspiring to omit from published law specific sections that the President identified?

(11) What rationale did Justice Kennedy provide for judicial enforcement of separation of powers vested in Congress and the President? What other structural provisions of the Constitution did he assert were subject to judicial enforcement on the same rationale?

(12) How did Justice Kennedy's rationale support his conclusion that Congress may not voluntarily surrender its own powers to the Executive?

(13) Other than prohibiting a transfer of power from Congress to the Executive, what other intra-governmental power transfer did Justice Kennedy find implicit in the design of the Line Item Veto Act? Are such transfers consistent with, or in opposition to, democratic theory? Did the Line Item Veto Act actually make any such transfer?

(14) What constitutionally-permissible mechanisms did Justice Kennedy identify for control of federal spending?

(15) After reviewing the dissent, consider whether a majority of the Court would have upheld provisions in the Balanced Budget Act of 1997 and the Taxpayer Relief Act of 1997 permitting the President to spend federal funds on behalf of the claimants "not exceeding" the tax liabilities otherwise due from them, and authorizing the claimants to use such sums to off-set any tax liability. Stated otherwise, does it matter to the analysis whether the statute addresses the expenditure of funds rather than the collection of tax liabilities? If that distinction does not make a difference, does it matter that the statutory authorization for the President's action was contained in a separate statute, the Line Item Veto Act?

(16) After *Clinton v. City of New York* and *Bowsher v. Synar*, what alternatives remain for Congress in seeking to facilitate balancing the budget short of a constitutional amendment?

WHITMAN v. AMERICAN TRUCKING ASSOCIATIONS, INC.

531 U.S. 457 (2001)

Justice Scalia delivered the opinion of the Court.

. . . .

In a delegation challenge, the constitutional question is whether the statute has delegated legislative power to the agency. Article I, § 1, of the Constitution vests "[a]ll legislative Powers herein granted . . . in a Congress of the United States." This text permits no delegation of those powers, *Loving v. United States*, 517 U.S. 748, 771 (1996); *see id.* at 766–777 (Scalia, J., concurring in part and concurring in judgment), and so we repeatedly have said that when Congress confers decisionmaking authority upon agencies *Congress* must "lay down by legislative act an intelligible principle to which the person or body authorized to [act] is directed to conform." *J.W. Hampton, Jr., & Co. v. United States*, 276 U.S. 394, 409, Treas. Dec. 42706 (1928). We have never suggested that an agency can cure an unlawful delegation of legislative power by adopting in its discretion a limiting construction of the statute. . . . Whether the statute delegates legislative power is a question for the courts, and an agency's voluntary self-denial has no bearing upon the answer.

. . . .

The scope of discretion § 109(b)(1) allows is in fact well within the outer limits of our nondelegation precedents. In the history of the Court we have found the requisite "intelligible principle" lacking in only two statutes, one of which provided literally no guidance for the exercise of discretion, and the other of which conferred authority to regulate the entire economy on the basis of no more precise a standard than stimulating the economy by assuring "fair competition." *See Panama Refining Co. v. Ryan,* 293 U.S. 388 (1935); *A.L.A. Schechter Poultry Corp. v. United States,* 295 U.S. 495 (1935). We have, on the other hand, upheld the validity of § 11(b)(2) of the Public Utility Holding Company Act of 1935 which gave the Securities and Exchange Commission authority to modify the structure of holding company systems so as to ensure that they are not "unduly or unnecessarily complicate[d]" and do not "unfairly or inequitably distribute voting power among security holders." *American Power & Light Co. v. SEC,* 329 U.S. 90, 104 (1946). We have approved wartime conferral of agency power to fix the prices of commodities at a level that " 'will be generally fair and equitable and will effectuate the [in some respects conflicting] purposes of th[e] Act.' " *Yakus v. United States,* 321 U.S. 414, 420, 423-26 (1944). And we have found an "intelligible principle" in various statutes authorizing regulation in the "public interest." . . . In short, we have "almost never felt qualified to second-guess Congress regarding the permissible degree of policy judgment that can be left to those executing or applying the law." *Mistretta v. United States,* 488 U.S. 361, 416 (1989) (Scalia, J., dissenting); *see id.* at 373 (majority opinion).

It is true enough that the degree of agency discretion that is acceptable varies according to the scope of the power congressionally conferred. *See Loving v. United States,* 517 U.S. at 772–73; *United States v. Mazurie,* 419 U.S. 544, 556–57 (1975). While Congress need not provide any direction to the EPA regarding the manner in which it is to define "country elevators," which are to be exempt from new-stationary-source regulations governing grain elevators, *see* 42 U.S.C. § 7411(i), it must provide substantial guidance on setting air standards that affect the entire national economy. But even in sweeping regulatory schemes we have never demanded, as the Court of Appeals did here, that statutes provide a "determinate criterion" for saying "how much [of the regulated harm] is too much." In *Touby* [*v. United States,* 500 U.S. 160 (1991)], for example, we did not require the statute to decree how "imminent" was too imminent, or how "necessary" was necessary enough, or even — most relevant here — how "hazardous" was too hazardous. 505 U.S. at 165–67. Similarly, the statute at issue in *Lichter* [*v. United States,* 334 U.S. 742, 783 (1948)], authorized agencies to recoup "excess profits" paid under wartime Government contracts, yet we did not insist that Congress specify how much profit was too much. 334 U.S. at 783–86. It is therefore not conclusive for delegation purposes that, as respondents argue, ozone and particulate matter are "nonthreshold" pollutants that inflict a continuum of adverse health effects at any airborne concentration greater than zero, and hence require the EPA to make judgments of degree. "[A] certain degree of discretion, and thus of lawmaking, inheres in most executive or judicial action." *Mistretta v. United States,* 488 U.S. at 417 (Scalia, J., dissenting) (emphasis deleted); *see id.* at 378–79 (majority opinion). Section 109(b)(1) of the CAA, which to repeat we interpret as requiring the EPA to set air quality standards at the level that is "requisite" — that is, not lower or higher than is necessary — to protect the public health with an adequate margin of safety, fits comfortably within the scope of discretion permitted by our precedent.

We therefore reverse the judgment of the Court of Appeals . . . .

[The opinion of Justice Thomas, concurring, the opinion of Justice Stevens joined by Justice Souter, concurring in the judgment, and the opinion of Justice

Breyer, concurring in the judgment, are omitted.]

Exercise 11:

The U.S. Supreme Court has never overruled either *Panama Refining Co. v. Ryan*, 293 U.S. 388 (1935), or *A.L.A. Schechter Poultry Corp. v. United States*, 295 U.S. 495 (1935). Nonetheless, the Court has not since those cases found any statute to violate the non-delegation doctrine. The cases in this chapter summarize many of the statutory standards that the Court has determined satisfy the "intelligible principle" test. If either of the 1935 cases remain good law, they must be distinguishable on some basis.

Does the Court continue to refer to these precedents as good law or to cast doubt upon them? What bases for distinguishing the cases are suggested by the Court in *Mistretta*, by Justice White in *Chadha*, by Justice Breyer in *City of New York*, and the Court in *American Trucking*? Incorporating one or more of those suggested bases for distinguishing cases that found a violation of the non-delegation doctrine, formulate a test for distinguishing permissible from impermissible legislation.

TABLE OF CASES

[References are to pages]

A

B

C

D

E

F

G

H

I

J

K

[References are to pages]

FEDERAL CONSTITUTIONAL LAW

[References are to pages.]

[References are to pages.]

D

E

F

[References are to pages.]

[References are to pages.]

Q

R

S

[References are to pages.]